Peter H. Felker

The Grocers' Manual

Containing the natural history and process of manufacture of all grocers' goods.

Also, their adulterations, and how to detect them; rates of tare, as allowed by

custom and law

Peter H. Felker

The Grocers' Manual
Containing the natural history and process of manufacture of all grocers' goods. Also, their adulterations, and how to detect them; rates of tare, as allowed by custom and law

ISBN/EAN: 9783337348052

Printed in Europe, USA, Canada, Australia, Japan

Cover: Foto ©Suzi / pixelio.de

More available books at **www.hansebooks.com**

THE

GROCERS' MANUAL,

CONTAINING

THE NATURAL HISTORY AND PROCESS OF MANUFACTURE
OF ALL GROCERS' GOODS.

ALSO,

THEIR ADULTERATIONS,

AND HOW TO DETECT THEM;

RATES OF TARE,

AS ALLOWED BY CUSTOM AND LAW;

TABLES OF WEIGHTS, MEASURES, MONEYS, ETC.

THE WHOLE

BEING DESIGNED AS A GUIDE TO AID IN THE
PURCHASING OF GOODS.

BY P. H. FELKER.

––––––

CLAREMONT, N. H.,
PRINTED BY THE CLAREMONT MANUFACTURING COMPANY.
1878.

.

THE CLAREMONT MANUFACTURING COMPANY,
CLAREMONT, N. H.,
BOOKMAKERS AND STEREOTYPERS.

PREFACE.

THE preparation of this manual was suggested to me by my own need of one while in the trade. Great care¹ has been taken in the description of the various articles, to have the information up to date. Technical terms have been avoided as much as possible in a book designed for popular use. The sharp competition in trade and the many adulterated goods now manufactured render some such guide as this manual a necessity to all intelligent tradesmen.

P. H. FELKER.

Grand Rapids, Michigan, July, 1878.

THE

GROCERS' MANUAL.

Adulteration. The adulterating of goods of all kinds is extensively carried on, and so general has become the practice that it is almost impossible to obtain pure manufactured goods. Even the articles used for adulterating purposes are themselves adulterated, and the evil has no limit. Just where to lay the blame for this evil is hard to determine. The great competition in trade has led manufacturers to fall in prices, and to do this they must sell impure materials. In England and other European countries, severe laws are in force against adulterating. Many of the states of the Union have similar laws but they are generally a dead letter. The matter is an important one and should be under control of the officers of the public health. We give some of the most important articles of the grocers' goods which are adulterated :

1. COFFEE. This is adulterated largely with chicory, this latter being itself adulterated with roasted corn, beans, lupine seeds, peas, pulse, horse-chestnuts, spent coffee, and various roots, such as carrots, parsnips, mangel-wurzel, dandelion, etc. It is said that spent tan-bark and dried bullock's liver have been employed for the same

purpose. The test for these adulterations is the different appearance of the tissues when examined under the microscope; also the infusion of chicory does not become discolored when treated with iodine, as it contains no starch. Ground coffee is of such a greasy nature from the presence of oil that when thrown on water it will float, while the adulterating materials will readily sink, and rapidly discolor the water, giving it a brown appearance, while pure coffee does not readily discolor the water. A rough test may thus be made of the amount of impurities in coffee; by stirring the ingredients in water the coffee will rise to the top and the amount can thus be determined; or it may be more accurately determined by chemical analysis. There is a machine patented in England for making spurious berries out of common vegetable substances, and thus the green coffee is itself adulterated.

2. TEA. This is extensively adulterated in China by means of exhausted tea leaves, and leaves of other trees, to the amount of millions of pounds annually. Mineral matters are also used for coloring or facing teas; China clay, fine sand, iron filings, etc., are used to the extent of 20 to 40 per cent. The tests for these adulterations are very simple. The common test is by infusion; this is poured off the leaves and examined for color, taste and odor, all of which are characteristic. The leaves are also examined for size, color and for special botanical peculiarities. Impurities, like sand, iron filings and dirt, may be seen among the leaves or at the bottom of the cup. The leaves, too, betray by their coarseness and botanical character, the nature and quality of the tea; for although

the leaves of genuine tea differ much in form and size, yet their venation and general structure are very distinctive. The young leaves are narrow, downy and convoluted; those next in size and age have their edges delicately serrated, and the veins are scarcely perceptible; in leaves of large size the venation is well marked, there being a series of loops along each side of the leaf extending from the midrib to the edge. Chemical examination of the ash will also determine the mineral impurities; iron filings may be discovered by the use of the magnet.

3. BREAD. The chief adulterations of bread are with alum or sulphate of copper for the purpose of giving solidity to the gluten of damaged or inferior flour; or with chalk or carbonate of soda to correct the acidity of sour flour; or with boiled rice or potatoes to enable the bread to carry more water, and thus to produce a larger number of loaves.

4. FLOUR and other farinaceous matters are adulterated with plaster, potato starch, etc. The granules of the different kinds of starch can be determined by the use of the microscope.

5. BUTTER and LARD may be adulterated by mixing with inferior fats, or by the addition of water, salt and starch. If impurities are added they may be detected by melting in a glass and allowing to stand; the fat will float while the impurities will settle. Foreign fats in butter are recognized by the granular look of the butter, by its gritty feel, by its taste, and by its odor when warmed.

6. MUSTARD is so acrid and so powerful in its flavor that it is commonly diluted with flour or other farinaceous matter, turmeric being added to improve its appearance.

The genuine material contains no starch, and the addition of starchy matter may be detected by the iodine test.

7. SPICES, as pepper, cinnamon, ginger, cloves, cayenne, etc., are all subjects of large adulterations, which can readily be determined by the microscope. In some cases of so called ground pepper the specimen examined consisted of gypsum, buckwheat husks, mustard husks and starch, and no pepper. Ginger is adulterated with sago meal, ground rice and turmeric. In cayenne we have ferruginous earths, brick dust, and even vermilion and red lead.

Exhausted spices are also re-ground and used to adulterate.

Among the adulterations which are practiced for the purpose of improving the appearance of the article, and giving it a false strength, are the following : the addition of alum and salts of copper to bread ; the facing of black tea with black lead, and of green with a mixture of indigo or Prussian blue, with turmeric and China clay ; the treatment of pickles and preserved fruits with a salt of copper which has the property of mordanting and brightening the green coloring matter of vegetables. *Ferruginous earths* are added to sauces, anchovies, potted meats and the preparations of cocoa. *Mineral pigments*, such as yellow and orange chromate of lead, green arsenite of copper, etc., are frequently used in coloring confectionery, and have produced serious effects in those eating it. Sulphuric acid is added to vinegar ; black jack or burnt sugar to coffee and chicory, etc.

Of minor adulterations we have flour and terra alba added to baking powders ; starch and flour to chocolate ;

gum arabic added to licorice ; common plaster to cream tartar, as high as 80 per cent. ; starch and farinaceous matters to indigo ; flour to powdered sugar ; syrups made from corn starch and sulphuric acid ; tapioca made from potatoes ; foreign leaves and paper added to tobacco ; liquors of all kinds artificially manufactured ; maple sugar made from muscovado ; nutmegs boiled and recoated ; artificial honey and jellies ; and indeed the catalogue embraces about all manufactured goods.

Alcohol. This substance has long been known as alcohol or spirits of wine. It is obtained as a result of the fermentation of sugar, and is extracted by distillation from spirituous liquors, such as wine and brandy. Alcohol is the essential element in all intoxicating drinks. Pure or absolute alcohol is a colorless fluid, with a pungent and agreeable taste and a fragrant odor. It is very combustible and burns with a pale blue flame, without smoke. The action of alcohol on the system is that of a powerful and dangerous stimulant. Its composition is C_2H_6O.

Alden Dried Fruit. A name applied to fruit dried by what is known as the Alden Process of Evaporation. This process consists in extracting the water from the fruit, without impairing its flavor or freshness. The fruit is dried in a chamber constructed for this special purpose, and the water extracted by means of hot air blasts. All kinds of fruits and vegetables are dried by this process, and are now extensively sold in our markets, bringing a much higher price than fruit dried by the old methods.

Allspice, the dried fruits of *Eugenia pimento*, a native of the Carribee Islands, and also cultivated in the East

Indies. It is a handsome tree about thirty feet high and is extensively cultivated in Jamaica, where the trees are planted in rows which are called pimento walks. Soon after the tree has blossomed the berries become fit for gathering, not being allowed to ripen, as, when ripe they are difficult to cure, and become black and tasteless when dried. The berries are dried by spreading on a terrace exposed to the sun for about seven days, during which time they gradually lose their green color and become of a reddish brown. They have a fragrant odor which is supposed to resemble a mixture of cloves, cinnamon and nutmegs; hence the name of allspice by which they are known. Their taste is warm, aromatic, pungent, and slightly astringent. The berries are used as a spice in cooking, and as a carminative in medicine. For the year ending June 30, 1875, there were consumed, in the United States, 1,721,683 pounds of allspice, valued at $ 83,151, exclusive of duty.

Almond (*Amygdalus.*) A genus of plants of the natural order Rosaceæ, composed of trees and shrubs, closely allied to the peach. The tree from which the common almond (*A. communis*) is obtained is a native of Barbary and grows to the height of 25 to 30 feet. Almonds are produced throughout the whole of Southern Europe, Syria, Persia and Northern Africa, but our supply is largely from Spain and the South of France. They are distinguished as bitter and sweet almonds, the latter being used as an article of food. There are two varieties of the sweet almond, known in commerce as Jordan and Valentia almonds. The former are imported from Malaga, are longer, narrower, more pointed and

more highly prized than the latter, which are shipped
from Valentia. The kernels of the sweet almond are
used, either green or ripe, as an article in the dessert.
They are also much used in confectionery, cooking, per-
fumes and medicine. When young and green they are
preserved in sugar, like green apricots. They also furnish the Almond Oil of commerce, which is used in the
arts for the same purpose as olive oil. The bitter almond is injurious to animal life, on account of the large
quantity of hydrocyanic or Prussic acid which it contains. This species is but little used in domestic economy, but is sometimes employed in flavoring confectionery, and should only be used with the greatest caution.
According to the statistics of 1875, there were consumed,
in this country, almonds to the value of $ 487,524.

Alum, a double sulphate of alumina and potash. It
has a sweet, astringent taste, and crystallizes in the form
of octohedrals. Its chemical formula is $K_2 4 S O_4 24 H_2 O$;
it contains one pàrt by weight of sulphate of potash, one
of tersulphate of alumina, and twenty-four of water. Alum is extensively manufactured, and is used in preparing
skins, and as a mordant in calico printing. It is sometimes used by bakers in the adulteration of bread. Ammonia alum, containing ammonia instead of potash, is
now largely manufactured, on account of the cheapness
of the ammonia sulphate.

Ammonia, a chemical compound in the form of a
transparent, colorless and pungent gas. Its formula is
$N H_3$, one atom of nitrogen and three of hydrogen. The
name is derived from sal-ammonia, which was formerly
obtained near the Temple of Jupiter-Ammon, in Libya,

by burning camel's dung. It is now manufactured in connection with the distilling of bituminous coal in making
gas, and from various refuse animal matter. It combines
with acids to form salts. A solution of this gas in water
is used in medicine, and is known as hartshorn. Smell-
ing salts is the carbonate of ammonia. Ammonia combined with sulphuric acid forms a white salt, the sulphate
of ammonia.

Anchovy, (*Engraulis encrasicolus*), a small fish of the
herring family, from five to seven inches in length, and
found in the Mediterranean sea and on the Atlantic shores
of Europe. Anchovies also abound on the Atlantic and
Pacific coast of the United States. They are largely
taken in the Mediterranean, and salted and packed in
small barrels for exportation. The fish are used largely
in the manufacture of pastes and sauces, and anchovy
paste and sauce is quite common in our markets.

Anise-seed ; the fruit of *Pimpinella anisum*, originally from Egypt and the Levant; but now cultivated all
over Europe. The seeds have a fragrant odor, and a
sweet, warm, aromatic taste. They are used in medicine,
and also to flavor liquors, and as a condiment. The seeds
contain a volatile oil, which is obtained by distillation,
and used as a substitute for the seeds. The star anise
oil of commerce is the product of *Illicium anisatum*, a
small tree of the order of Magnoliaceæ, a native of Eastern Asia. It is imported from Anam and China. In
1875 there were imported 90,956 pounds of anise and star
anise seed.

Annotto, or **Annatto,** is a red dyeing drug produced
from the red pulp which covers the seeds of *Bixa orellana*,

a shrub growing wild in South America, and cultivated in the West Indies. The method of manufacture is as follows: the pulp and seeds together are bruised in wooden vessels, and hot water poured on them; they are then left to soak for several days, and then pressed through a close sieve to separate the seeds. The matter is then left to ferment for about one week, when the water is gently poured off, and the solid part is left to dry in the shade. When it has acquired the consistency of a solid paste, it is prepared for market. Besides being used in painting and dyeing, it is largely employed as a coloring matter in the manufacture of butter and cheese. In 1875 there were imported into this country, of annotto in various forms, 212,259 pounds.

Apple. (*Pyrus malus.*) This most useful of all fruits is a native of the temperate regions of Europe and Asia. It is a member of the natural order Rosaceæ, and grows to a height of from fifteen to thirty feet, with spreading branches forming a bushy top. It is a hardy tree, slow of growth, and attains a great age—instances being known of trees over 200 years old. The blossoms are very fragrant, and a tree in full bloom is a very beautiful object. It flowers in May, and fruits from July to November. The number of varieties under cultivation is over 200, and is rapidly increasing. According to the time of ripening of this fruit it may be divided into three classes: summer, autumn and winter apples. Among the best varieties of summer apples for commercial purposes are the Early Harvest, Red Astrachan, Summer Queen and Golden Sweet. Among fall apples are Maiden's Blush, Rambo, Fall Wine and Fall Pippin. Of winter fruit we have the Baldwin, Ben Davis, Northern Spy, White Pippin, Belleflower, Swaar, Peck's Pleasant, Roxbury Russet, Winesap, Rhode Island Greening and Hubbardston Nonesuch. Large quantities of apples are annually exported from the Northern United States to Great Britain. When sliced and dried the apple forms an important article of commerce. For the year ending June 30, 1875, there were exported from this country 759,574 bushels of green apples, and 4,053,696 pounds of dried apples. The finest fruits are produced in New York and other states of the same latitude. The wood of the apple tree is very fine grained, and when green weighs from 48 to 56 lbs. per cubic foot, and when dried loses about one-tenth. The wood is used in the manufacture of shoe lasts, plane handles, cog-wheels, etc.

THE SIBERIAN CRAB (*Pyrus voccata*), a native of Siberia, is cultivated in Europe and in the United States. It is largely used in the manufacture of jelly and preserves.

THE AMERICAN CRAB is *Pyrus coronaria*, and grows wild in this country. The fruit is of little value.

The wild crab of Europe is the parent of all our cultivated varieties of apples, which have been produced by careful selection and cultivation. At present the standard varieties are propagated by grafting, and are much superior to those raised from the seed, which are known as natural fruit.

Apricot, (*Prunus armeniaca*), a small tree of the natural order Rosaceæ. It is a native of Armenia, but is cultivated in both Europe and America. The fruit is mostly of a yellow color, with the side exposed to the sun of a reddish tinge ; and in many of its qualities it closely re-

sembles the peach. In the East it is dried in the same
manner as figs, and used as an article of food. It may
be propagated by budding on the peach, plum and wild
cherry. With us it flowers in April and fruits in July.

Argol, (See Cream Tartar.)

Arrow-root, (*Maranta arundinacea*) is a native of
the West Indies, from which large quantities of the prepared root are imported into the United States and Europe. It is also cultivated in Georgia and Florida. In
Cayenne the natives eat the root roasted for the cure of
intermittent fevers; bruised, it is applied to arrow
wounds whence the origin of the English name. It is
from the root stocks of this plant that the finest Bermuda
or West Indian arrow-root is obtained. When a year
old, the root-stocks are taken up and well washed, and
afterward beaten to a pulp in wooden mortars; it is then
thoroughly washed in water till the fecula is removed
from the fibre. The fibrous portion is then removed by
hand, and the white, milky-looking fluid is strained
through a coarse cloth, and allowed to stand till the fecula subsides. The water is again poured off and fresh
water added; this water is then run off and the starch,
which has settled to the bottom, is dried in the sun on
sheets. Prepared arrow-root is almost pure starch, but
is very frequently adulterated with potato starch. This
adulteration may be detected by the use of the microscope. The starch granules of the genuine arrow root
are of an ovate-oblong, convex shape, nearly equal in
size and with very fine concentric rings, increasing in
size from the apex; while the granules of the potato
starch are very irregular in size and streaked and fur-

rowed on the surface. Another test for genuine Maranta arrow-root is to mix a portion with twice its weight of strong muriatic acid, when it will form an opaque paste ; perform the same operation with potato starch and the result will be transparent and jelly like. The fecula of many other plants is used as a substitute for arrow-root or for its adulteration. Potato starch is the most common adulterant, and from it is manufactured the English arrow-root. East India arrow-root is obtained from the roots of different species of *curcuma*. Under the microscope the starch grains appear united to each other, and surrounded with rings. Brazilian arrow-root is prepared from a species of euphorbia, (see Tapioca.) For the year 1875, 1,032.062 lbs. of arrow-root were consumed in the United States.

Artichoke, (*Cynar oscolymus*), a perennial herb of the natural order Compositæ, and nearly related to the thistle. It is cultivated in the gardens as a vegetable—the part used being the fleshy receptacle of the flower head, gathered before the flower expands, and boiled or made into a salad. It flowers in August, and fruits in September.

The **Jerusalem Artichoke,** (*Helianthus tuberosus*), is a species of sunflower, and is cultivated for the fleshy tubers found at the root. These tubers are pickled and used as a condiment. They are also used in the feeding of stock. The plant is a native of Brazil, and flowers with us in August and September, and fruits in October.

Asparagus. (*Asparagus officinalis.*) A species of plant belonging to the Lily family and largely cultivated in gardens as an article of food. The young plants are

raised from seed and then transplanted into beds prepared in rich soil. The perennial roots send up, every
spring, a crop of shoots which are cut just below the
soil, when a few inches in length, and tied in bunches
and sent to the market.

Axle Grease, a compound for greasing the axles of
wagons, etc. It is prepared from the pitchy remains of
fatty acids, petroleum or lard oil. Tallow, tar, lime
water, whiting, flaxseed, flour, venetian red and rosin
are the ingredients of one of the patent axle greases.
Another is given as black oil, hard tallow, wood ashes,
white lime, salt, sulphur, and black lead. It is generally packed for market in small boxes or tin cans.

Baking Powder, a compound of an acid and alkali
and used as a substitute for yeast. It is commonly made
from cream tartar, and carbonate of soda or ammonia;
the phosphate of ammonia has also been employed. The
acid and alkali in baking powders should be used in such
proportions as to just neutralize each other. The materials necessary to form the baking powder are generally
mixed with flour, or some other cheap material. The
addition of flour is of no injury, but in the cheap baking
powder the flour largely predominates. One of the best
baking powders we have, on analysis, yields as follows:

Cream tartar, bicarbonate of soda and water,	85.416
Flour, - - -	9.522
Sand, etc, - - -	5.062
	100.000

Chlorine and Sulphuric acid, trace.

Another " yeast powder" yielded as follows:

Cream tartar, and bicarbonate of soda,	63.267
Flour, - -	32.568
Sand, etc, - -	4.165

100.000

Trace of Chlorine and Sulphuric acid.

In using baking powder it is mixed with the dough, the moisture in which is sufficient to cause the acid to act on the soda, and carbonic acid gas is evolved which causes the dough to rise. The great advantage of these powders over yeast, is the rapidity with which it forms the gas, thus enabling baking to be done very much quicker.

Banana, (*musa sapientum*) is the fruit of a species of palm, a native of India, but now generally cultivated throughout the tropics of Asia, Africa, and America. It is regarded by some botanists as merely a variety of the plantain (*musa paradisica.*) The banana forms a principal article of food to the inhabitants of the tropics. The tree which bears this fruit has an herbaceous stalk, about five or six inches in diameter at the surface of the ground, and tapering upward to the heights of fifteen or twenty feet. The leaves are in a cluster at the top; they are very large, being six feet long, and two feet broad, with a strong midrib. The spike of flowers rises from the centre of the leaves to the height of about four feet. The fruit is about an inch in diameter, eight or nine inches in length, and bent a little on one side. As it ripens it turns yellow, and is filled with a pulp of a luscious sweet taste. These clusters contain from one hundred to two hundred specimens, and weigh from seventy to eighty pounds. The banana is very productive and on the same amount of ground will yield of nutritious material in proportion to wheat as 132 to 1, and of potatoes as 44 to 1. The banana is now cultivated in Florida and bears continually, the shoots from the main stalk coming into bearing as the old one dies.

Barley, (*Hordeum vulgare*) is a plant belonging to the grass family, and extensively cultivated in all temperate climates and used as an article of food. In this country the grain is raised almost exclusively for the use of breweries. When the skin has been removed and a portion of the berry cut off and rounded by passing through millstones of a peculiar kind, the kernels having been previously steamed and dried, it forms what is known as the *Pearl Barley* of commerce, a food much used for invalids. In 1875, there were consumed of imported barley, 6,229,688 bushels.

Bath Brick, a preparation of calcareous earth in the form of a brick, and used for scouring knives. It is imported from France, and also manufactured in this country at Joliet, Illinois.

Bean, (*Phaseolies nanus.*) A leading vegetable of our market gardens, and extensively cultivated in all sections of the country. It is used as food in both the green and ripe state. In the green state they are known as string beans, and the pod and seed are both eaten. When ripe they are shelled and are then known as dry beans. In the early spring, string beans are largely shipped from the south to the northern markets where they find a ready sale. In the dry state beans form an important article in the produce markets. The white marrowfat is the variety generally cultivated to sell in a dry state. Besides the bush bean, we have the pole bean, *Phaseolus vulgaris*, which grows to the height of ten feet and requires support. The Lima is the best known of this class. The bean is originally a native of India.

Beer, a beverage in common use, the fermented infusion of malted barley, flavored with hops. The first operation in the making of beer, is the manufacture of the malt (which see.) The color of the malt depends on the temperature of the kiln at the time of drying, and the different colored malts are used for the various kinds of beer. In the brewing of malt it is first ground or crushed by passing between iron rollers. It is then placed in the mash tub with warm water and the temperature gradually raised to about 167° F., when the starch of the malt is converted into glucose and dextrine which are dissolved by the water. One barrel of beer requires from one to four bushels of malt, and when malt is high, other saccharine substances are sometimes substituted for it. After the infusion has been allowed to settle, the clear wort is drawn off into a copper vessel when it is boiled with hops ; from one to five pounds of hops being added, according to the strength and quantity of beer being made, the boiling liquor is then strained and run into coolers, where it is cooled as rapidly as possible, and it is then put into the fermenting vats or tuns. The next process is that of fermentation by the addition of one gallon of yeast to one hundred of wort; and during this process a part of the saccharine matter is converted into alcohol and carbonic acid, the latter rising to the top carrying with it particles of yeast and forming a scum. After fermenting several days the beer is separated from the yeast, and transferred to the cleansing butts where it is purified by the addition of finings. The beer is then transferred to casks and set away, where it developes its qualities and is ready for use. The quantity of alcohol found in beer is in varying quantity, according to the strength of the beer.

ALE is prepared from pale malt and contains a large percentage of sugar. . *Pale ale* is made from malt dried in the sun or by steam. *Scotch ale* is a strong, sweet ale. *Small beer* is made from the remainder, after the wort for ale has been drawn off, by the addition of more water. *Porter*, is a dark colored beer made from a mixture of pale, amber, brown and black malt. *Stout*, is a variety of porter. *Lager beer* is beer fermented at low temperature with bottom yeast. It can be kept a long time, and is extensively used. It was first manufactured in Bavaria. Beer is a stimulant and tonic, and also contains nutritious matter derived from the malt.

Beeswax, the material secreted by bees and of which their cells are manufactured. The wax, separated from the honey, is an important article of commerce. The honey being separated from the comb by pressure, or by means of the honey extractor, the residual wax is heated with water and stirred until it melts. It is then strained into a vessel of cold water and solidifies on the surface into a thick, yellowish cake. It is rendered white by the action of the sun and moisture. Purified beeswax is tasteless, colorless and odorless. It is insoluble in water and fuses at 145° F. It enters largely into the manufacture of candles and tapers.

Beet, (*Beta vulgaris*). This is one of our most largely cultivated vegetables. It has a large, esculent root,
rich in saccharine matters. In France and Germany
large quantities of sugar are manufactured from the variety known as the sugar beet. The boiled roots are a
common article of diet in nearly all civilized countries.
The young leaves are also boiled and eaten as greens.
The red beet is the best variety cultivated in gardens.
The best market varieties are, Short-top Round, Bassano,
Pineapple and Long Smooth Blood. During the early
season, beets are largely shipped from the South to the
northern markets. Swiss Chard (*Beta cicla*) is only
grown for its leaves ; the midrib is boiled like asparagus
and the remainder of the leaf used as spinach.

Blackberry, the common name of several species of
Rubus, natives of the United States. The plant is shrubby in its growth, and some species reach the height of six
feet. *Rubus vilosus*, our common blackberry, grows a-
bundantly in all parts of the United States, along the
borders of fields, and in woods. In some of the Southern States, large quantities of the berries are dried and
sent to market. They are also canned to some extent,
but the fruit is rather insipid. The fruit of the blackberry is not a true berry, but a collection of drupes or
stone fruits on a fleshy receptacle.

Blacking, a preparation used for the blacking of boots,
shoes, etc. The essential ingredients are ivory black,
vinegar or sour beer, sugar or molasses, a little sweet oil,
and sulphuric acid. Blacking appears in the market both
in the form of paste and of a liquid. Many varieties are in
use and differ in the proportions of the various ingredi-

ents used. Any blacking which will retain its oily consistence of a paste when exposed to the air, is superior to that which dries and becomes harsh. An excess of blacking is injurious to leather on account of the acid present. For the production of a polish a fine brush is necessary as a coarse one will scratch the polish.

Bloater, herring slightly dried and smoked and intended for immediate use. (See Herring.)

Blue Fish, (*Temnadar saltator*), a fish allied to the mackerel, but larger and found in abundance off our Atlantic coast. It is a very voracious fish and feeds on mackerel and smaller fishes. Its weight varies from five to ten pounds; as a fish for the table it is of superior quality.

Blueing, an article used in the laundry for the coloring of clothes. It is sold in either the dry or liquid form. The latter is sometimes a dilute solution of the sulphate of indigo in water; but it is generally made from Prussian blue (ferrocyanide of iron), dissolved in water by means of oxalic acid. The dry blueing may be prepared from the acid solution of indigo, by precipitating the indigo by means of a solution of salt. Another method is by neutralizing the acid solution by the carbonate of soda; indigo appears as a precipitate, which is washed on a filter with a solution of salt and sold as a paste, or as a dry powder.

Blue Vitriol, the commercial name for sulphate of copper ($CuSO_4$). It is obtained by oxidizing at a low temperature the native sulphides of copper, as in the roasting of ores from which a considerable amount may be obtained by treating the roasted ores with water. It may also be formed by treating oxide of copper with dilute sulphuric acid and is an accidental product in various operations in the arts, as in the refining of gold and silver. It exists in large rhomboidal crystals of a beautiful sapphire blue color which are soluble in four parts of water. It is slightly efflorescent in dry air. Blue vitriol is very extensively used in dyeing and in calico printing. It has some application in medicine and is used to some extent as a preservative of timber, etc. It has also a quite important application in a certain class of electrical batteries.

Borax, a compound of boracic acid and soda, and is found free in nature as a saline incrustation on the shores of lakes in Thibet, Persia and India ; also in South America and in lakes on our Pacific coast. Borax is a white salt of a sweetish alkaline taste. It is very fusible and is much used as a flux in metallic mixtures and in welding iron. It is also used as a blowpipe reagent, from the facility with which it forms colored glasses with metallic oxides.

Borecole, or **Kale,** one of the varieties of the common cabbage and is grown in the vicinity of New York, not having come into general cultivation. It is said to be the most delicate and tender of all the cabbage tribe. BRUSSELS SPROUTS. This vegetable has never come into general use, probably owing to its being too tender to stand our northern winters. This is distinguished from all other varieties of the cabbage tribe by the sprouts or buds about the size of walnuts which grow thickly around the stem ; these sprouts are the parts used and are equal in flavor and tenderness to cauliflower or broccoli.

Brandy, a spirit that should be distilled from wine, but in the United States is distilled from the fermented juice of other fruits, as the pear, apple, cherry and peach. The flavor of the brandy depends on the quality of the wine from which it is manufactured, and good judges can tell from its flavor, the wine from which it was made. The best brandies are those obtained from the white wines of the regions of Cognac and Armagnac, districts of France. Brandies are distinguished as pale and dark. When first distilled the liquor is without color, and the pale amber tint it acquires is derived from the wood of the cask in which it is kept. Burnt sugar is added to new brandy which gives it the color of old brandy. Large quantities of common whiskey are exported to France from this country and returned as a sort of fictitious brandy. In France, rum, beet-root spirits and spirits from potatoes are largely used in its manufacture. The brandy made in the United States is derived from rectified whiskey made from Indian corn. Its flavor is given it by adding ascetic ether, oil Cognac, tannin, and burnt sugar to give it color.

Brazil Nuts, also called Para nuts, are the seeds of *Bertholletia excelsa*, a beautiful tree of 100 feet in height growing in Brazil and Guiana. The fruit is a thick, hard, woody capsule, like a pot with a lid, about four inches in diameter and five, six, or more in height. It contains many triangular nuts, laid over each other in a regular manner; when fresh these nuts are sweet and pleasant to the taste. They yield large quantities of oil which is used for the purposes of illumination. The large capsules when falling in the forests are said to be a source of great danger to travellers. For the year 1875, there were consumed in the United States 2,647,682 pounds of Brazil nuts.

Bread. An article of food prepared by the thorough mixture of flour, water and salt in proper proportions, and then baked. In the United States, bread is almost wholly made from wheat flour. Unleavened bread is that made without fermentation, or the employment of yeast, and is simply formed into a dough and baked. Raised or fermented bread is that which has been made porous and spongy, by the aid of some gas produced before or during baking. Fermented bread is prepared by the addition of leaven or the use of yeast. When leaven is used a portion of each baking is set aside for the next batch. It is difficult to make good bread from leaven on account of the trouble of mixing the leaven uniformly throughout the dough, so as to have it equally porous when baked. In the manufacture of home-made bread, yeast is the fermenting agent generally employed. It can be obtained from the brewers, and in the cities the German or compressed yeast may be had fresh daily. This yeast is thoroughly mixed with the dough, and much kneading is very essential to the making of good bread. This yeast sets up fermentation in the dough and carbonic acid is evolved which penetrates the dough making it light and porous. The carbonic acid is generated from the sugar contained in the flour. During the process of baking there is a loss of weight of about 25 per cent., chiefly water. In the baking of bread a high temperature is necessary but the heat should be raised gradually so as to have the loaf baked throughout; it

can be baked at 212° F. but no crust will be formed.
Sour bread arises from the flour being partly spoiled, or
from too old yeast or leaven, or from letting the dough
stand too long before baking ; bitter bread, from too much
or bad yeast ; heavy, from too little kneading or yeast :
and mouldy, from flour kept too long in a damp place. The
use of yeast or leaven in the fermentation of bread may be
dispensed with, and the gas generated by the addition of
baking powder (which see.) Graham bread is made
from the unbolted meal of wheat and is a mixture of bran
and flour. Rye bread is used to some extent but is
darker and harder than that made from wheat. Wheat
flour makes better bread on account of the large quantity
of gluten found in the flour, which retains the gas, making the bread light and porous. Alum is sometimes
added to flour in the making of bread, for the purpose of
increasing its weight, as the alum retains a large proportion of water ; a mixture of potato starch and boiled
rice is sometimes added for the same purpose. Alum in
bread may be detected by dipping a piece in a watery
solution of logwood, when a claret color will be produced
if alum is present.

Brimstone, the common and commercial name for
sulphur, (which see).

Broccoli, a garden vegetable closely resembling the
cauliflower and is a variety of the cabbage (*Brassica
oleracea*). It is grown as a fall crop, and as an article of
food is about equal to the cabbage.

Broom, a domestic utensil for sweeping, made of various materials, most commonly, with us, of broom corn,
a species of sorghum introduced from Africa. The han-

dles for the brooms are made by a broom handle lathe, out of either hard or soft wood. The corn is stripped of its seeds by a machine, the broom corn seed-stripper, shaped something like a comb, through which the corn is pulled. The stripped corn is then sorted and cut into proper lengths for the broom. The sewing of the broom is done by hand and by machinery, cheap brooms being made by the latter process; whisk brooms are simply small brooms with short handles used as substitutes for brushes.

Brush. An assemblage of hair, hogs bristles, strips of whalebone or short wire fastened to a handle either collectively or in separate tufts. The smallest kind of brushes are called *pencils,* and are made from the hair of the camel, badger, squirrel, goat, etc. Hogs bristles are, however, the material principally used, the white and better kinds being employed for hair, tooth, clothes and hat brushes, and also for the better class of paint brushes. The bristles are first sorted according to color, and then as to their size, by a series of combs with the teeth of varying width. The paint brush, the simplest form of brush, is made by inserting full length bristles between two projecting prongs in the handle and securing them by a wrapping of twine which is afterwards protected by a coating of glue mixed with red lead. Hair brooms, dusters, etc., are made by inserting tufts of bristles into a stock or head, previously bored for their reception. These are frequently bored triangularly to the face, or the face itself is rounded so as to give the tufts an outward splay when inserted; the root ends are first dipped into melted pitch, bound with thread, again dipped, and then inserted with a sort of twisting motion. Brushes of this description are generally made with bristles of full length ; but where stiffness is required as in hair or scrubbing brushes, the tuft of bristles is doubled so as to present both ends outward, and are then cut off square and even. The stocks or brush boards are cut from pieces of requisite thickness, so as to get two out of each width of board.

The holes are drilled through a pattern board to insure uniformity. *Drawing*, the next step in the manufacture is performed by clamping the drilled stock to a table, and passing a loop of brass wire through the first hole in the first row, inserting a tuft of bristles and drawing on the wire so as to bring it to its place ; then inserting another tuft and so on. The bristles are then cut the requisite length. The drawing wires are covered with veneering to strengthen and improve the brush ; it is then finished with a spoke shave and scraper, sandpapered and varnished. Brushes are also made by machinery. Woodbury's brush-making machine will make an ordinary scrub brush in one minute ; as the holes do not pass through the wood no back is required.

Buckwheat, (*Fagopyrum esculentum*) an annual plant, with purple stem two to four feet high, much branched. It is a native of Asia, and is believed to have been introduced into Spain by the Moors. It is now largely cultivated in the temperate regions of Europe and America. It grows well on poor soil, matures rapidly, but is very sensitive to the frost. The crop is sometimes raised for the purpose of ploughing it under as a manure, and also for the flowers which serve as a bee pasture ; but the honey is of inferior quality.　But the principal use of the crop is in producing of flour from the seeds ; it furnishes a white flour, from which a popular gruel is made in Germany and Poland.　In some parts of France, it is made into a dark bread and also cakes.　In this country and England the flour is almost entirely used in the making of breakfast cakes, or buckwheat cakes as they are commonly called.　It forms an extremely nutritious diet for winter consumption, but if used in excess is apt to cause eruptions on the skin.

Butter, no article is of more importance to the retail grocer than good butter, and it is a difficult matter to maintain a standard grade, unless it is the product of a factory.　Butter is the fatty substance extracted from milk, in this country the milk being that from the cow. The composition of the milk and consequently of the cream varies with the breed, age, and food of the cow, all of which circumstances must be taken into consideration in the making of butter.　When milk is allowed to stand, the globules of fat rise to the surface and form a layer of cream.

Dr. Voelcker gives the composition of cream as follows :

Fat (butter)	33.43
Caseine	2.62
Sugar	1.56
Salts	0.72
Water	61.67
	100.00

To procure the cream for the manufacture of butter, the milk is placed in a cellar at a temperature of from

55° F. to 60° F. After the cream rises, which takes place in from twenty-five to thirty-six hours, it is skimmed off and put into a stone jar until sufficient cream is accumulated to perform the process of churning. Care should be taken not to keep the cream too long, as it impairs the quality of the butter, giving it a cheesey taste. The process of *churning* consists of a violent agitation of the cream by means of a dasher, which causes the fat globules to unite in larger masses, and finally to separate entirely from the watery residue called butter-milk. No form of churn has yet been invented which is superior to the old-fashioned dasher churn. From forty-five minutes to one hour should be occupied in churning. If the butter comes much sooner it is apt to be frothy, and if much longer it is apt to be badly flavored. The butter is then washed in cold water, thoroughly worked or kneaded to expel the water, and made into rolls or prints when required for immediate use. If it is desired to be kept some length of time, it is packed in stone jars or wooden firkins ; the latter being preferable for shipping, which will contain, generally, 56 or 100 lbs. of butter. About one ounce of salt is used to a pound of butter for packing purposes. Only the purest salt should be used, such as the Ashton or Syracuse salt, made expressly for dairy use. Sometimes sugar and saltpeter are added to increase its keeping qualities. At the Orange County factories in New York, the following receipe is used : For every 22 pounds of butter, 16 oz. of salt, one tea-spoonfull of saltpeter, and a table-spoonfull of the best powdered white sugar. Butter made from cows fed on rich pasture, is of a deep yellow color. Hence poorer butters

are often colored with annatto, turmeric, or the juice of
carrots.   Manufactured butter has the following average
composition.

Pure fatty matter - . -	83.00
Water - - - - -	12.50
Common Salt - - - -	3.50
Milk Sugar - - - -	.60
Caseine and Albumen - -	.40
	100.00

The most common way of adulterating butter is by the
addition of an excess of salt, or water is allowed to remain in too large amounts.   The rancidity of butter is
due to the development of *butyric acid*, readily recognized by taste or smell, both being equally offensive.

ARTIFICIAL BUTTER.   A large factory is now in operation in New York for the manufacture of this butter, or
"oleo-margarine," as it is called.   Butter contains the
three fats, oleine, palmitine and stearine.   The same is
true of suet, with the exception of less oleine, and by removing the excess of palmitine and stearine, a mixed fat
remains, of the consistence of butter ; this fat or oleo-margarine is then poured into a churn, while still liquid, with
about half its volume of fresh milk and nearly as much
water.   A little annatto is then added for coloring and the
whole is then churned, yielding a sweet, palatable butter
which is treated in the same manner as ordinary butter.
This butter is difficult to distinguish from the genuine article ; it is cheap, clean, healthy and equal to genuine
butter ; but on account of prejudice is not used extensively as yet.   In New York a law has been passed compel-

ling all parties selling this butter to label it as " oleo-margarine."

Butternut, is the fruit of *Juglans cinerea,* a beautiful tree of from 20 to 30 feet in height. The fruit is oblong and clammy. The nut is thick furrowed and sharply ridged, and about two inches in length. The kernel is sweet and pleasant, but from its abundance of oil soon becomes rancid unless well dried. The half green fruit gathered in June, and with its down removed, is used for making pickles.

Cabbage, a well known garden vegetable and a variety of *Brassica oleracea,* a member of the mustard family. The other varieties of this species are the cauliflower, broccoli, borecole and brussels sprouts. The original of all these varieties grows wild on the rocky shores of England and in this condition has no appearance of a head. The cabbage is distinguished into two kinds according to the period of ripening, as early and late cabbage. Of early cabbages the best are the Early York, Jersey, Wakefield and Early Winningstadt. Of late ones we have the Drumhead, Flat Dutch, Mason, Drumhead Savoy, and Red Dutch. The cabbage is a biennial plant, during the first season perfecting its growth, and in the second the seeds are produced, when the whole plant perishes. As an article of food, cabbage is not very nutritious, but eaten cold in the form of a salad it is very wholesome.

Camphor, is a concrete, volatile product obtained from many different plants, especially those of the Laurel family. The greater part of the camphor of commerce is obtained from the camphor laurel or camphor tree (*Camphora officinarum*) a native of China, Japan, and Formosa and which has been introduced into the West Indies and Java. The tree grows to a large size, has evergreen leaves, yellowish white flowers in panicles and a fruit somewhat resembling a black currant. All parts of the tree possess the odor of camphor, and yield this article when cut into small pieces and distilled. The process is conducted in large iron kettles furnished with dome-shaped covers in which is placed a quantity of straw. The wood of the tree cut into chips is placed in the kettles together with a small quantity of water, and a moderate degree of heat applied when the camphor is vaporized, and rising is condensed upon the straw placed for the purpose in the tops. After separation from the straw, it is packed and sent into market constituting the crude camphor of commerce. This has to be further purified before it is fit for most uses to which it is to be applied. The art of refining was long monopolized in Europe by the Venetians and afterward by the Dutch. The crude article is introduced together with about 1-50 of its bulk of quick lime into iron retorts, over which are placed sheet iron covers connecting with the retort by a single small opening. A number of these retorts are placed in a sand-bath, and the temperature raised until the melting point of camphor is reached, when they are kept at a uniform temperature that the process may go on quietly. The lime takes up the moisture which would otherwise interfere with the condensation of the camphor vapor which takes place in the cover, and from which the pure camphor is removed in the form of a circular cake having a hole through its centre.

Borneo or Sumatra camphor, also called hard camphor, is obtained from the *Dryobalanops camphora* a very large tree, native of Sumatra and Borneo. The camphor is found in the solid state in fissures and cavities in the heart of the tree, from which it is obtained by felling the tree and splitting it into small fragments, from which the gum is picked by means of a sharp pointed instrument. It is sometimes found in masses as large as a man's arm, but usually in small particles, the largest trees rarely yielding more than twenty pounds of the crude material, whilst many trees contain none at all. The gum is of better quality than the common officinal camphor, and the Chinese ascribe to it marvelous medicinal properties, and will pay for it from fifty to one hundred times the price of ordinary camphor, for which reason it is almost never seen in Europe or America, being all consumed by the Chinese. The same tree produces, when young, a pale yellow liquid known as oil of camphor, which is generally supposed to be the camphor before acquiring by age a concrete state. It is considered valuable as an external application for rheumatism.

The composition of camphor is represented by the formula $C_{10}H_8O$. Its specific gravity is 0.987; its melting point 288° F., and it boils at 400° F. It is a semi-transparent, white substance crystallizing in hexagonal plates. It is soft, friable, but tough, being difficult to reduce to powder. It is very slightly soluble in water, but readily soluble in alcohol, ether, chloroform, and the essential oils. It has a somewhat bitter and pungent taste, a strong, fragrant, and highly penetrating odor which is exceedingly noxious to troublesome insects; and it is consequently much used in preserving specimens in natural history, as well as clothing, furs, etc. Exposed to the air it quite rapidly vaporizes. It is highly inflammable, burning with much smoke and light. Camphor is used in medicine internally and externally as a stimulant; in small doses it is an anodyne and antispasmodic, in large doses, it is a narcotic poison. Its alcoholic solution, and liniments in which it is an ingredient, are much used as external applicants for sprains, bruises, chilblains and chronic rheumatism. The importation of crude camphor into the United States, in 1875, amounted to nearly 1,000,000 pounds.

Canary-seed, is the product of the canary grass, *Phalaris canariensis*, a native of the Canary Islands. It is cultivated for its seed in England and Continental Europe; it is also sparingly cultivated in the United States. The seed is used as the food of cage birds. In the Canary Islands it is used by the natives as an article of food, as it contains a large quantity of farina which is very nutritious. Of imported canary seed there were consumed, in 1875, 49,217 bushels.

Candles, are made from tallow, wax, spermaceti, paraffine and other fatty substances formed into small cylinders round loosely twisted wicks and used for portable lights. They were formerly prepared chiefly from tallow and spermaceti by the process known as dipping. The wicks were first dipped into the warm semi-fluid tallow until saturated and then lifted and hung upon frames until cold when they were again dipped, and the process continued until the desired size was reached. This process has been replaced by that of moulding, in which the melted material is poured into moulds of tin or other metal, or glass, in the centres of which the wicks have previously been stretched. Wax candles have been found difficult to mould on account of the wax adhering to the interior of the moulds; they are consequently made by dipping, and by pouring the wax over the wicks, until a sufficient thickness is obtained, and then forming the candles by rolling between marble or hard wood slabs. They are also sometimes formed by drawing through a machine constructed for the purpose, much as wire is drawn. It has, however, recently been found that wax candles may be moulded by the use of glass moulds, which, when the candles are to be withdrawn, are dipped for a moment in warm water which causes the glass to expand sufficiently to loosen the candles and allow of their being readily extracted. The best candles in common use are made of spermaceti. This substance is found ready formed in the head cavities of the Sperm whale, existing there mixed with oil in a liquid form, which when removed becomes a white crystalline mass consisting of a liquid oil and a white solid, which is the pure spermaceti. The oil is removed by placing the mass in hempen bags and subjecting them to heavy pressure, after which the spermaceti is further purified by boiling with lye, and sometimes by other means, before being used for candles. Great improvements have been made in the manufacture of tallow candles since the investigations of M. Chevreul and others have led to a knowledge of the composition of animal and vegetable oils and fats. These consist of several distinct kinds of fats of different degrees of fusibility, chiefly oleine, stearine and palmitine, which are compounds of the fatty acids, oleic acid, stearic acid and palmetic acid, with a peculiar base called glycerine. The base glycerine adds but little to the inflammability of the acids with which it is combined. Oleic acid is a fluid oil at ordinary temperature, and its presence in the tallow adds fluidity and a tendency to run, whilst stearic and palmitic acids are solid and when freed from glycerine and oleic acid form a most excellent material for candles. Such a mixture of stearic and palmitic with also usually a quantity of margaric acids is known in commerce as stearine.

A method of obtaining stearine free from oleic acid and glycerine was first successfully employed by Messrs. De Milly and Motard in 1831, and in 1873 the manufacture had grown to such proportions that 130,000 tons of this article was prepared in Europe. The process as at present conducted consists essentially in first decomposing the fats into fatty acids and glycerine, by a continuous automatic commingling of water and steam with the fats under a pressure of ten to twenty atmospheres during a period of from twelve to twenty hours. Other methods of decomposition are however in use: e. g., by treating with superheated steam and lime, by digesting with sulphuric acid, etc. After the decomposition is effected the oleic acid is removed by placing the crude material in strong sacks and submitting it to heavy pressure between metallic plates in a hydraulic press. The remaining mixture, principally stearic and palmitic acids, is the well known stearine of commerce, and is ready for manufacture into candles. Pure stearic acid melts at 158° F. and palmitic acid at 140° F. Commercial stearine melts at

130° to 132° F. Candles made from this material are known as Stearine, Adamantine, Belmont sperm, or from the fact that they were first manufactured near the *Barriere de l'Etoile* in Paris they are recognized the world over as *Bougies de l'Etoile* or star candles.

Paraffine has recently been largely introduced in the manufacture of candles. By itself paraffine makes a candle of great beauty, but is objectionable from its too great fluidity and liability to droop in warm weather; when however from five to twenty per cent. of stearine is added to it, candles are produced having the appearance of wax and but little more fusible than are stearine candles. Paraffine is also largely used for "breaking the grain" or preventing crystallization in stearine candles.

Stearine, paraffine and wax candles are made of almost any color by the use of aniline colors of the desired tint.

The character of the wick is of great importance in the manufacture of candles, and much care is needed to adjust the size of the wick to the weight of the candle and to determine the character of wick which shall give the best results with each variety of candle made. Various devices have been employed to induce the complete combustion of the wick and obviate the necessity for removing the charred end which decreases greatly the light obtained by "snuffing." Cambacérès, in 1825, introduced a system of plaiting and twisting the wicks so that when burning the free end should be deflected in such a way as to bring it to the outside of the flame and into contact with the air where its complete combustion can take place. This system is still in use; the wicks are made of plaited cotton woven by a machine which lays up eighty or ninety strands in such manner as in burning to cause the wick to open at top and spread out to the edge of the flame. Wicks are also made of two parts twisted in opposite directions and wound with a fine thread. In burning they untwist and deflect the end of the wick outward. A twist is also sometimes given to wicks by winding them round a small cylinder, and in this condition saturating them with the melted stearine. When the candle is burned the wick uncoils, thus carrying the end to the outer side of the flame. A more important discovery, however, was that of De Milly, that by soaking the wicks in a weak solution of boracic acid the formation of a mushroom of unconsumed wick might be entirely prevented. The wicks are soaked for two or three hours in a bath holding in solution one and one-half per cent. of boracic acid and one and one-half per cent. of ammoniac sulphate, after which the wick is dried and singed in a lamp flame to remove the little filaments of adhering cotton. This discovery has been of great importance to the candle-making industry, increasing as it does to a great degree the value of the candles and the extent to which they are used.

Canning. The preserving of fruits and vegetables by the process of canning has of late years reached to an almost incredible amount. Domestic canning has become a necessary part of household economy, but the canning for market is what is of interest here. Canning for market is conducted on a large scale, and such is the division of labor and the employment of machinery that the products can be turned out at very low cost. These factories generally put up a variety of fruits and vegetables, so as to be in operation during the whole season.

In all canning operations the exclusion of the air from the cans is of the greatest importance and all the operations tend to this end. In all these factories a large number of people are employed and the operations are rapidly conducted. In some of the peach canning factories the fruit is piled on the upper floor and thrown into hoppers and conducted to tables on the lower floor, and the cans filled by placing them under the hopper and pressing the fruit in with the fingers. The cans are then passed to another table where syrup—about one pound of sugar to the gallon of water—is filled in and time given to allow the air between the peaches to escape. The cans are then cleaned from the syrup spilled on the sides, and passed to the tinmen who put on the circular covers, rapidly soldering them down. Each can has a small hole in the top to allow the air to escape and after the cover is on this hole is soldered up. The cans are then placed in a rack and lowered into a tank of water which could be heated by steam. As the temperature increases the imperfect cans can be told by the escape of air and are taken out. The water is then raised to boiling which is continued for half an hour, more or less, according to the size and kind of the peaches. After being boiled the cans are allowed to cool slightly, and are then vented by opening the prick hole in the cap, which allows the steam to escape, and immediately closing it again, when the cans have cooled if all right, the head will snap in by a slight pressure showing that there is a good vacuum, The cans are then placed in the store room and labels put on them when sold. In canning tomatoes they are first slightly scalded so as to remove the skin, and when peeled are thrown into pans to allow some of the watery portion to drain off. They are then packed in cans and a little syrup added, made of water, sugar and salt. They are then sealed, tested and boiled as above described. The canning of corn is more difficult though similar in operation. The corn is boiled, cut from the cob, put into cans, and the spaces being filled with a little syrup of sugar and salt, the can is soldered tight. The cans are then boiled in a solution of chloride of calcium, or refuse from salt works ; this solution has a much higher boiling point than water. After being boiled for several hours the cans are taken out and vented, again soldered up and returned to the bath for another boiling of several hours duration, when they are taken out and the process is complete. The canning of all fruits and vegetables has a general resemblance to the above process, varying of course in the details, and in the kind of materials canned. The number of articles canned for food is very large and constantly increasing ; all kinds of fruit, vegetables, meats, many kinds of fish, oysters, etc., etc., are now in the market and find a ready sale.

Caper, the common name of the pickled flower buds of *Capparis spinosa* of Southern Europe and Barbary. It is generally found wild on walls and rocks ; it is found growing on the walls of Rome, Sienna and Florence, and is especially cultivated in the south of Europe ; but our greatest supply is from the island of Sicily. In the early part of summer the plant begins to flower, and they continue to appear successively till the beginning of winter.

The young flower buds are picked every morning, and as they are gathered they are put into vinegar and salt ;

this operation continues as long as the plants are in a flowering state. When the season closes the buds are sorted according to their size and color, the smallest and greenest being the best. These are again put into vinegar and then packed in jars and are ready for sale and exportation.

Caraway Seeds are the fruits of *Carum Carui*, a plant of the family Umbellifereæ, and cultivated in Europe and America for its aromatic seeds, which are used for flavoring purposes in cooking and confectionery.

Carrot. (*Daucus carota*). The common carrot is a biennial plant, a native of the East, but now naturalized in this country. It is cultivated for its root which is of a deep yellow, and is much used in soups and other culinary preparations. A French variety of carrot, quite small, is put up in cans and jars and to some extent imported into this country. Carrots are raised principally as food for animals.

Cassia is furnished by *Cinnamonum Cassia*, a tree growing from forty to fifty feet in height, and cultivated in China and other eastern countries as well as in Brazil. The China cassia is the best of all the cassias. The bark resembles true cinnamon, but is thicker, coarser and is used to adulterate the true article. Cassia bark is distinguished from cinnamon by being more brittle, and of less fibrous texture ; it is not so pungent and has more of a mucilaginous or gelatinous quality.

Cassia Buds are the dried flower buds of the cassia tree. The best come from China and are round, bearing some resemblance to a clove but smaller, and have a rich cinnamon flavor. Of imported cassia, there were consumed for 1875, 1,665,636 lbs.

Castor-oil, *Oleum ricini,* a fixed oil obtained from the castor-oil plant, (*Ricinus communis*). The plant is a native of Asia, but has become naturalized in most warm parts of the earth. It varies much in size and habit ; in Africa it is a tree, whilst in Europe and the Northern United States, it is an annual, growing but from three to ten feet in height. It is often cultivated in gardens, where it is very ornamental from its stately growth, large palmate-paltate leaves and glaucous purple stems. The seeds are about the size of a small bean, oval, the surface smooth, shining, and beautifully marbled. The oil is obtained from the seeds by heat or pressure, or by both combined. It is of better quality when obtained by pressure without the aid of heat, and is then known as cold pressed oil. The quality also depends upon the greater or less maturity of the seeds, and the variety of the plant from which they are obtained. In India large quantities are extracted by boiling the seeds, but the oil is dark in color, irritating, and unfit to be used in medicine, but is extensively used there as a lamp oil. When pure, castor oil is of a light yellow color, slightly viscid, the best being almost limpid, of nauseous odor and oily taste. The best castor oil is one of the mildest of purgatives ; in doses of one or two tea-spoonfuls it is a gentle laxative, whilst a dose of a table-spoonful will almost always open the bowels freely. The chief objection to its use is its repulsive taste. Some attempt to obviate this difficulty by floating it upon hot coffee, or spiced syrup, or by making it into an emulsion with liq-

uor potassae and spicing; others take it in " soda water."
The manufacture of castor oil is extensively carried on in
St. Louis; the beans being grown in Southern Illinois
and Missouri.

Catsup, Catchup, or Ketchup is made from tomatoes,
mushrooms, or walnuts, by boiling until soft, rubbing
through a fine sieve, and seasoning to taste with a variety of spices and condiments. It is put up for market
either in bottles, or in bulk.

Cauliflower, a well known garden vegetable: a variety of *Brassica oleraceœ*. Unlike its nearly related varieties its leaves are not the parts eaten; but the parts used
are the flower buds, and the stalks of the plant transformed by cultivation into a compact, rounded head, of a
white color, and of a delicate flavor. Besides being boiled for the table, it makes excellent pickles, and is almost
always found in the mixed pickles of the shops. Two
crops of cauliflower may be raised during the season, one
in June and the other in the fall.

Caviare, an article of food prepared from the roe of
large fishes, especially the sturgeon. It is chiefly made
in Russia, though it is made to some extent in this country and exported. In the process of manufacture, the
roe is thoroughly cleaned from its membranes, mixed with
salt, and the liquor pressed out. It is then dried and
packed for sale. The best kind, which is most thoroughly
freed from the membrane, is packed in kegs, while the
inferior is made into small cakes. It is largely consumed
in Russia, Italy, Greece and Turkey.

Cayenne, a commercial product derived from *Capsicum* a genus of plants belonging to the Night-shade fami-

ly, and has no relation to the family which furnishes the real pepper. Cayenne pepper is derived from four species, viz. : *C. annuum*, *C. frutescans*, *C. cerasiforme*, *C. Groisum*. The first two only are of importance. The first is an annual herbaceous plant, a native of tropical countries, growing in very poor soil, and cultivated in most parts of the world. It grows two or three feet high, and bears a pod of a conical form, recurved at the end, green when immature, but bright scarlet or orange when it ripens. It is used in the green state for pickling, and in medicine when ripe, dried, and ground into powder to make cayenne pepper. In England, the dried berries kept in the shops are called *chillies*. This variety is imported from the West Indies, as well as raised in our own gardens. *C. Frutescans* furnishes the so called bird or guinea pepper, a hotter and more pungent, as well as a better flavored variety. The plant is a shrub, with berries scarcely an inch long and quite narrow. The berries are used in making pepper vinegar, or pepper sauce. In Mexico and other warm countries of this continent, the red pepper is almost one of the necessaries of life. The common people living mostly upon vegetable food, use this stimulant freely, and it forms an accompaniment to every meal. The cayenne of commerce is shamefully adulterated. Red lead and vermilion, or sulphuret of mercury, are the worst materials introduced, both being deadly poisons, and having the property of aggregating in the system, when taken in small quantities. They are added to keep up the color, and also to increase the weight. Ochres are employed for similar purposes ; salt also to improve the color, and add to the weight. Ground rice and turmeric are more harmless additions. The popular varieties of pepper, cultivated in our gardens, are the Bull Nose, an early variety of mild flavor, and used in the crude state, and for pickling; the Squash pepper, the sort most generally grown; Sweet mountain, large and of mild flavor, and used to make stuffed pickles.

Celery. (*Apium graveolens*). A vegetable grown for the succulent and spicy petioles of the radical leaves, which are used as a salad. In order to render them palatable they require to be blanched, which is accomplished by ridging the plants with earth till they become whitened. The smaller or dwarf varieties are much superior to the large kinds. It is sometimes marketed as early as August but reaches its prime late in the season. Celery has a sweetish and aromatic taste and deserves to be more widely used as an article of food.

Ceresin wax, Fossil wax, a general name for several distinct mineral hydrocarbons of the general formula $Cu H_2n$ of which one, Agucerite, has recently assumed considerable economic importance as a substitute for beeswax, which in physical properties it much resembles. Ozocerite is found in large deposits in connection with the coal measures in Galicia in Spain and at Gresten in Austria, which deposits have, since 1872, been extensively explored and the ozocerite industry is already attaining large proportions, a single establishment in Vienna having facilities for working up 6,000,000 pounds of the raw wax annually. It is used for all purposes to which beeswax is applied and from its higher melting point, 140° F, it is capable of being applied to many uses to which the former is not adapted.

Chalk is a soft, friable, earthy mineral, consisting chiefly of carbonate of calcium. It is entirely of animal origin consisting in part of the finely ground remains of shells and corals and the excrement of shell fish and certain gregarious fishes but principally of the shells of microscopic marine animals of which by far the most abundant are the rhizapods. According to Ehrenburg a cubic inch of chalk often contains more than a million of these minute organisms. Chalk is very abundant in England occurring in immense rock foundations and constituting cliffs of great height along the shores of the North Sea and the English channel. Chalk is burned in great quantities and used for lime. Whiting or Spanish white consists of finely powdered chalk which has been carefully purified and its harder particles removed. Chalk when thoroughly purified is used in medicine as an absorbent in diarrhœa and as an antacid; and also as a dentrifice. Cylindrical crayons for drawing upon the black-board are made in great quantities from chalk ground and formed into a paste, to which consistency is given by adding small quantities of gum or wax. Any desired color is given by the addition of various pigments. The paste is then run into moulds where it is allowed to solidify when the crayons are removed, packed with sawdust in small boxes and sent into market.

Cheese, is the compressed curd of coagulated milk consisting of the caseine and butter with part of the water and salts of the milk, together with any coloring matter and salt, which may have been added in the process of manufacture. Caseine plays an exceedingly important part in the manufacture of cheese and is apparently much the most abundant constituent, but in " whole -milk" cheese, it exists usually in less quantity than the butter. An analysis by Volcker of an average sample of good milk gave :

Water, - - - - -	87.30
Butter, - - - - -	3.75
Caseine, - - - - -	3.31
Milk, sugar and extractive matter, -	4.86
Mineral matters, (ash) -	0.78
	100.00

The cheese made from this milk had the following composition :

Water, - - - - -	37.85
Butter, - - - - -	28.91
Caseine, - - - - -	25.00
Extractive matter, lactic acid, etc., -	4.91
Mineral matter, containing common salt, -	3.33
	100.00

The proportion of butter in cheese is subject to very great variations due to the richness of the milk, and the method of manufacture. Caseine is the coagulable element in milk, and belongs to the group of albuminoid or proteine compounds which compose the principal part of the nitrogenous material of plants and animals. The process of cheese-making consists essentially of gently warming the milk, and causing the curd to coagulate by the use of some acid, and the separation of the whey by draining, and finally forming the curd into a fine mass by pressure in suitable moulds. The variations of the details of this process, are however, almost as numerous as the number of manufacturers. In Holland the milk is coagulated by Chlorhydric acid, whilst in this country and England, the dried rennet or fourth stomach of the calf, is used for this purpose. The rennet is prepared for use by long continued steeping in brine, or whey, which has been previously boiled, to free it from albuminous matter. The brine liquor is considered better if left to stand for weeks before being used. Much the greater proportion of cheese, in this country, is made at factories which are owned or supported by an association of farmers, and which use the milk of from one hundred to upward of fifteen hundred cows each. The process of cheese-making adopted in the factories is in a general way usually nearly as follows :

The evening's milk is kept in coolers during the night, at a temperature of about 60° and in the morning is added to the morning's milk, the whole being then placed in a suitable vat, and raised to a temperature of from 80° to 100° F., by means of a warm water bath. When the milk has reached the desired temperature, a sufficient quantity of rennet is added to cause the milk to coagulate in about forty minutes : some makers add, at the same time, a quantity of sour whey, to facilitate the development of lactic acid which is held to prevent the species of fermentation which results in the formation of gaseous and other objectionable products. When the curd has become sufficiently firm to divide with a smooth fracture, when the finger is drawn through it, it is cut by means of curd knives, one set having perpendicular, and another horizontal blades, into cubes of from $\frac{1}{4}$ to $\frac{1}{2}$

inch in diameter, in order to hasten the separation of the whey. After standing fifteen or twenty minutes the curd is broken into still smaller pieces, by an instrument called the wire shovel breaker, and the temperature is still further raised, and, soon after, the whey is drawn off and the curd heaped in one end of the vat to drain. It is now allowed to stand until it becomes quite coherent, forming a partially solid mass which is next cut into thin slices, and allowed to cool, and as it becomes more firm it is broken up, and turned and stirred, care being taken not to handle whilst still so soft as to cause the buttery particles to be removed with the whey. In about an hour from the time the whey is drawn off it should have become cooled to about 70° and have become of a peculiar mellow, flaky appearance, which can only be judged of by experience, when it is, by some, placed in a hoop and gently pressed for ten or fifteen minutes to express more of the whey and arrest the process of fermentation. It is then taken out and broken into pieces about the size of peas, by means of the curd mill, after which it is salted, about two and a half or three pounds of salt being used to one hundred pounds of curd, with which it must be very thoroughly incorporated. After salting the curd is again placed in a hoop and subjected to quite heavy pressure for from twelve to twenty hours when it is removed, and the sharp edges pared away; after which it is carefully bandaged with cotton cloth, turned, and again placed in the press, where it is subjected to still heavier pressure preferably for one or two days longer, though in many of our factories the cheese is kept in press no more than twenty-four hours altogether. The temperature at which it is placed in the press is of very great importance, for if too high, gaseous fermentation takes place rendering the cheese very porous. Many of our factory cheeses are injured in this way. The temperature at which Chedder cheeses are placed in the press, is always between 60° and 65° F., and this point is considered by the makers, as of prime importance in the production of good cheese.

Very great care is needed to preserve the most perfect cleanliness in all parts of the process in cheese making, milk being such an exceedingly sensitive fluid as to absorb with the greatest readiness any taint, not only with which it may come in contact in the containing vessels, but which may exist in the air. The air of the dairy should accordingly be pure and cool, and all vessels used should be scalded in boiling water as soon as emptied, and if possible frequently allowed to stand in the direct rays of the sun. After the cheese is pressed, it is taken to the curing room, where it is rubbed thoroughly with fresh melted butter, and is then turned once a day, and repeatedly rubbed with butter until it is cured. The curing room should be kept at a constant temperature of about 70° and should be but dimly lighted, not only for the purpose of excluding flies, but to avoid the chemical action of light upon the curing cheese, at the same time it should be well ventilated and the air kept pure.

Aside from the "whole milk" cheese whose production we have described, there are many "skim milk" cheeses made at the creameries and elsewhere in this country, in which the evening's milk is set, and the cream skimmed from it in the morning, and used to make butter, whilst the skimmed milk is added to the morning's milk and made into cheese. Skim milk cheese is also made from milk all of which has been skimmed, but it is hard and of very poor quality. It is largely manufactured, however, in England, and is used by the laborers in some countries as a substitute for, and to the almost entire exclusion of meat.

Cream cheeses are sometimes made of pure cream, as the famous Neufchatel made in France, of cream thickened by heat, and compressed in a mould. It is esteemed a great delicacy, but is difficult to preserve in good condition. Cream Chedder is made by adding the cream from one milking, to the whole milk of the next in the proportion of one quart of cream to ten of milk, and the whole is then treated much the same as in the process of making whole milk cheese, but is handled with still greater care and when placed in the hoop is pressed by its own weight only being turned four or five times a day until sufficiently firm to be bandaged and taken to the curing room.

All varieties of cheese are frequently colored, annatto being very commonly used to give an orange yellow color, while many English cheeses are given a greenish hue, by the use of sage and various kinds of grass. Of the more famous varieties of cheese the Chedder, Gloucester, Stilton and Wiltshire of England; Gonda, Edam and Limburg of Holland; Gruyere of Switzerland; and Neufchatel and Bris of France, are among the more noted, all of which are, however, successfully imitated in this country, those sold under these names although usually of American manufacture are perhaps equally good and frequently very difficult to distinguish from the imported. In 1872, it is estimated that 2,000,000 pounds of Limberg cheese were made and sold in this country. Cheese itself, especially when taken in considerable quantities, is generally considered, and without doubt justly, to be difficult of digestion, but when taken in small quantities it is undoubtedly an aid to the digestion of other and especially rich varieties of food. It accordingly forms a very proper accompaniment to dessert. The amount of cheese produced annually in the United States is about 200,000,000 of pounds, much the larger portion of which is made in factories, of which there are upward of two thousands.

Cherries, the fruit of many different trees belonging to the Rose family, genus Prunus. Cultivated cherries are of many varieties and come from two distinct species, (*Prunus aviura* and *P. vulgaris*) both of which are found growing wild in the woods of England. Of the numerous varieties the Kentish or early Richmond, May Duke, Gov. Wood, Purple Guigne, Morello and late Kentish are among the most valuable. Cherries are a very useful dessert fruit, and are dried and canned extensively, and are also used in the manufacture of a variety of liquors.

Chestnut, (*Castanea vesca*) a very handsome tree found in Europe, Asia and North America. The tree attains a great size, reaching the height of sixty or eighty feet in fifty or sixty years. Its timber is very valuable and used for many purposes. The wood makes excellent casks and in this country is used in the manufacture of cigar boxes. The nuts are enclosed in a hard and prickly four-valved involucre; these burs contain from one to three edible nuts, often compressed or flattened on one or both sides. Chestnuts form an important article of food in some parts of France, and in many of the mountainous regions of Europe where wheat cannot be raised. The nuts are eaten either steamed, boiled or roasted ; they are sometimes kiln-dried so as to preserve them for seasons of scarcity. Ground and reduced to a powder they make good bread, and highly washed they make a good substitute for chocolate. A chestnut tree on Mt. Etna is said to be 200 feet in circumference ; and one in France is over 1,000 years old and is still very productive. The fruit of the American Chestnut is smaller than that of the Spanish and the kernels much sweeter. With us the chestnut flowers in June and fruits in October.

Chicory or **Succory**, (*Cichorium Intybus*) a plant belonging to the same family as the dandelion, and growing wild in most parts of Europe and especially in England. In some parts of the latter country it is cultivated and when well grown the roots resemble large white carrots. The yield per acre is from three to five tons. It is naturalized in this country and grows along the fences in fields and roads. It grows to the height of from one to three feet and bears quite a handsome blue flower. The root is the part for which it is cultivated, and is used as a substitute for coffee, and for adulterating it when roasted. After being dug the roots are washed and cut into pieces about half an inch in length and placed in a kiln to dry, after which it is placed in a revolving cylinder with the addition of a little butter and roasted the same as coffee. Its use in England is legalized for the adulteration of coffee but the packages must be marked mixture of coffee and chicory. Notwithstanding its cheapness, chicory itself is adulterated with carrots, turnips, oak bark tan, mahogany, sawdust, etc. By a chemical analysis, it has been found that chicory has but few of the qualities of coffee, and when used alone is often very deleterious to the system. In the year 1875, there were imported of chicory in its various forms 4,561,545 pounds at an average value of about four cents per pound.

Chocolate, a substance used as a beverage and prepared from the seeds of the cacoa, (*Theobroma cacoa.*) a tree native of South America, Mexico, and the West Indies. The tree is an evergeen and grows to the height of from twelve to sixteen feet. The fruit of the cacoa resembles a cucumber and is five or six inches in length, and about three in diameter, and contains twenty to forty beans, arranged in five rows in the pinkish white pulp. Their size is about that of the sweet almond. The fruit matures for gathering in June and December. It is at first of a dark green color, and dull red on the side next the sun; but as they ripen the green turns yellow and the dull red becomes more bright and lively. They do not all ripen at once, but for three weeks or a month in a season. The overseers of the plantations go every day to cut those that are turned yellow; they are then laid in heaps till they have heated and are then opened by hand, the seeds extracted and spread out on mats in the sun to dry. Before the Spaniards landed in Mexico, the natives made a sort of beverage of the seeds and flavored with allspice or vanilla. From them the Spaniards introduced it into Europe. The Mexicans called this drink *chocalat* from which we derive our word chocolate. In manufacturing chocolate the beans are slightly rosted in an iron cylinder similar to that used in roasting coffee. After roasting they are cooled, freed from their husks by sifting and fanning. They are then reduced to a paste by trituration, at a temperature of 130° F., in a mortar or a mill, and the paste is then mixed with from one half to equal quantities of sugar and a small quantity of vanilla bean added for flavoring ; the proper temperature having been observed, it is turned into moulds and formed into cakes and rolls of various shapes. Chocolate is used in solution with hot water as a breakfast beverage. The addition of milk does not injure but rather improves its quality. Good chocolate is smooth, firm, soluble, aromatic, not viscid after having been boiled and cooled, but oily on the surface and leaves no sediment. Chocolate is often adulterated with rice meal, oat meal, flour, potato starch, roasted hazel nuts, etc. All of.these adulterations may be determined by means of the microscope. The *cacao nibs* of commerce are the bruised and broken seeds of the cacao, but the mass is more difficult of solution than chocolate. *Cacoa* shells, improperly spelled cocoa, is the thin shell or pellicle that covers the beans, and which is separated before they are ground and powdered. These shells are used as a substitute for chocolate and are preferred by many. In the year 1875, there was imported in this country, cacoa, in the form of crude, leaves and shells, 5,216,556 pounds, valued at $ 583,011. *Broma*, is the name given to a certain preparation of chocolate.

Cider. This is the juice of the apple, either unfermented or fermented, and is largely manufactured in this country and Europe. The process of manufacture is very simple. The apples are ground in a mill, the pulp subjected to pressure, and the expressed juice is stored away in barrels; its further treatment being similar to that of wine. Vinous fermentation converts the sugar of the juice into alcohol. Fermented cider contains from 5 to 10 per cent. of alcohol, and is intoxicating in its qualities. New or sweet cider is often boiled to a thin syrup, which may be preserved in bottles for a long time. With us cider is largely used in the manufacture of vinegar, and is the essential element in the manufacture of fruit butter. It is also said to be converted into champagne and sold for the imported article.

Cigars. A small roll of tobacco used for smoking. In the manufacture of cigars, the tobacco is first dampened in a trough, so that the water can run off. The first process is stemming the fillers, which is done by removing the midrib from the smaller and inferior leaves, the larger and whole ones being used for wrappers, and are stemmed in a similar manner. Cigars are composed of two parts; the wrapper and filler. The former must be a perfect, smooth leaf, while the latter is simply the pieces which are made into a bundle, and forms the interior of the cigar. In hand made cigars, the operation is essentially as follows: taking a leaf in his hand, the workman spreads it out before him on a table, smoothing it carefully to remove all creases; then with his knife he cuts it into a peculiar, nearly semicircular shape. He then picks up the material for his filling in his left hand, making it into a kind of bundle; this operation requires considerable experience to get the right amount. As soon as he has enough leaves, he presses them together and lays them on the wrapper before him. Then by a peculiar sort of twist, he brings up the edges of the latter, and with a quick roll envelopes the loose bundle; the form of the cigar is at once apparent. He now finishes off the end for the mouth, by carefully trimming the leaf, and smoothing it to a point; fastening the extremity with a little paste; the other end he cuts off smooth; a few more rolls between his flat knife and the table, and the cigar is done. A good workman will make from 200 to 400 in a day. After the cigars are finished they are sorted by workmen into different lots according to their color, or strength, each grade being known by a specific name, viz:

Madura.

Madura Colorado.

Colorado.

Colorado Claro.

Claro.

Madura is the darkest and strongest, and the Claro the lightest and mildest. Flor, applied to cigars means "flower," or the best of tobacco; below this comes *bueno*, good, and superior. A *concha* is a short, thick cigar. *Espanado* takes its name from the ribbons with which it is tied, being red at the end of the bundles and yellow in the middle, making the colors of the Spanish (*Espanol*) flag. *Partagos*, are a long cigar. *Regalia*, indicates a large sized cigar, finely made, and usually high priced. In regard to the filling, they are said to be long fillers, or scraps; Havana fillers from Havana tobacco.

Cigars are also made by machinery. A machine cuts the tobacco into wads of cigar length from a chute filled

with leaves; these are pressed into moulds, and afterward wrapped by machinery. The tip is finished separately, and the end cut square off. Cigars are adulterated
by using other material than tobacco, such as various
kinds of leaves and brown straw paper. In using the
latter, it is soaked in the juice of tobacco stems and other
waste, rolled, veined and printed with spots to imitate the
natural leaf; in this state it is used both for fillers and
wrappers. It is said this paper tobacco is shipped to
Havana, where it is converted into cigars and returned to
this country as genuine Havana cigars. *Cigarettes* are
small cigars, or fine tobacco rolled in paper.

Cinnamon. True cinnamon is produced by *Cinna-
momum Teglonicum*, a member of the Laurel family, a
tree twenty to thirty feet high and twelve to eighteen
inches in diameter. It is a native of Ceylon, but is now
cultivated in South America and the West Indies. The
whole plant has the same aromatic properties that is
found in the bark; the root yields camphor by distillation. The bark is obtained from the branches of four
or five years growth, and of from one half an inch to
three inches in diameter. The bark is removed from the
branches by making longitudinal incisions, and is then
taken off in strips. The strips are placed one above the
other in parcels eight or ten inches thick and allowed to
ferment by which process the pellicle and green bark
are easily removed and the inner bark remains. As this
dries in the sun, it rolls up in the form of quills, the
smaller being packed into the larger. Good cinnamon is
known by the thinness of the bark, the thinner and more
pliable the finer the quality; when it is broken the frac-

ture is splintery. The tree is raised from the seed and produces bark in five or six years. Two crops are gathered in a year, one in May and June, and one in November. These trees sometimes attain the age of two hundred years. Most of what is sold for cinnamon, in our markets, is simply cassia. The amount of true cinnamon consumed in the United States for the year ending June 30, 1875, was valued at $4,013 while that of cassia was $279,250 or nearly seventy times the amount of cinnamon.

Citron, the citron of our shops is the preserved fruit of *Citrus medica*, a tree closely related to the orange and lemon. The citron is a native of Asia, but is extensively cultivated in Southern Europe. The fruit is frequently as much as six inches long, ovate, uneven on the surface, and with a protuberance on the top. The curing of the citron is briefly as follows : it is first pickled to extract the bitter flavor and absorb the oil, then boiled and placed in a solution of sugar until it becomes saturated, when it is placed on racks to dry. It is then packed in thin boxes for the market, known as quarter and half boxes. There are a number of varieties of citron, and the fruit of some reach the weight of twenty pounds. In its native country it is constantly in bloom, and fruit and flowers are found hanging on the trees together.

Clams, a name affixed to many bivalve mollusks of different genera. The common clam of the United States, (*Mya arenaria*) is much used for food, and is considered one of the greatest delicacies furnished us by the sea. It is dug from the sands of the shore, between the limits of high and low water, being usually found at a depth of from six to eighteen inches. It is found also in Europe and Asia, and upon the shores of Alaska. The round clam, or quahaug (*Venus mercenaria*) is also largely used for food, but is much inferior to the preceding. The clam loses, to a great degree, its delicacy of flavor by any method of preservation, and is consequently rarely shipped or used, otherwise than fresh from its sandy bed. They are however, to some extent, put up in cans, shipped in cold weather and sold in our markets.

Clover Seed, seeds of the plants of the genus Trifolium, of the order Leguminoseæ, including numerous species, several of which are common and very valuable. All of the species have herbaceous, more or less procumbent stems, with trifoliate leaves, and flowers borne in roundish heads, or oblong spikes, and seeds in pods containing one and rarely three or four seeds each. The most important and valuable species is the common red clover (*Trifolium pratense*) a native of Europe, but which is grown extensively in all temperate climates, as a forage plant. The seed should be sown in very early spring usually in connection with some cereal crop as wheat, barley, oats, etc., when it will furnish a full crop the second year. This is cut first when in full bloom in June for forage when a second growth comes rapidly forward and ripens its seeds in September. The first crop if allowed to ripen, rarely produces any seed and is much injured for forage. Clover has in recent years acquired additional importance from its value when plowed under as a means of preparing the soil for the growth of winter wheat.

White clover (*Trifolium repens*) is a native of America,

and is found in fields and open woods everywhere. It is invaluable for pasturage and mixed with grasses is exceedingly desirable for lawns. It is also one of the most valuable of honey producing plants. Alsike clover (*Trifolium Hybridum*) has recently been introduced into this country from the south of Sweden and has attracted much attention. Buffalo clover (*Trifolium reflexum*) native of our western plains is worthy of greater attention.

Cloves, are the dried unexpanded fruit buds of a small tree, the *Carophyllus aromaticus* of naturalists. It is a native of the Moluccas but now cultivated all over the East Indies, and also in the West Indies, Guiana and Brazil. The flower buds are gathered by hand or beaten with rods so as to fall upon cloths which are placed under the trees to receive them ; they are either dried in the sun or by the heat of a fire. They are slightly smoked so as to give them a uniform brown color. The fruit, which is a dry berry, also contains aromatic properties and appears in market under the name, mother cloves. Water extracts the odor of cloves, with comparatively little of their taste. The aromatic qualities of cloves depend on an essential oil which may be obtained by distillation with water, and is sold as the oil of cloves. The value of the cloves consumed in the United States for the year ending June 30, 1875, was $ 213,965, and the number of pounds was 1,235,572.

Cocoa-nut, the fruit of the *Cocos nucifera*, a tree of the palm family, and one of nature's richest gifts to man. Without this tree the islands of the Pacific Ocean would be uninhabited, and the uncivilized races of the tropics would be left to perish of hunger and thirst, without clothing or shelter. The tree delights in regions bordering the sea shore, and attains the height of 60 or 100 feet or more, with a crown of leaves at the summit. Every part of the tree is useful to the natives. It furnishes them with their food, with cooking utensils, their dwellings, their clothing, their medicines, their ornaments and their drinks. The fruit is a very important product of this tree. When it acquires full size it is filled with a white liquid, generally called milk, but which in reality is the albumen in a liquid form. When the fruit has attained maturity, this milk is absorbed, or becomes hard, and forms the hard, white, solid albumen which we eat in this country. Each tree yields from 80 to 100 nuts yearly and will continue to bear during two generations of men.

DESICCATED cocoa-nut is the prepared albumen of this nut; water, sugar and carbonate of soda being used in its preparation, the process being a patent. It is put up in packages and sold as shelf goods. It is largely used in making puddings and pies.

MACERATED cocoa-nut is prepared from the same fruit by boiling till in a semi-fluid state, and scaling in cans. It is used for the same purposes as the above.

Cod, a genus of soft rayed fishes belonging to the family *gadidae*, characterized by an elongated smooth body, compressed towards the tail; three dorsal fins; ventral fins pointed; abdominal line white; two fins behind the vent; the lower jaw with one barbule on the chin. In North America there are found eight species. The American cod (*Marrhua Americana*) is found along the New England coast from New York to the St. Lawrence River. The color of the back in the living fish is a light olre green, becoming pale ash in dead specimens, covered with numerous reddish or yellowish spots ; the lower part being a dusky white, but the colors of the species vary considerably. They sometimes reach a weight of over one hundred pounds, their average weight being about eight pounds. The common or bank, cod (*M. vulgaris*) well known as an article of food is taken on the Grand bank, in the deep water off the coasts of New Foundland, Nova Scotia, and Labrador. It is a thick, heavy fish sometimes reaching a weight of 90 pounds. The color varies considerably but is generally a greenish brown, fading into ash in the dead fish, with numerous reddish yellow spots ; the belly is silvery opaque white, the fins pale green and the lateral line dead white. The tom cod is a small species, found along the coast from New York to New Brunswick. It is caught from wharves and bridges, by almost any bait ; it is from 6 to 12 inches in length. The cod is abundant along the North Pacific coast, especially in the region of Alaska. It is also plentiful on the west and north shores of Norway and Sweden, and on the south-west of Iceland. It is an exceedingly voracious fish, devouring indiscriminately everything in its way in the shape of small fish, crustaceæ, etc.

The cod is very prolific, and specimens of the female have been caught with upwards of 8,000,000 eggs ; but as only a small portion of these are fertilized and a still smaller portion ever reaches maturity, the numbers remain about stationary. The cod is of slow growth and is about three years of age before it begins to propagate. The exhausting of the cod fisheries is a question of much interest ; but as yet there is no perceptible decrease in the

bank fishcries after three and a half centuries ceascless
fishing. But it is claimed that at certain points in the
shore fisheries there is beginning to be a scarcity of the
fish. These fish are not migrative as was once supposed,
but merely move from the feeding to the spawning
grounds, and from deep to shallow water. It seems that
the cod lives in colonies in certain places adapted to them
and here they live and die without mixing with the adjoining colonies. In fact the peculiarities of the fish enable it to be told from what particular locality it is caught.

Cod fishing is an important branch of industry; the
cured fish finding a ready sale in all parts of the world.
The great resort of the American, Nova Scotian and
French fishermen is the Grand Bank of New Foundland,
and the banks east and south-east of Nova Scotia; the
most western of these banks being known specifically as .
the Western Bank. Massachusetts ranks first in its cod
fisheries, Maine coming next. Gloucester is the great
fishing port of the country. South-east of Massachusetts
is a fishing bank known as George's Bank, from which
we derive our Georgia Bank cod. The cod is taken by
means of a hook and line, and on favorable occasions a
single man will take from 300 to 400 in a day. Most of
the Massachusetts vessels use trawls which are set and
hauled periodically. The trawl consists of a long line,
anchored and buoyed at each end, with hooks, generally
several hundred in number, adjusted at intervals. The
trawlers use fresh bait, herring, mackerel, or squid.
The hand-liners use salted clams for the first part of the
season, but afterwards obtain squid. The fish when
brought aboard the vessel are dressed and sealed in the

hold. Upon arrival home they are taken out, washed and dried on flakes or platforms of wickerwork on the shore. The process of dressing them is reduced to a system, and is performed with great rapidity. The throater, usually a boy, cuts the throats and rips them open ; the header removes the entrails and the head ; the splitter splits the fish, removing a portion of the back bone ; while the salter piles them in tiers and sprinkles them with salt. The dried fish are sold by the quintal of 112 pounds. Codfish are sometimes cured by being kept in a pile for two or three months, after salting, in a dark room, covered with salt grass, after which they are opened and again piled in a compact mass for about the same length of time. They are then known as dun fish, from their color, and are highly esteemed. From the liver of the cod, oil is obtained, which is useful in pulmonary complaints. The tongue and sounds are frequently preserved in pickles. From the sounds, preserved and dried, isinglass is obtained.

BONELESS COD is a form prepared for market by taking out the bones, and packing them in boxes, in strips or in rolls. Much of this form of fish is inferior in quality and consists of the hake and haddock, fish closely related to the cod. Dried haddock may be distinguished from the cod by its lateral line being black, that of the cod being white. The number of persons engaged in the cod fisheries in the United States is from 12,000 to 15,000, and in Canada and New Foundland from 40,000 to 50,000. The quantity of cured cod brought in by American ships for the year ending June 30, 1875, was 756,543 cwt., valued at $ 3,664,496. The fishing grounds on the high seas are free to all nations, but the coast and river fisheries are regulated by special treaties.

Coffee, the name applied to the seeds of the plant *Coffea Arabica*, and also to the beverage prepared from the infusion of the seeds in boiling water. It is a native of Abyssinia where the plant grows wild in great profusion and has been in use from remote times. It is now naturalized in many tropical countries. The coffee-producing region is widely distributed, the principal countries being Brazil, Java, Ceylon, Sumatra, the western coast of India, Arabia, Abyssinia, the West Indies, Central America, Venezuela, Guiana, Peru, Bolivia, Mexico and some of the Pacific Islands. The plant is an evergreen, with opposite, shining leaves, and white, fragrant flowers, which grow in clusters in the axils of the leaves. It reaches a height of 20 feet, but in cultivation is kept down to about five feet, by pruning, to increase its productiveness, and for convenience in gathering the fruit. The plants are raised from seed in nurseries, and when a year old are transplanted and set out in rows. They begin to bear fruit at three years of age, but do not acquire maturity till the fifth year; the trees continue in bearing for twenty years. Where the climate is dry abundant irrigation is necessary, and the water is shut off as the fruit begins to ripen as its quality is thereby improved. The coffee tree blooms for eight months in the year, so that the ripe coffee may be gathered at almost any season; but the real harvests are two and sometimes three in the course of a year. The fruit when ripe becomes red and finally purple. It much resembles our red cherry, and the fleshy portion surrounding the seeds is sweet and palatable. Each berry contains two seeds; the flat sides are opposed to each other in the centre of the pulp and are separated by it and by the tough membrane which closely envelopes them both. Sometimes one seed is abortive and the remaining one then becomes round. As the fruit dries the pulp forms a sort of shell or pod, which is removed by a process of curing in order to prepare the seed for market. In the West Indies the fruit is picked by hand at intervals during the seasons of harvest; but in Arabia where no rains prevail which would beat it from the trees, it is allowed to remain till nearly ready to fall, and is then shaken off upon cloths spread upon the ground; its perfect ripeness may be one reason of its superior quality. In the West Indies and South America the curing is usually performed by exposing a layer of fruit several inches in thickness to the heat of the sun so that fermentation takes place. When the moisture has disappeared the dried fruit is passed between wooden rollers, and sometimes pounded in wooden mortars, and the pulp is then washed away. The tough membrane is separated after the seeds are dry, by a similar process, with a pair of heavy rollers. The chaff is next removed by winnowing. The following is a description of the gathering of the crop in Ceylon.

" In the height of the crop the fruit is taken to the pulping-mill at mid-day, and again in the evening. The task given to the Coolie is to bring a bushel of berries at each collection. From good bearing coffee trees, some quick hands will gather as much as four bushels a day, for which, of course, they get extra pay. The cherries are very much like our cherries, and it would puzzle most people to distinguish a heap of coffee berries from the edible fruit. Instead of the stone, as in our cherry, the coffee fruit contains two seeds. These coffee beans are enveloped in a thick, leathery skin which gets the name of parchment. After the thick pulp has been removed, the seeds are left in a cistern till such time as fermentation sets in ; the mucilage is easily worked off, and the coffee is then in a fit state to be carried to the drying ground. The drying of the coffee is a most important process ; a shower of rain will discolor the bean, and depreciate its value much. A constant watch must therefore be kept for the signs of rain clouds, and dreadful is the noise and hurry when such appear and threaten in a few minutes to break over the precious parchment coffee on the barbecues. When thoroughly dried the parchment is put into the bushel bags and dispatched to Colombo. It there undergoes another drying preparatory to being relieved of its husk, which is done by being placed in circular troughs, where heavy rollers touch the coffee sufficiently to break the skin without injuring the bean. The coffee is then sized, that is, the large beans, the medium size, and the small are separated. This is done for the sake of having an equable roasting. A small bean would be burnt into charcoal by the time a large one was sufficiently roasted. This is a very important point and much care is given it by the Colombo merchant who undertakes this part of the preparation for market. The quality of the coffee depends very much on the district, and the elevation at which it has been grown. The greater the elevation, the finer the quality. Maturalto has long been famous for the superior quality of its coffee, and the plantations are all upwards of 4,000 feet above the sea level."

The use of coffee was introduced into Persia from Ethiopia as early as A. D. 785, and into Arabia from Persia about the fifteenth century. In 1554 it is said to have been publicly sold in Constantinople and reached Venice in 1615. The first coffee-house was opened in London, in 1652, by a servant of a Turkey merchant, and at the close of the century, the annual consumption of coffee reached to one hundred tons. Its culture was introduced into Java by the Dutch between 1680 and 1690, and it was then extended throughout the East Indian islands. In 1720, it was introduced into Martinique, where it succeeded so well that in a few years all the West Indies could be supplied. In some places an infusion of the raw coffee is used as a beverage, but the general custom is to have it roasted, which developes its aromatic properties. The ob ject therefore of roasting is not only to render it friable, so as to be easily ground, but to create or develope this aromatic, volatile oil, and care is required to limit the operation so that the good effect of the latter may not be destroyed by burning the substance of the bean. The roasting is effected by placing a quantity of coffee in an iron cylinder, which is slowly turned round over a fire so that all the beans may in turn be exposed to the same heat. The natural color of the bean is a dull pale green ; (coffee beans are often artificially colored and polished to improve their appearance) but it acquires three colors in roasting, yellowish brown, chestnut brown and black. The first is not considered sufficient, and induces a loss of 12½ per cent. in the weight, and the loss is increased in the chestnut brown to 20 per cent., and in the black to about 23 per cent; 112 pounds of raw, when fairly roasted, will yield 92 pounds of roasted coffee.

The composition of raw coffee is as follows:

Caffeine,	-	-	-	-	0.8
Casein or legumin,	-	-	-	13.0
Gum and sugar,	-	-	-	15.5
Fat and volatile oil,	-	-	-	13.0
Mineral matter,	-	-	-	6.7
Coffeo-tannic acid, }	-	-	-	5.0
Coffeic acids, }	-	-	-	
Woody Fibre,	-	-	-	34.0
Water,	-	-	-	-	12.0

Roasted coffee contains about 1 per cent. of caffeine and a small proportion of volatile oil and tannin. The proper degree of roasting is that of a chesnut brown, and when the color approaches to a black it gives a burnt, dry flavor to the infusion. After roasting, coffee deteriorates by exposure to the air, and should be kept in tight cans. It may be injured by absorbing the odor of other substances, and even raw coffee is liable to be damaged in the same way; a few bags of pepper have been known to spoil a whole cargo of coffee. It is a singular fact, that the same peculiar principle is found in the three great beverages of the world, viz. tea, coffee and chocolate, and the same principle is recognized in those plants used as a substitute for tea. This seems to suggest that it has a peculiar adaptation to the wants of the human system. In coffee this principle is called caffeine, in tea, theine, and in chocolate theo-bromine.

The annual consumption of coffee in England is about one pound per head; in the United States, eight pounds, and in Holland and Germany, it is fourteen pounds. The best coffee of commerce is the Mocha, and next to this the Java. Mocha coffee is brought from Arabia; the seed is small, yellowish, and often almost round, which is caused by the frequent abortion of one of the two seeds, the one that is left assuming the shape of the berry. It is packed in large bales, each containing a number of smaller ones, and when good appears fresh and of a greenish olive color. Much of the coffee sold under the name of Mocha is produced in the East Indies and Brazil; it is sent to Mocha and then reshipped as the genuine article. It is estimated that one half of the coffee exported from Brazil, is consumed in Europe as Java, Ceylon, Martinique, St. Domingo and Mocha. Prof. Agassiz says of the coffee of Brazil: "More than half of the coffee consumed in the world is of Brazilian growth; and yet the coffee of Brazil has little reputation and is even undervalued. Why is this? Simply because a great deal of the best produce of Brazilian plantations is sold under the name of Java or Mocha, or as the coffee of Martinique or Bourbon. Martinique produces only six hundred sacks of coffee annually. Gaudaloupe whose coffee is sold under the name of the neighboring island, yields six thousand sacks, not enough to supply the markets of Rio de Janeiro for twenty four hours, and the island of Bourbon hardly more. A great deal of the coffee which is bought under these names or under that of Java, is Brazilian, while the so called Mocha coffee is often nothing but the small, round beans of the Brazilian plant found at the summits of the branches and very carefully selected.

JAVA coffee is distinguished into the pale yellow, which is new and cheapest, and the brown, which is old and more valuable. The seeds of the Java are of good size, and the suture quite large. At the Centennial exhibition in Philadelphia, coffee from Brazil was exhibited as "Imitation Java," which is the kind commonly sold in our markets; it differed materially from the Java coffee on exhibition from the Dutch East Indies. *Bourbon* coffee is larger and not so round as the Mocha. *Martinique*, is large, long, and of a greenish color, covered with a silvery skin which comes off in roasting. *St. Domingo* coffee is very irregular, has rarely any skin covering it, and is of a pale green or whitish color. In the commercial quotations, a large number of coffees are quoted by names applied to them according to the port from which they are shipped, or the country in which they are raised. Brazilian coffee is generally sold as *Rio* and is commonly divided into the following grades; Fancy, Choice, Prime, Good, Fair, Ordinary and Common.

The total amount of coffee imported into the United States in 1875 was 317,970,665 lbs., and its value was $50,591,488. The consumption of coffee for the same year was 317,017,309 lbs., valued at $50,414,320.

The chief countries from which coffee was imported into the United States in 1875, were as follows:

COUNTRIES.	POUNDS.	VALUE.	PRINCIPAL PORTS OF EXPORT.
Brazil,	229,701,637	$ 35,099,274	Rio Janeiro.
Venezuela,	25,781,256	4,498,140	Laguyra and Maracaibo.
Dutch East Indies,	16,883,358	3,258,121	Batavia.
Central Amer. States,	11,932,157	1,885,631	San Juan de Nicaragua.
Hayti,	9,545,410	1,584,484	Santa Dom. & P't au Prince.
U. S. of Colombo,	5,446,992	950,976	Cartagena.
British W. I. and Brit. Hond.,	3,433,250	528,517	Kingston and Truxillo.
Dutch W. I. and Dutch Guiana,	3,295,401	597,967	Paramaribo.
British East Indies,	3,113,381	519,776	Acheen and Colombo.
Mexico,	2,691,889	485,489	Vera Cruz.

Coffee Extract. A preparation largely sold to be used in connection with coffee. The compounds are generally patented, and one we had analyzed was composed of chicory, burnt bran and molasses. A genuine extract of coffee may be prepared from an infusion of coffee, but the patent compounds lack the genuine article.

Confectionery, a term of wide significance and embracing all preparations which have sugar for their basis or principal ingredient. Under this definition would come fruits preserved in sugar, jams, jellies, pastes, etc. ; but we can here only notice the branches of the manufacture of sugar preparations, such as lozenges, comfits, etc., which now constitute an extensive industry. The simplest form in which sugar is prepared as a sweet for eating is in the form of a lozenge. They are prepared from refined sugar, ground to a very fine powder, mixed with dissolved gum, and flavored with essential oils, or other ingredients. In the making of these lozenges on a large scale the operations are somewhat similar to those used in biscuit making. The fine loaf sugar is ground to an almost impalpable powder between a pair of millstones, after which it is mixed with dissolved gum-arabic sufficient to form a very stiff dough, and the whole is then thoroughly mixed by machinery. The doughy mass is then reduced to a uniform cake by repeatedly passing pieces backward and forward between a pair of heavy metal rollers, the surfaces being kept from adhering by being dusted with starch flour. The cake is then transferred to a piece of tough wet paper, and passed by an intermittent motion under a frame of cutters of the size and form of the lozenge to be formed. These punch out and take up the lozenges, and when the tube of the cutters is well filled, the whole frame is turned over and the cut lozenges emptied into a tray. The trays are then placed in heated apartments, and the lozenges allowed to harden These lozenges are colored and flavored with a great variety of ingredients which are added in proper portions with the dissolved gum.

Hard confections, or comfits, constitute the second leading variety of confectionery. To make these a core or centre is necessary and may consist of some seed, or of a small lozenge. Around this centre successive layers of sugar are added till the required size is attained. The cores are placed in large copper pans or vessels which are geared to revolve at an inclined angle, so that by their revolution their contents keep constantly in motion, tumbling over each other. The copper pans are kept revolving by steam or other power, and are kept hot by a steam jacket or double casing into which steam is admitted. A pure strained syrup of sugar is prepared, a quantity of which is periodically applied to the contents of the pan as they appear to get dry, and after receiving a certain coating the comfits in process of manufacture are removed for some time and allowed to dry and harden. The comfits thus receive alternate coatings and dryings, till they attain the proper size, when they are finished with a coating of thin syrup, which may be colored if required, and long friction in the pan. They are then hardened in a drying apartment and are fit for use. For the core or centre of these comfits a great variety of seeds is used, as almonds, caraways, coriander, cloves, cassia, and perfumed cherry kernels.

Sugar candy is prepared from a solution of sugar boiled to the point of crystallization. It may be prepared from either brown or refined sugar, to the latter cochineal or some other coloring ingredient being added. These solutions, when boiled to a proper degree, are poured into moulds, across which at sufficient intervals are stretched pieces of strings. The sugar gradually crystallizes from its solution on the sides of the mould and on the strings—it being in the meantime kept in an apartment heated from 90° to 100° F. When sufficiently deposited the remaining liquor is drained off, and the crystals removed and dried in a high, uniform heat. Sugar drops are made from fine sugar mixed with a small portion of water, and coloring and flavoring material as desired. The mixture is dissolved by heat but not allowed to boil, and is then poured in separate drops on a sheet of paper, on which they quickly set and harden.

What is termed boiled sugar, that is sugar which has been boiled until cooling and hardening it assumes a glassy appearance and fracture, is the basis of another variety of confectionery. Of this class *barley sugar* is the type and simplest example. It merely consists of sugar boiled as above indicated, flavored, cut into strips and rolled or twisted into sticks. Boiled sugar is prepared in various fancy forms by passing it while still in a viscid condition through small machines in which pairs of brass rollers having patterns sunk in the surface, stamp these patterns into the material. It is also worked up in the form of balls, plaited into coils, and formed into many-colored sticks, etc. Most of the candy now manufactured is largely adulterated with starch, plaster, etc. The coloring matter is cochineal for red, and various dyes and pigments for the other colors, most of them being poisonous in their nature.

Copperas, Green Vitriol, the commercial names for the hydrated protosulphate of iron ($FeSO_4$ 7 H_2O). It occurs in pale green prismatic crystals which are very soluble in water. It is largely used for dyeing black and in the manufacture of common black writing ink; and is also valuable as a disinfectant. It is usually produced by dissolving iron in dilute sulphuric acid, filtering and evaporating the solution and setting it aside to crystallize. Large quantities are made in this way from the refuse sulphuric acid which has been used in the refining of petroleum. It is also largely obtained from the oxidation of native sulphides of iron, or pyrites, which after being roasted absorb oxygen spontaneously from moist air and are slowly converted into copperas.

Coriander Seed. The fruit of *Coriandum Sativum*, a low annual plant of the south of Europe. It is of very easy cultivation, and is used for flavoring curries and other culinary preparations. In 1875 there were consumed in the United States 881,103 pounds of coriander and caraway seeds.

Cracker, a hard biscuit. In the manufacture of plain and fancy biscuits, the operations are largely carried on by machinery. The mixing of the dough and water, the kneading, the rolling out, the cutting and panning, are all done by machinery; and in the patent ovens the biscuit is gradually carried through on a traveling stage. The rate at which biscuits of different sizes and degrees of richness must travel the whole length of the oven, varies from about 5 to 45 minutes, and the temperature of the oven is modified to suit the various qualities. There is an endless variety in the form and composition of plain and fancy biscuit. In the making of fancy biscuit, milk, eggs, sugar, butter or lard, and flavoring essences are extensively used, and in these cases the proportion of the various ingredients are roughly mingled before being put in the mixer. In the richest class of biscuit the dough for which is necessarily soft, they are cut by hand, and fired on trays in common ovens. Cracknells are made without either milk or water being used to mix the dough, eggs alone being employed for the purpose; certain proportions of butter, sugar and sesquicarbonate of ammonia, are added to the mixture of flour and eggs, and the dough is baked in the usual way. Many other varieties of biscuits are rendered light and spongiform by the use of the sesqui-carbonate of ammonia or of carbonate of soda with sour milk. Many hundred kinds of plain and fancy biscuit are manufactured and named from the kind of flour used, or the flavoring, or as fancy may dictate.

Cranberry, (*Vaccinium Macrocarpum*) is cultivated for its fruit, which is a small, red, acid berry. The plant is a shrub and grows best in lowlands where there is plenty of decayed organic matter. The cranberry is almost exclusively a northern plant. In northern Europe it has been highly appreciated for centuries, and immense quantities are annually brought into the English markets from Russia and Sweden, in addition to those produced in Britain. The first settlers in this country found such an abundance of cranberries that there was no necessity for cultivation ; but about 40 years ago the demand became so great that attention was turned to its cultivation. It is now extensively raised in the region of Cape Cod, Mass., in New Jersey and in Wisconsin. The three varieties recognized in the markets are the cherry, bugle and bell varieties. The best of the cherry varieties are very dark colored.

The soil required for cranberry culture is usually found in low peat bogs, where the requisite amount of water can be applied as necessary. A deep ditch is dug around the bed to drain off the water so that the ground may be cleared. This is accomplished by clearing off all trees, logs, brush, etc., and burning them on the ground and scattering the ashes. Some cultivators remove all of the surface soil to the depth of six inches or a foot and fill in with sand. The whole bed is made level and is surrounded by an embankment so that it can be flooded when necessary. After the plants are up, the bed must be kept clean for two or three seasons when the plants will be so thickly grown as to prevent other vegetation from springing up. The water is let on the beds at the approach of winter and should be deep enough to keep the plants from freezing. The fruit ripens in October and is sometimes gathered by means of a rake, but is mostly picked by hand. The berries are packed in crates and barrels and shipped to all parts of the country. Those shipped to Europe are packed in small kegs filled with water, or in bottles. The cranberry can also be cultivated on the uplands and considerable experiments are being made in that direction.

Craw Fish, a species of crustacea of the genus *asta-*

cus, and resembling the lobster, but smaller. It is esteemed as a very delicate food, and is eaten fresh or preserved by canning.

Cream of Tartar, Acid Tartrate of Potassa, a compound existing already formed in the juice of the grape and in other vegetable juices. Its chemical composition is indicated by the formula $K H C_4 H_4 O_6$. In the juice of the grape it is held in solution by the saccharine matters present, but, as it is less soluble in alcohol, when the sugar is transformed into alcohol by the process of fermentation it is deposited in the casks forming an incrustation upon the inside of the wine barrels, which, when removed, constitutes the *argol* or crude tartar of commerce. Argol is imported from wine producing countries, the best coming from Italy and the south of France. It is the source from which we obtain tartaric acid and the various tartrates. Commercial argol contains from 5 to 45 per cent of tartrate of lime and other impurities, including some of the coloring matter of the wine, rendering it red or white according to the kind of wine from which it was deposited. It is refined by treatment with boiling water in which the cream of tartar dissolves and from which it crystalizes out upon cooling. It is then redissolved in water to which 4 or 5 per cent of pipe clay has been added to precipitate the impurities, after which the clear solution is drawn off and evaporated until crystallization again takes place. Thus prepared, cream of tartar consists of colorless, rhombic crystals which usually contain from 2 to 5 per cent of tartrate of lime. It has a pleasant acid taste, and is quite freely soluble in water. It is quite extensively used in connection with bicarbon-

ate of soda as a substitute for yeast in bread raising.
(See Baking Powder.)   It is also used as a mordant in
dyeing wool and to some extent in medicine.   Cream of
tartar as found in market is adulterated to a frightful degree.   Prof. Chandler says, that in samples purchased
from several grocers in New York in 1872, flour, chalk,
alum, sawdust, clay, gypsum and sulphate of potash,
were found to have been used for this purpose.   Gypsum
was found in many cases in great quantity and of one
sample constituted as much as 70 per cent.   In samples
analyzed for this work by Prof. Robert Kedzie of Lan-
sing, Mich., over 79 per cent. of common plaster was
present ; and this is the stuff sold for cream tartar !

Cucumber, (*Cucumis sativus*).   Our common cucumber is a native of Middle and Southern Asia, and its culture dates from earliest times.   In the form of a pickle
it is an important article of food in Europe and the
United States.   The small, young cucumbers made into
pickles, are known as Gherkins.

Currant, a name applied to certain species of shrubs
of the genus Ribes ; the name currant was applied to them
from their resemblance to the Zante currants.   The red
currant (*Ribes rubrum*) is a native of Europe, Asia and
North America, and is extensively cultivated for its pleasant acid juice.   It is extensively used for the making of
jellies and conserves, and is often manufactured into wine.
They are dried for market and also canned in the green
state.   The black currant is *Ribes nigrum*, but it is not
much cultivated as yet in this country.   The number of
varieties of currants in cultivation is very great ; they are

propagated by cuttings and are of easy culture. It flowers in April and fruits in June and July.

Currants, (from Corinth in Greece), a common name applied to the dried fruit of the Corinth grape. English or Zante currants are not true currants but a kind of small raisin, exported from Zante and the other Ionian Isles. They are simply dried in the sun on the ground, and then packed into casks. This accounts for the great quantity of foreign matter found among them. These currants are used in cooking as an ingredient in cakes and puddings. For the year ending 1875 there were consumed in this country Zante currants and others, to the value of $ 771,384.

Curry, Curry Powder, a very highly seasoned aromatic condiment, which is in universal use in India and the East, but which varies in composition with each manufacturer. It is usually so strongly pungent as not to be greatly relished in temperate climates. Simmonds' Dictionary of Trade Products gives the following as the composition of Ceylon curry : " A piece of green ginger, a few coriander and cardamom seeds, one dry capsicum pod, six or eight black pepper corns, two cloves of garlic, six small onions, half a cocoanut, half a lime, a small piece of turmeric, and half a dessert spoonful of butter, well mixed together." The following table contains five recipes for making curry :

Turmeric,	6	4	6	3	2
Black Pepper,	5	4	2	2	½
Cayenne Pepper,	1	1	...	¾	6
Ginger root,	...	2	3	...	½
Fenugreek,	3	2	...	1	½

Cumin seeds, ...	3	2	2	4	..
Coriander seeds, ...	...	6	8	12	6
Cardamom seeds,................	...	...	½	½	..
Pimento, ...	...	...	½	¼	¼
Cinnamon, ...	...	...	...	¼	¼
Cloves, ...	...	...	...	¼	1
Nutmeg, ...	...	...	...	...	½

Cusk, a fish belonging to the Cod family, characterized by an elongated body, a single dorsal fin extending the whole length of the back, fleshy ventral fins and one barbule at the chin. The American cusk is considered a distinct species from the European. The length of the fish varies from two to three feet or more, and it weighs from four pounds upward. It is generally taken on the middle bank with the hook, by the deep water cod fishers. In spring it is seen in the Boston markets, when it is less esteemed than cod ; but in winter it brings a higher price. The European species, called tarsk or tusk, is plentiful among the Shetland Isles where it forms quite an article of trade. It is caught, salted and dried, in much the same manner as cod, to which it is considered superior.

Dates, the fruit of the date palm (*Phoenix Dactylifera*) a tree growing native throughout the East and the greater part of Northern Africa, and which is cultivated in Spain, Portugal, Italy and Sicily. The tree grows to a height of from forty to eighty feet, but is easily ascended as the trunk is covered with cavities, left where fallen leaf stalks have become deta ched, having horizontal even surfaces, which form excellent rests for the hands and feet, making the tree as easy to climb as a ladder. The tree is diœcious, that is the male and female flowers occur upon separate individuals, and in Africa where the female trees are cultivated, the natives gather male flowers from the wild date trees and shake them over the female flowers when at maturity, the pollen thus distributed rendering the female flowers fruitful. The tree comes into bearing when from six to ten years of age, each female tree yielding annually about an hundred pounds of fruit.

There are many varieties of the fruit, varying much in size and quality. The fruit ripens in the tropics about the end of August, but in Spain and the northern limits of its cultivation, not until about Christmas. Dates form an extensive article of food in countries where it is native, many of the inhabitants of Persia, Arabia and Egypt subsisting almost entirely upon them. Upwards of two and a half millions of trees are registered and taxed in Egypt, where they constitute one of the important sources of revenue. The fruit is dried either in the sun or in ovens, and then buried in the sand for future use. They may be kept in this way for two or three years. They are prepared for market by pounding and pressing in large crates, in which form they are shipped, and form an extensive article of commerce. The tree furnishes many other articles of value. From the leaves are manufactured baskets, brushes, mats, coverings for the roofs and walls of houses, and innumerable utensils ; the stem furnishes timber for houses, fuel, fences, etc. ; the fibres from the base of the leaves are spun into cordage, whilst, when the heart of the leaves is cut, there exudes a thick, honey-like juice which by fermentation produces wine or vinegar.

Dandelion, a well-known plant of the order *Compositae*, with a perennial root and spreading, toothed leaves, which are sometimes bleached, and also used as a salad. Under cultivation the plants attain a large size, and are sold in the spring for a popular and much esteemed pot herb under the name of greens. The root is sometimes roasted and used as a substitute, or for the adulteration, of coffee.

Eels, a name applied to many elongated fishes of more or less serpentine appearance, but properly belonging only to members of the family *Anguillidæ*, of which the type is the common fresh and salt water eel (*Anguilla Bostoniensis* or *A. vulgaris*). This species has many varieties, some of which are by many writers regarded as distinct species. It inhabits both salt and fresh water, from the British provinces to the Gulf of Mexico, and is also found in European waters. It varies in length from twelve to thirty inches, is greenish or olive brown above and yellowish white beneath. It is a very voracious feeder, preferring for its feeding grounds muddy bottoms and extensive flats and shallows near the shore, where it is taken in great numbers with hook and line, by bobbing and spearing. In winter, eels bury themselves in the mud to a depth of about a foot, where they remain quite torpid, breathing scarcely at all, and taking no food until spring. While in this condition they are speared in great numbers, through holes cut in the ice. They are fine-flavored and make an excellent article of food, but from their snake-like appearance (though the resemblance is only in form, they being true fishes) many persons are strongly prejudiced against their use.

Eggs. This well-known animal product is of the utmost importance as an article of food, and is of universal use. The eggs of all birds may be used as an article of food, but our supply is obtained from the common fowl. The quality of an egg is no doubt influenced by the food on which the fowls feed, the richer the food the better the egg. The composition of all eggs is nearly similar, for there is always a white portion and a yolk, the former consisting of nearly pure albumen with water, and the latter of albumen, oil, sulphur and water. The weight of an ordinary fowl's egg is from one and a half to two ounces, while that of the duck is from two to three ounces. It is estimated that New York city consumes annually over 300,000,000 eggs, valued at over $ 6,000,000. The estimated value of the product of our poultry yards for one year is over $ 200,000,000.

There are several factories in this country that now manufacture what is known as *Desiccated eggs*, by a process of extracting the water, leaving the residue dry and of a mealy appearance. It is sent to market in cans, boxes and barrels. It answers all the purposes of fresh eggs in cooking, and may be kept for any length of time. As an article for winter consumption, or for use on journeys it must certainly come into extended use.

Egg Plant, (*Solanum Melongena*) an annual herbaceous plant belonging to the same genus as the potato and nightshade, is a native of India and Northern Africa. The plant grows to a height of about two feet, has a prickly stem and large ovate prickly leaves, flowers of a purplish color of some beauty, fruit a globose or egg-shaped berry about four inches in diameter, but varying much in size with the conditions under which it is grown. It is much cultivated and is a favorite article of food in India

and other warm countries and is also used to a considerable extent in the United States. The plant flourishes in
New Jersey, where it is extensively grown, but does not
do as well further north. It is sown in hot beds in March
or April and transplanted late in May or in June to a
warm, rich soil. There are several varieties of the plant,
producing respectively purple, white and red fruit. It is
prepared for the table in many different ways.

Epsom Salt, the common name for hydrated magnesium sulphate ($Mg\ S\ O_4\ 7\ H_2\ O$), so called from its having
been first obtained by evaporating the water of mineral
springs at Epsom, England. The commercial supply of
the salt is now chiefly obtained from sea-water and from
magnesian limestone. When sea water is used the
greater part of the common salt is first removed by evaporation and the remaining *bittern*, consisting chiefly of
magnesium chloride and magnesium sulphate, is boiled
down with the addition of sulphuric acid or sodic sulphate, by either of which magnesium chloride is converted
into sulphate. When magnesium limestone is used, it is
first calcined, and the lime and magnesia are then converted into hydrates by sprinkling with water, after which
both are converted into sulphates by treating with sulphuric acid, and, as sulphate of magnesia is much more
soluble than sulphate of lime, the separation is easily effected. An excellent quality of the salt is also made at
Baltimore and Philadelphia from the mineral magnesite a
silicious hydrate of magnesia. This is reduced to powder and treated with sulphuric acid, and the sulphate
thus formed is separated from the accompanying iron
and other impurities by crystallizing and separating and

washing the crystals. Epsom salt is also found in the form of an inflorescence incrusting the walls of caves, in many of our Western States. In the Mammoth Cave, Kentucky, loose masses of it like snow balls are found adhering to the roof. Epsom salt crystallizes in four sided prisms with reversed dihedral summits, having a specific gravity of 1.75. The crystals effloresce slightly in the air and those found in commerce are often deliquescent from containing magnesium chloride. They are soluble in about their own weight of water. In taste they are saline and bitter.

The salt is much used as a cathartic and, being mild and cooling, is well adapted to the treatment of fevers and inflammatory diseases. The average dose is one ounce, but its laxative action may be much increased by diluting it with a large amount of water, the same dose dissolved in a quart of water, producing a much greater effect than if dissolved in but a half pint. Owing to its nauseous taste it is most easily taken in "soda water" with lemon syrup. The action of many of the celebrated mineral waters depends largely upon the presence of this salt. The salt is frequently mixed with ordinary white-wash, it giving a fine pearly appearance to the walls. It also forms an excellent addition to starch for laundry use, materially increasing its stiffening properties. Epsom salt is frequently adulterated with sulphate of soda, the presence of which may be detected by dissolving 100 grains in water and precipitating with a boiling solution of carbonate of potash. If this precipitate when dry weighs less than 34 grains, sulphate of soda is probably present in fraudulent quantities.

Essence, as now used, is very loosely applied in its meaning. Sometimes it is equivalent to *fluid extract* or *volatile oil*, and at other times to strong solution, to *concentrated preparation*, to *infusion*, to decoction, and to tincture. Among the large number of essences now sold and used for flavoring purposes in beverages, perfumery or pastry, are the essences of apple, allspice, almond, bergamot, caraway, cedrat, celery, cinnamon, cloves, jasmine, jonquil, lavender, lemon, lemon peel, myrtle, nutmeg, orange, pear, peppermint, pineapple, rose, vanilla, verbena, violet, etc. Animal essences are those made from animal substances. Artiffcial essences are now manufactured by the skill of the chemist, from the petroleum compounds, and so closely imitate the natural flavor of fruits as to defy detection. Essences as commonly prepared are simply the solutions of the essential oils in alcohol; the oil is added to the rectified spirit and shaken till a uniform mixture is obtained; thus essence of lemon is simply a solution of the oil of lemon in rectified spirit; it may be still further diluted by the addition of water.

Extracts of Meat. These are prepared in two forms—in a thick semi-fluid state, and as a solid. The extracts are prepared by boiling down the flesh of animals so that thirty-two pounds of flesh are said to be required to produce one pound of Liebig's extract. During the process, all the fat and as much of the gelatine and albumen as can be extracted are removed from the solution of flesh, whilst the fibrine, being insoluble, is left behind. Hence there remain water, salts, osmazome and the extractives of flesh; or in general terms the flavoring matters and the salts of meat, thus leaving out all that is popularly regarded as nutritious. This substance varies in value according to the amount of water allowed to remain in it. The intense flavor of meat which it possesses is like that of roasted flesh, and is always the same. This substance is of but little value as a nutritive, as the nutritious portions have been removed and nothing remains but the salts and the flavor. But used as an addition to other food, or mixed with white of an egg, gelatine, bread and other cooked farinaceous food, it is of considerable value as a stimulant. The solid preparations contain a considerable proportion of gelatine, and do not putrefy, because the gelatine has been dried. On account of the presence of gelatine this is more nutritious than the semi-fluid form.

Fluid Meat is a preparation of lean meat which differs from the various extracts of meat, in its retaining the fibrine, gelatine, and coagulated albumen. This is effected by dissolving them as they would be in the process of digestion in the stomach, and thus both advancing them a stage in the process of digestion, and enabling them to resist decomposition. One pound of the fluid meat is obtained from four pounds of lean flesh, and assuming that all the nitrogenous compounds in the flesh, as well as the salts, are present in it, it must be a convenient as well as a valuable food. Fluid meat is prepared by the action of pepsin and hydrochloric acid upon lean meat, finely sliced, with the addition of water, at a temperature of 96° to 100° F., until the whole fibrine of the meat has disappeared. The liquid is then filtered, separating small portions of fat, cartilage, or other insoluble matters, and neutralized by means of carbonate of soda. It is finally evaporated to the consistence of a soft extract.

Farina. A name applied to any powdered cereal grains, and even powdered pulse. In a wider sense it includes all starchy foods prepared from various roots and stalks, such as arrowroot, sago, tapioca; as these substances abound in starch, starchy food is often called farinaceous.

Figs, the fruit of the *Ficus carica*, a deciduous tree of the Artocarpeæ or bread-fruit family, native of Asia and Barbary. The tree grows to a height of from fifteen to twenty feet and has a large, spreading top, resembling an apple tree, when grown in its native climes, but when grown in cold climates it is shrubby in habit and attains but a small size. It is thought by many that the fig tree is a sort of anomaly in nature bearing its fruit without ever producing any blossoms. The error has arisen from the peculiar manner in which its flowers are produced, they being borne upon the inside of a hollow receptacle which first appears in the axils of the leaves and in form much resembles a little bud. Upon being cut open this will be found to contain a large number of minute apetalous flowers each bearing both stamens and stigmas. When the flowers have become impregnated, the enclosing receptacle, which has been at rest for some time, begins again to increase in size, becomes sweet, succulent, very pulpy, and, when ripened, constitutes the edible portion of the fig. The seeds formed from the development of the flowers are to be found in large numbers upon the inside. This so called fruit is accordingly like the strawberry, not a true fruit but a peculiarly developed edible receptacle upon which the true fruit is borne, not as in the strawberry upon the outside but upon the inside. The tree produces two or more crops in a season, the first from the axils of the leaves of the preceding year, and a later and longer continued one from the axils of the leaves of the season. In warm climates the second crop is much more abundant and valuable ; they receive the name of summer figs and are the ones chiefly exported. The fig is cultivated in warm, temperate climates, but can be well ripened only where the summer and autumn are warm and dry. It is grown throughout southern Europe and to some extent even in England. In the eastern United States the great difficulty encountered in its cultivation is the severity of the winters which sometimes kills the trees as far south as Florida.

It may, however, be successfully grown if afforded winter protection. There are several varieties of figs, comprising fruits which are white, brown, green, and yellow in color. The brown Turkey, white and brown Ischia, and white Marseilles are among the more valuable varieties. Fresh figs form a very important article of food in many parts of the Levant and of Africa. For exportation they are dried in the sun or in stoves and are known as " natural" when not compressed in packing but retaining their original shape, or as "pulled" when after drying they are made supple by kneading and then packed by pressure into drums or boxes. " Eleme" figs are merely those of a superior quality, so called from a Turkish word meaning hand-picked. In packing the best quality of figs a few bay leaves are placed in the top of the box to exclude insects. Until recently nearly all the figs used in the United States and Great Britain were grown in Turkey, Smyrna being the great fig mart from which they were exported. For the year ending September 30, 1877, there were consumed in this country 5,889, 011 pounds of figs, valued at $398,982. Recently however California figs have become of much importance in commerce.

Filberts, the nut of the European Hazel (*Carylus Avellana*) a shrubby bush growing six to ten feet in height and which is extensively cultivated for its nuts. The round varieties are commonly called cobnuts the name filbert being applied only to the elongated sorts. The American hazel-nut has sometimes received the name of filbert. The *Carylus Caluma* of Turkey produces large and very oily filberts, used principally for the production of oil. Barcelona nuts are filberts which have been kiln-dried to increase their keeping qualities. Filberts are much used as dessert nuts, and also for the production of an oil, known as nut-oil, of which they yield about half their weight. Nut-oil is much used by artists as a drying oil, and is also employed by the makers of choice varnish, and by druggists as the basis of fragrant oils.

Gelatine, an azotized semi-solid substance of soft, tremulous consistency, obtained from various parts of the animal body, such as the white-fibrous tissue, the skin, and cartilage, by boiling in water. The substance as it usually exists contains much water which may be dried out, leaving a brittle, glassy mass which swells but does not dissolve in cold water but dissolves readily in hot

water. When pure, gelatine is colorless, transparent, in-
odorous, and of insipid taste. It may be tested for odor
by dissolving in hot water, as, when dry, glue, if present,
does not reveal itself by its characteristic odor. It consists according to Scheerer, of 50.05 parts carbon, 6.9
hydrogen, 17.4 nitrogen, and 25.65 parts oxygen. It is
claimed by others to contain a small amount of sulphur.
It is prepared for market from the skin from calves' heads,
and from other thick pieces which are unfit for the tanner.
These are first cleaned of hair and bits of flesh and fat,
and well washed, after which they are cut into small
pieces and reduced to pulp by machinery, being washed
during the process by cold water to remove all impurities.
The pulp is then subjected to a temperature of 240° to
250° F. and passed through crushing rollers, by which
means the gelatine is obtained in solution. The methods
employed differ however considerably among manufacturers. The gelatine solution is purified by the addition
usually of ox blood, and allowed to settle, after which it
is drawn off into shallow coolers and dried. Gelatine is
used to a considerable extent as food, more commonly in
the form of soups, but has not a high nutritive value It
forms the basis of many jellies used upon the table as
appetizers. It is extensively used in the arts as a dressing for silk and other fabrics, for the manufacture of
cements, for clarifying liquors, for preparing tracing
paper, etc. The French make from it artificial flowers of
great beauty. It has recently been used with striking
success as a material in which to take very delicate casts.

Gin or Geneva, an alcoholic liquor, distilled from rye
and barley and flavored with Juniper. It was first man-

ufactured in Holland, from which it is sometimes called
"Hollands." At Schiedam in Holland there are nearly
300 distilleries of this liquor. Gin, unlike all other ardent
spirits, may be said to be a purely artificial compound
and prepared by recipes adopted by each distiller, with
the unknown addition of the retailer. It consists of any
spirit distilled in the ordinary manner, (but usually from
inferior spirits, and containing much fusel oil) of which
about 80 gallons of proof strength is distilled with 10
gallons of water, $3\frac{1}{2}$ lbs. of common salt, and five fluid
ounces of turpentine, with or without essence of juniper
berries, and creosote. A strong, acrid, fiery spirit, is
prepared by adding to gin various aromatic essences, as
coriander, capsicum, caraway, cardamoms and lemon, or
creosote, sulphuric acid, and salts of tartar. Gin is very
largely the drink indulged in by the lower classes in England, and is probably adulterated more than any other
liquor.

Ginger (*Zanzibar officinale*) is a native of India and
China, but is now extensively cultivated in tropical America and west Africa. It has an annual stem which
grows from a tuberous root-stock, to the height of two or
three feet. Its flowers are yellowish and emit an aromatic odor. The ginger of commerce is derived from the
fleshy, creeping root-stocks ; these are dug up when a
year old, generally in January and February after the
stems have withered. After being properly cleaned, they
are scalded with boiling water to prevent sprouting, and
then rapidly dried. This is known as black or East India ginger. In Jamaica the best sorts are selected and
deprived of their outer skin, or epidermis, and then care-

fully and separately dried in the sun. This gives them a beautiful white color, and it is known in commerce as white or Jamaica ginger. Calcutta exports the principal part of the ginger of commerce, and also much ginger root which is boiled and then cured with sugar. In commerce the whole ginger is known as *race* ginger. Ginger is used as a flavoring for food, and is also employed in medicines. The popular aromatic stimulant sold as Jamaica ginger is a concentrated alcoholic tincture. Ginger is commonly sold in the powdered state and is largely adulterated with starch, wheat flour, mustard husks, etc. The value of the ginger consumed in the United States for 1877 was $ 158,277.

Glauber's Salt, so named from its discoverer, J. R. Glauber (1604–68), is the hydrated neutral sulphate of soda, ($Na_2So_4H_2O$). It is found native in sea-water, in mineral springs, and very abundantly in the alkaline soils and waters of the western plains and mountains of the United States. It is made in enormous quantities by the decomposition of common salt by sulphuric acid in the process of manufacturing common soda. It forms large transparent monoclinic crystals which are highly efflorescent, and if exposed to dry air for some time lose all their water of crystallization and fall down in a bulky white powder. Glauber's salt is a mild saline cathartic and was formerly much used in medicine but is now but little employed except in veterinary practice.

Glue, a hard, brittle form of dried gelatine, containing impurities which give it a brownish color. It is made from the hoofs, scraps of hides etc., of animals, in the same manner as gelatine. For use as a cement it is dissolved

by a gentle heat in a water bath. Prepared or liquid glue
is the ordinary solution, kept liquid by the addition of nitric or commercial acetic acid.

Gooseberry, (*Ribes Grossularia*) a low, deciduous
shrub ; stems mostly bearing thorns at the base of the leaf
stalks ; the fruit is smooth or prickly. The gooseberry has
been cultivated in Europe for the last two or three hundred
years, and the varieties are very numerous. It is also a
native of this country, from which our cultivated varieties
are derived. The European species will not thrive in
this country on account of its being attacked by the mil-
dew. The fruit is used, when unripe, for making tarts and
pies, and when ripe is a good dessert fruit, and is also
made into jam and preserves. It also enters into the
manufacture of wine and vinegar, and, put up in cans, is
found on all grocers' shelves.

Grape, the fruit of woody vines belonging to the genus
Vitis of the order Vitaceæ. Grapes for our purpose may
be divided into two classes—European and American
grapes. The former species is the *Vitis Vinifera* of the
naturalists, and from it are derived the many varieties
cultivated in Europe and Asia. The European grape cannot be successfully cultivated in this country east of the
Rocky Mountains ; but in California it is of easy growth,
and grape culture in that state is assuming large proportions. Of the American grape there are four described
species, viz. V. Labrusca, V. Aestivalis, V. Cardifolia,
and V. Vulpian. From these species have been derived
by cultivation all our varieties of grapes. From the
grape we have, as commercial products, wine and raisins
(which see), while the fruit itself is largely consumed as

a dessert for the table. Among the best varieties for table grapes may be mentioned the Concord, Delaware, Iona, Hartford Prolific, Isabella, Catawba and Diana; of these the Concord, Delaware and Catawba take the lead.

Grass Seed, a term generally applied to the seed of the timothy (Phleum pratense), although it may be applied to the seed of any grass. Timothy is one of the most valuable of all crops for the production of hay. It grows to a height of from two to four feet, and the flowers are arranged on a spike, one head to each stem. When cut for seed, the timothy is allowed to ripen, which impairs its feeding qualities. As high as thirty bushels of seed have been raised from one acre of ground. Large quantities of seed are raised in Illinois and Wisconsin and shipped to the east.

Gum, Chewing, an article of unknown benefit, and of equally mysterious composition. The natural gum of the spruce is largely used in the manufacture of chewing gum; various other gums and resins are also used. Paraffine is also largely used in its preparation.

Gumbo, Okra, the pods of the *Hibiscus esculens*, a plant of the Mallow family, native of the West Indies, where, as also in the Southern States and most warm climates, it is much cultivated. The green pods are very mucilaginous, and excellent in soups or cooked and served with butter. They are also extensively made into pickles.

Gunpowder, is an explosive material formed by the intimate mechanical admixture of nitre, charcoal and sulphur. The knowledge of the explosive property of such

a mixture is of very great antiquity, some writers placing
it even anterior to the beginning of the Christian Era.
It was certainly in use in China as early as the ninth century, but we are not certain of its having been employed
with firearms until the early part of the fourteenth, and it
was not until the sixteenth century that it came into general use in warfare.   The proportions of the several ingredients in gunpowder are always nearly the same, and
correspond quite closely with the proportions required by
the theory of combining equivalents, were the combination a chemical one instead of simply mechanical.   The
following are the proportions usually employed :

	Nitre.	Charcoal.	Sulphur.
By atomic theory,	74.64	13.51	11.85
U. S. Military,	76.	14.	10.
Sporting,	78.	12.	10.
Blasting,	62.	18.	10.

In blasting powder the proportion of nitre is reduced
to make it cheaper, and for the same reason nitrate of
soda is frequently substituted for the nitrate of potash.
This makes an equally strong and very cheap powder,
but it has a strong affinity for moisture and is consequently difficult to preserve without deterioration.   The
most important ingredient of gunpowder is the nitre or
saltpetre, the nitrate of potash, which is chiefly obtained
from the East Indies, where it occurs as an efflorescence
upon the surface of the ground.   The charcoal for gunpowder is made by the destructive distillation of the lighter kinds of wood in iron retorts.   In this country willow
and poplar wood are principally employed, and in Europe
the common and black alder and white birch are chiefly

made use of for the purpose. Only sticks of small size, not over an inch in diameter, and for sporting powder even much smaller are used, and these must be peeled and well seasoned before charring.

The quality of the charcoal depends upon the heat at which it is distilled; if it be about 1800° F., at which temperature the process takes about six hours, the result is black charcoal. If a temperature of about 500° is continued for twelve hours there results brown charcoal. Brown charcoal makes a stronger and more inflammable powder, but one which is more difficult to preserve, from its liability to absorb moisture. Sulphur for the manufacture of gunpowder is obtained by purifying crude sulphur by distilation, and afterward pulverizing it in a mill. Flowers of sulphur produced by sublimation are not suitable upon account of containing a quantity of sulphuric and sulphurous acids.

In the process of manufacturing gunpowder the ingredients are first pulverized, the charcoal and sulphur being rolled for this purpose in barrels with zinc balls. The barrels in which the charcoal is crushed are made of cast iron and those for the sulphur are of leather stretched over wooden frames. The materials after being thoroughly pulverized are next incorporated together by first mixing them in rolling barrels and after grinding them under heavy cast-iron wheels following each other in a circular cast-iron trough. Each wheel weighs from four to eight tons, and the operation is continued for from three to twelve hours and is one of the most important in making gunpowder, for, the more thoroughly the materials are mixed the more complete will be the combustion. It is

also the dangerous operation in powder making, explo-
ions of the wheel mills as they are termed frequently occurring, though such precautions are now taken that they are
seldom very disastrous. The powder, when taken from
the wheel mill, is very lumpy and irregular and is consequently next reduced to meal under rollers, after which it
is spread in layers upon brass plates and submitted to
very heavy pressure in an hydraulic press, which reduces
the layers from about four inches in thickness to cakes of
an inch or less in thickness. The mildness or violence of
the explosive power of the powder depends very much
upon the degree of pressure to which it has been subjected, as the pressure determines the density and rapidity
of combustion of the grains.

The cakes, after removal from the press, are next submitted to the process of graining, which consists in breaking up the cakes by passing them through fluted rollers
and passing the product over a succession of sieves of
varying mesh. The grains as thus produced have sharp
angles and require to be rounded and smoothed to prevent
the formation of dust in transportation and handling. This
is done by rolling the powder in barrels for from six to
twenty-four hours, after which it is dried in rooms heated
by steam to from 130° to 180° to remove the moisture
which has been purposely introduced in the previous operations. The fine dust and minute grains are next removed by the use of fine sieves and bolting cloths, after
which the powder has but to be graded to be ready for
market. It is classified, according to the size of the
meshes through which it is sifted, into eleven numbers,
from 0 to 10, No. 10 being the finest rifle powder whilst

0 is mammoth powder for artillery. Instead of numbers the letters F, FF, and FFF, and C, CC, CCC, are sometimes used. In classifying according to quality each maker has his own system and nomenclature.

Haddock, a soft rayed fish of the cod family, and genus Morrhua (*M. aeglefinis*). The species vary in length from 1 to 2 feet, and weigh from two to six pounds. It is found everywhere on the American coast from New York to the Arctic regions ; they occur in immense shoals, changing their grounds as their food becomes exhausted. It is an excellent fish when eaten fresh. It is a voracious eater and is easily caught; the fishery is valuable to New England and the British provinces, and is pursued in the same manner as for cod, and in deep water. Haddock may be distinguished from cod by its having a black lateral stripe instead of white, as in the cod.

Hake, a name applied to fishes of the cod family of the genus Merlucius ; also applied to the American hake, a fish belonging to the genus Phycis. The hakes may be distinguished from the cod by having only two dorsal fins. The European hake is abundant in the ocean and in the Mediterranean sea, and on the coasts of Ireland and Cornwall. It grows to a length of 1 to 2 ft. and is caught and cured like the cod in northern countries. The white or common hake reaches a length of from 1 to 3 ft. and is taken along the coast from New Jersey northward. It is a valuable fish when salted and is largely exported from the British Provinces. The hake, haddock and pollock are often sold as cod to those unable to distinguish them.

Halibut, (*Hippoglossus vulgaris*) a fish found on the

coast from New York to Greenland, and also on the northern shore of Europe. It reaches a length of from three to six feet, and varies in weight from one hundred to five hundred pounds. The fish has a flat, oblong body, compressed vertically, the right side dark brown, and the left a pure white ; the eyes are on the right or colored side. Large quantities of these fish are caught on George's bank and Nantucket shoals ; it is also abundant in the bay of Fundy and in the waters of Nova Scotia. The flesh of the halibut is coarse and dry but much esteemed by some. Large quantities of the flesh are dried, salted or smoked, and largely consumed in northern countries. In England it is but little esteemed, but in this country brings a higher price than cod. Our fresh water sturgeon is said to be smoked and largely sold for halibut.

Hazel Nut, the fruit of a small shrub, the *Corylus Americana*, belonging to the oak family. The nuts are small and not so good as those of the European hazel or filbert. It is found in thickets, along borders of fence rows etc., throughout the United States. It flowers in March and April and fruits in September.

Hemp (*Cannabis sativa*) is a plant belonging to the family of nettles. The true hemp is a native of the East, but is now cultivated throughout Europe and in the United States, and used in the manufacture of cordage and textile fabrics. The seed of the plant is the part that enters into the grocers' economy, being sold as food for cage birds ; it is said to greatly increase the brilliancy of their plumage, and, in the case of the bullfinch and some others, to cause it to turn black. Hemp seed upon expression yields hemp seed oil, the commercial supply of which comes principally from Russia.

Herring. Two species of herring are of importance as furnishing large quantities of food, the American and European. The common American herring, or blue back, is the *Clupea elongata* of naturalists. It varies in length from twelve to fifteen inches, and is found on the coasts of New England, New Brunswick, and Nova Scotia, and is generally most abundant from March to May. It is captured by means of seines and sweep nets to the amount of a hundred barrels or more in a single night. The common herring of Europe is *C. Harengus*, and is from ten to thirteen inches long. Herrings are eaten fresh, salted, and smoked, and in the value of its fishery it ranks next to the cod. The food of the herring appears to be chiefly minute crustaceans or worms, and sometimes its own young and other small fish. The young of the herring is said to be the celebrated white bait. It was once thought that the herrings migrated to the Artic regions in the winter, when they reappeared in immense shoals during the spring, summer and autumn, along the coasts of Europe, Asia and America. But it is now maintained by modern observers that the fish merely retire to the deep waters and return to the shores during the spawning seasons. Whenever they do appear they come in vast shoals covering the sea for miles, and are followed by large flocks of sea birds which devour them for food. Immense quantities of the fish are taken annually, but there seems to be no diminution of their numbers. The regularity of their appearance, their value as food, and the ease with which they are taken has led to their capture from the earliest times. The French herring fishery dates from the eleventh century, and the English three centuries earlier. The Dutch also engaged in the fishery at an early period and it was a source of much prosperity to them. Amsterdam was the great center of the trade, and it has been said that the city was built on herring bones. The quantity of cured herrings brought in by American vessels for the year ending June 30, 1875 was 124,215 cwt., valued at $ 265,463. Large quantities are also consumed fresh which are not included in the above. The fishing is carried on during the winter and spring. An important winter fishery is along the coast of Maine and in the bay of Fundy. The fish are taken through holes in the ice by means of nets ; they are preserved frozen and sold in the eastern cities. The herring is cured both gutted and ungutted ; when pickled and packed in barrels they are known in Great Britian as white herrings ; salted and smoked, they are called red herring ; when partially cured and smoked they are known as " bloaters." The Dutch fisheries have greatly declined, but Dutch or Holland herring still command the highest price in the continental markets.

Hickory Nut, the fruit of the trees of the genus *Carya*. *C. Alba* furnishes the common shellbark or shagbark hickory nuts of the markets. The bark of the trunk is shaggy, coming off in rough strips or plates. The tree is tall, reaching a height of 60 or 80 feet, with irregular and scattered branches. The nut is white, flattish globular, barely mucronate, the shell *thinnish*. The delicious flavor of its fruit is not excelled by any foreign nut. *C. Sulcata* is the western shellbark hickory. In this the nut is large, from one and a half to two inches long, and usually angular, dull white or yellowish, *thick walled,* usually strongly pointed at both ends. The shellbarks are found from Pennsylvania to Wisconsin and southward. The wood of both species is very valuable and is largely used in the turning of axe helves, spokes, handspikes etc.

Hominy (See Indian corn).

Honey. The saccharine material collected from flowers by various kinds of insects as food for themselves and progeny, especially that collected by the honey-bee. Honey is a natural product of the plants from which it is obtained, the bees simply gathering and storing it, and not, as many suppose, making it from some other material. It consists esentially of a solution of several different kinds of sugar, but contains in addition small quantities of other substances peculiar to the plant by which it is produced, and its flavor and quality depend, consequently, very much upon the source from which it is obtained. That made from the flowers of the bass-wood and white clover is of the finest flavor. That made from many plants retains something of the poisonous quality of the juice of those plants, and, in consequence, many persons having delicate stomachs, are entirely unable to partake of this delicacy. The deleterious substances are, however, usually volatile, and honey which has stood some time is consequently much less liable to produce injurious effects than that just removed from the hive. The invention of the movable frame hive, together with the still more recent honey extractor, which removes the honey from the comb cells by centrifugal force, leaving the comb in condition to be again used by the bees, are improvements which have greatly added to the economy of honey producing. The extracted honey contains none of the bee bread and other impurities which render strained honey of so inferior flavor.

The total production of honey in the United States is about 50,000,000 lbs. annually, which is obtained from about 2,000,000 hives of bees kept by 70,000 persons.

Of this product about 4,000,000 lbs., or $1,200,000 worth is exported.

Honey is often adulterated with solutions of cheap sugars, especially the uncrystallizable or grape sugars (glucose), and starch, chalk, gypsum and pipe clay are also added to it to increase the weight.

Artificial honey is produced in considerable quantities, and usually consists of a solution of glucose, to which is added eggs and frequently cream of tartar. Flavorings of various kinds are employed, and a small quantity of genuine honey is sometimes used to improve the flavor.

Hops, the strobiles or cones containing the seed of the Hop plant (*Humulus lupulus*). The hop is a vine with perennial roots, from which spring up numerous annual shoots which climb spirally around any sustaining object to a hight of 20 or 30 feet. The plant is diœcious and its flowers apetalous, the staminate ones growing in large, axillary panicles, whilst the pistillate ones are clustered in short catkins made up of leafy scales, each of which bears two flowers. In maturing, the scales of the catkin increase much in size, and form the membranaceous cones or strobiles.

The scales are covered near their base with minute, yellow grains of an aromatic, resinous substance, known as lupuline. This constitutes about 10 per cent of the weight of the dried strobiles and contains the greater portion of the valuable constituents of the hops. The valuable constituents of commercial hops are a highly aromatic oil, residing almost entirely in the yellow lupuline, a bitter crystalline principle, tannic acid, and extractive matter which is soluble in water. The hop is found growing wild in North America and in Europe and has long been in cultivation. It is grown in Germany and elswhere upon the continent, whilst in England the county of Kent is found especially favorable to its growth, over 25,000 acres of land in the shire being appropriated to its production. In the United States the production has very greatly increased in the last few years, the total production in 1850 being about 3,500,000 pounds, in 1860, 11,000,000 lbs., and, according to the last census, 25,456,699 lbs. in 1870, of which New York produced 17,558,000, and Wisconsin 4,630,000 pounds.

Hops require a deep, rich soil, and it is especially essential that it should be well drained and comparatively dry at all seasons of the year. They are grown in hills from 6 to 8 feet apart, in which are set the " cuttings " which are the shoots from the crown of the plant cut into pieces containing two to four buds each. About one hill in 60 or 80 is set with male plants in order that the female flowers may be properly fertilized. The first year the vines are allowed to run upon the ground, or poles six or eight feet in height are set for them, but unless the soil is rich and strong no crop is to be expected. Some other crop

is however frequently grown upon the same ground the
first year. In the spring of the second year stakes 18 or
20 feet in height are set, usually two in each hill, and as
the vines start they are turned upon them. In sections
where poles are scarce, sawed stakes about eight
feet high are set and hempen strings are stretched from
the top of one to another for the vines to run upon.
During the summer it is only necessary that the ground
should be kept mellow and free from weeds. The hops
ripen about the last of August, when the poles are taken
down, the vines being first cut, and the hops are picked
by women and children. The harvest lasts several weeks
and employs a great number of hands. After being picked the hops are taken to the kiln, or drying house, where
they are placed upon screens of wire or hair cloth, or upon
hempen carpets, and dried at a temperature not exceed-
ing 180° F. When dry they are packed lightly in bales
by means of screw presses and are then sent into the market. The hop crop is a very uncertain one, they being
subject to the attacks of many enemies of which the blight
and aphis or louse are the most common. There are several varieties of hops cultivated, of which the Grape,
English Cluster and Pompey are considered the best.

Hops are used in enormous quantities in the manufacture of malt liquors to which they impart an agreeable flavor, add to their tonic and stimulating properties, and
greatly increase their keeping qualities, while the tannic
acid which they contain, by its action upon the albumen
in the liquors, is of value in clearing and settling them.

Hops are also used in the manufacture of yeast and to
some extent in medicine.

Horse Radish (*Nasturtium Armoracia*), a perennial plant belonging to the Mustard family, native of Europe, is cultivated in gardens for its root, which furnishes a pungent condiment for the table. When fresh it has a biting taste and pungent odor, due to the presence of a volatile oil which is dissipated in drying. This oil is very similar to if not identical with that of mustard. For use the root is grated and mixed with vinegar and should be used fresh as it deteriorates by standing. It is put up for the market in tightly sealed bottles. Both the root and leaves are to some extent used in medicine as local stimulants. The young leaves are much used as pot herbs and are excellent for the purpose.

Huckleberry, Whortleberry, Blueberry, names applied somewhat indiscriminately to the various species of the two genera, *Gaylussacia* and *Vaccinium*, of the Heath family. The name huckleberry is more appropriately used only for the genus Gaylussacia and blueberry for the Vaccinium, whilst whortleberry is the name in common use in Europe, but is falling into disuse in this country. These plants are found very widely distributed in temperate climes and differ much in their habits of growth. All are shrubs but vary in height from one to twelve feet. Several species grow only in dry, rocky, and mountainous regions, while others are found only in very wet, dark swamps. All produce edible berries which vary in size from that of currants to small grapes, and in color from light blue to black, many varieties being covered with a delicate white bloom. They ripen from first of June to last of August and are gathered in very great quantities and used as a dessert fruit and for pies and

puddings.   In many sections of the United States they
furnish much the most abundant fruit for midsummer use.
They are but little cultivated.

Indian Corn (*Zea Maze*).   One of the most valuable
of food-producing plants, and well known throughout all
this country.   It is a tropical plant but reaches its perfection in the south temperate zone, where the hot sum-
mers force it to maturity.   It is supposed to be a native
of America and was used as an article of food by the Indians at the time of the discovery of this country, whence
its name, Indian Corn.   From America it was carried to
Europe and its cultivation soon extended into Asia and
Africa.   Corn cannot be successfully grown in England
on account of the dampness of the climate.   The chemical composition of 100 parts is as follows : water, 14 ;
nitrogenous, 11.0 ; starch, 64.7 ; sugar, 0.4 ; fat, 8.1 ;
salts, 1.7.   From this composition it is seen that corn is
a very valuable food, it also being rich in the phosphates.
The varieties of corn have been much modified by cultivation and the higher varieties have nearly reached perfection.   The more improved varieties contain less
oil but more starchy material : rice corn contains most
oil, and Tuscarora most starch and no oil.

The many varieties of sugar or sweet corn furnish in
their green state a nutritious and delicious food ; the unripe grains then contain large proportions of sugar, which
is converted into starch as the grain ripens.   The ripe
corn may also be eaten in a parched state, as in some
eastern countries, but with us it is ground and used in
the form of meal.   The whole grain is ground and in this
state is sold as " unbolted" meal ; when it is sifted and

the bran removed it is known as "bolted" meal. The meal is largely used in the making of corn bread or "Johnny Cakes," or boiled and eaten in the form of a mush, when the grains of corn are roughly broken and the hull removed it is known as *hominy;* it is prepared for use by boiling with water. When the corn is finely broken or crushed it is known as *Samp*, and is used in the same manner as hominy. *Hulled Corn* is prepared by soaking the grains in lye to enable the hulls to be removed; it is then thoroughly soaked in water and afterward boiled until tender. Corn enters largely into the manufacture of whiskey and a great many distilleries are employed in its production.

Indigo, a vegetable dyestuff derived from numerous plants belonging to the order Leguminoseæ and natives of the tropical regions of Asia, Africa and America. The genus Indigofera contains over two hundred species, several of which yield the indigo of commerce. *I. tinctoria* is the species most cultivated in the East, and is also cultivated in the West Indies. It is a small shrub from two to five feet high, with pinnate leaves and rose colored papilionaceous flowers. In India the seeds are sown in drills about a foot apart, during the rainy season, and the crop, being kept free from weeds, in the course of two or three months will be ready for cutting; and during the rainy season a fresh crop may be cut every six weeks. The plants are not allowed to come into bloom as this would injure the quality of the indigo. It is therefore cut just before flowering, and tied up into bundles about five and a half feet in circumference, and carried as quickly as possible to the factory.

If kept, even for a short time, and particularly in heaps, a sort of fermentation takes place, completely destroying the indigo. When brought to the factory these bundles are thrown into a large vat and strongly pressed down by means of bamboos and a stout crossbar; the whole is then covered with water and allowed to steep for ten or twelve hours according to the state of the weather and the skill of the planter. This part of the process must be carefully watched, for if the steeping be continued too long the indigo will be much damaged or "burnt" as it is called, and if too short the full amount of indigo will not be procured. The liquor is then drawn off into another vat where it is beaten and stirred with bamboos till it granulates, which generally takes place in from one and a half to three hours, and requires the utmost attention to stop the beating at the proper time, for if continued too long the granules are again broken and liable to be lost. When the grains are properly formed a few pailfuls of cold water, or lime water, may be added to hasten the deposit, but the latter is said to injure the quality of the indigo by throwing down foreign matter in connection with it. After the coloring matter has subsided the water is drawn off and the deposit is removed to a copper boiler and allowed to remain till it begins to ferment. It is then placed on a bamboo frame covered with cloth to serve as a filter and all the liquor that will is allowed to drain from it. It is then placed in proper frames and strongly pressed by means of screws; it is now removed and cut into cakes of the proper size and placed in the drying house. In some districts it is ready for the market in this form; but in the interior of Bengal it is in this state loosely packed in boxes with hemp between the layers. It here undergoes a sort of sweating and is then removed to the drying house and, when thoroughly dry, repacked and sent to market.

Another method of preparing indigo is by gathering the leaves and drying them in the sun and then storing. When a sufficient quantity has been collected they are steeped with six times their weight of water and stirred for two hours, till all the leaves sink; the liquor is then drawn off and the indigo is procured as in the process above described. The species of indigo most cultivated in America are the *Indigofera Anil*, and the *I. Gautinala*. The former is a native of South America, but now grows wild in the southern states as the remains of a former cultivation. The use of indigo as a dye was known in Italy as early as the eleventh century, the supply being obtained from India. It was also brought back from America, the Mexicans knowing its use at the time of the discovery by the Spaniards. In the seventeenth century the trade with India assumed importance and considerable quantities were taken to Holland. But its use as a dye caused much complaint among the Germans on account of its superiority to the native woad. Its use was accordingly prohibited by the Diet in 1577, and it was denounced under the name of the " Devils Dye". Its use in both France and England was prohibited by law, and severe penalties were attached to its infringements, and in the reign of Elizabeth persons were authorized to search for it and logwood and, to destroy both : and it was not till the beginning of the eighteenth century that it came into general use.

Asiatic indigo is brought from several parts of India and from Java and Manilla. The best Bengal indigo shipped from Calcutta is the superfine or light blue, in cubical cakes, so light as to float upon water, friable, soft, of clean fracture and of a beautiful copper color when rubbed with the nail. Merchants recognize sixteen grades in the Bengal Indigo, and twenty one in the Java variety. The Benjal and Java range from 40 to 80 per cent. of Indigo blue ; the remaining varieties vary from 10 to 37 per cent. They are Caromandel, Onde, Madras, Manilla, Egyptian, Guatimala, Caraccas and Mexican. The best quality of indigo gives a glossy and purplish red streak when rubbed by the nail; when the streak is dull and furrows on each side the quality is poor. The best kinds will also float upon water. It is insoluble in water or alcohol, but is readily dissolved by sulphuric acid, which, without destroying its color, so far alters its nature as to render it freely soluble in water and thus affords a convenient method of applying it to the purposes of dyeing. A simple solution of this in water is known as *Saxon Blue*, which is used as a blueing for laundry purposes ; the sulphuric acid is rendered neutral by the addition of the acetate of soda. When carbonate of soda is added to a sulphuric solution of indigo a precipitate is formed which being filtered is sold as a paste or a dry powder, or dry blueing ; this is also soluble in water. Indigo is sometimes adulterated with starch, Prussian blue, rosin, ground dyewoods etc. The tests of the properties of indigo blue or " Indigotine " in samples of commercial indigo, are quite difficult and should be referred to the chemist for determination. In 1875 the United States imported 885,752 lbs., the majority coming from the British East Indies, the Spanish Possessions and Mexico. In 1871 the imports were 1,994, 752 lbs., showing a decrease in four years of over 1,000,000 lbs.

Ink, the name given to any colored fluid used for producing characters in writing or printing. From the essential difference, both in composition and use, inks are naturally divided into two classes, writing and printing inks. Writing ink as used by the ancients appears from the best knowledge which we are able to obtain to have closely resembled the ink which is at present in use in China and India, being either a combination of lampblack with glue or gum, or the black fluid secreted by the cuttle fish. Manuscripts written from the 5th to the 12th century, are generally found much more legible than those written in the 15th and 16th centuries, which is supposed to result from the use in the older manuscripts of ink of which carbon was the base, whilst the more recent ones were written with ink made from nutgalls and iron.

The writing inks in use in modern times are of great variety both in color and composition. The essential requisites of a good writing ink are permanency of character, close adherence to the paper, without a tendency to destroy it, a consistency which will allow it to flow freely from the pen, a good legible color, together with the negative virtues of not moulding, not corroding the pen if of steel, and not depositing a sediment upon standing. The black ink in most common use is made from the infusion of nutgalls and copperas with the addition of gum, sugar, or mucilage to hold the coloring matter in suspension. The nutgall contains two organic acids, viz. gallic acid and tannic acid, which unite with the iron of the copperas, (sulphate of iron) forming the tanno-gallate of iron. As the gallate of iron is of a much deeper black, and also much more permanent than the tannate, or gallo-tannate, it is usual to leave the infusion of nut galls exposed for some days to the action of the air, whereby the tannic acid is converted into gallic acid. When the infusion is then mixed with a solution of copperas, there is produced a deep black powdered precipitate of the gallate, and gallo-tannate of iron, which quickly settles to the bottom of the liquid in the form of sediment. It is consequently necessary in the manufacture of ink, that some means be adopted for holding it in suspension; this is usually accomplished by the addition of a small quantity of gum to the mixture. A few drops of carbolic acid, or some essential oil, are frequently added to prevent the formation of mould. The proportions in which the various materials are used are almost as various as the number of manufacturers, whilst the recipes for this class of inks alone, are simply without number. Drs. Lewis and Ribaucourt, seem to have been the first chemists to study carefully the character and composition of ink. They made extended series of experiments about the close of the last century, which added much to our knowledge of the subject, and led to great improvement in the quality of ink subsequently produced. Dr.

Lewis recommended the following proportions as giving the best ink.

Powdered copperas,   -   -   1 oz.
Ground logwood,   -   -   - 1   "
Bruised galls,   -   -   - 3   "
Gum-arabic,   -   -   - 1   "
White wine, or acetic acid,   - 1 quart.

Although a less proportion of galls gave an ink of good color when used, it subsequently turned to a yellowish brown ; and whilst water was found to answer for ordinary purposes, white wine, and still better, acetic acid, gave an ink of much blacker color. Dr. Ure, who made a careful study of the composition of ink, gives the following recipe for the best black ink.

Nutgalls,   -   -   - 12 pounds.
Copperas,   -   -   - 5   "
Gum Senegal,   -   - 5   "
Water,   -   -   - 12 gallons.

This makes an ink much stronger than most of that sold, and it will still be of good quality if the quantity of water be considerably increased. One of the great objections to this class of inks is their tendency to mould if gum be used in considerable quantity, and to deposit their coloring matter if it be not. To avoid this difficulty it is now usual to add sulphate of indigo which dissolves the coloring matter, producing a clear solution which flows freely from the pen, and retains its fluidity, especially when steel pens are used, to a much greater degree. Stark, after having manufactured ink for fourteen years, and tested 229 different kinds, declares his decided preference for the gallnut-copperas ink, made

clear by the use of sulphate of indigo.   He recommends
as the result of his experience, the following as the best.

Best gallnuts, - - -	12 oz.
Copperas, - - - -	8 "
Gum arabic, - -	4 to 6 "
Sulphate of indigo, - -	8 fluid "
Water, - - -	1 gallon.

As the use of steel pens injures the quality of iron
inks, he advises that legal, and other important docu-
ments, be written with gold or quill pens. All inks of
this character are lighter, usually blue or greenish, when
first written with, but rapidly turn black by exposure to
the air.   Arnold's and most of the other favorite fluids
of the day belong to this class of inks.   If these inks
become too thick for use, by long standing, the best fluid
with which to dilute them, is a strong decoction of coffee,
which will give an excellent color and lustre to the ink.
Vanadium black ink, was first proposed by Berzelius,
who recommended the use of vanadate of ammonia, with
infusions of nutgalls.   This furnishes a fine black ink
which flows freely from the pen, does not deposit any sediment, and will not corrode a steel pen.

Chrome black ink is made by adding one part of chromate of potassa to 1000 parts of strong decoction of logwood, prepared by steeping 22 pounds of logwood in a
sufficient quantity of water to make fourteen gallons of
the decoction.   The ink thus made is very black, cannot
be washed out with water, will not corrode steel pens,
and weak acids will not affect the writing.   It is however
liable to gelatinize.   Copying inks which are intended to
give an impression of the writing to a second or third

sheet of paper by moistening and pressing upon the original, are frequently made like the ordinary gallnut inks, with the addition of gum and sugar in much larger proportions. A great variety of other preparations is also used, one of the most highly esteemed being made of four parts by weight of logwood extract, dissolved in a mixture of 70 parts of water and 60 parts of vinegar, to which is added three parts copperas, two parts alum, two parts gum arabic, and four parts of sugar. This gives a fine violet ink. A valuable French coppying ink is made from 30 grammes of logwood extract, and 7.5 grms. of crystallized carbonate of soda boiled with 240 grms. of water, to which is added with vigorous stirring, 30 grms. of glycerine, and, after the liquid has become cold, one gramme of neutral carbonate of potassa and 7.5 grms. of gum arabic, previously made into a paste, are dissolved in it. When this ink is used the paper upon which the copy is to be made need not be moistened.

Colored inks of great variety have long been in use, but the introduction of aniline in recent years has greatly added to the permanence and beauty of tint to be found in such inks. Red inks have been made principally from cochineal and Brazil-wood, but aniline is now rapidly replacing them. The best carmine ink is made by digesting cochineal in water, to which is added a small quantity of cream of tartar and alum, and, after the impurities have settled, pouring off the clear fluid and allowing it to stand a considerable time to settle, when the sediment is removed and dissolved in caustic ammonia. The ink thus produced is very brilliant, but rapidly fades when exposed to the air, and must be kept in closely closed bottles. The older blue inks were usually made by dissolving Prussian blue in oxalic acid and water. The production and use of aniline colors is a growth entirely of the last twenty years, yet they have already to a great extent replaced the coloring matters previously in use in most of the arts. The most beautiful red, purple, violet and green inks are already made from it, whilst very much remains yet to be done to develop and perfect them, for which there are materials which promise the most striking results. These inks are mostly prepared by simply dissolving the anilines of commerce, of the required color, in water. Green aniline ink is the most strikingly beautiful.

Printers' ink is made of lamp-black held in suspension in linseed oil, to which is added rosin, turpentine, and a small quantity of soap. The oil must be clarified with great care and is boiled for a considerable length of time and at the same time burned by setting fire to the vapor which escapes from it. After burning a short time the flame is extinquished by covering the boiling oil. After the oil is prepared, the lamp-black and other materials are mixed with it and the whole thoroughly ground, when it is ready for use.

Indelible ink, used for marking clothing, is usually a carbon ink, the base being lampblack, which is prepared for use in a variety of ways. A good indelible ink is also prepared from aniline, and the juice of the anacardium nut is also used for the same purpose.

Jellies, a term applied to the evaporated juice of fruits, or meats, boiled with sugar to a consistency between solid and fluid. Jellies are made from almost all fruits, that of the currant being especially desirable. Jellies are generally put up for market in small glass cups of any desired size. Almost all of the jellies in market are of artificial manufacture. Gelatine is the base generally used in the manufacture of these jellies, flavored by the various extracts, (many of these latter being also artificial), and are then labelled currant, strawberry, etc., as the demand may be.

Kerosene, is a mixture of several liquid hydrocarbonates used for purposes of illumination. It has the consistency of the essential oils, a burning taste, and aromatic odor. When properly refined it is nearly or quite colorless by transmitted light, but quite fluorescent by reflected light, giving beautiful violet-blue tints. It is at present obtained in immense quantities from crude petroleum, by a process of refining which consists simply in separating it from other related products with which it is found combined. It may, however, be produced by the destructive distillation at low temperature of almost any organic or mineral product containing carbon and hydrogen, and was in fact so produced in considerable quantities before petroleum had been discovered in sufficient quantities to render its preparation from that material of any importance commercially. It was in fact the production and use of kerosene from other sources which first called attention to petroleum (which had long been known but made almost no use of) as a source of supply for this already valuable illuminant.

Kerosene has been produced in quantity from bituminous coal, bituminous shale, asphalt, malthas, wood, rosin, and various oils, especially menhaden oil. The

first mention which we find of the possibility of thus pro-
curing this material is in the specification of a patent
granted in England to Thomas Hancock, Martin Eele
and William Portlock in 1694, for "a way to extract and
make great quantities of pitch, tar and oyle out of a sort
of stone." The stone thus referred to was a bituminous
shale found in considerable quantities in England and
Wales. These men do not, however, seem to have made
use of their process to extract oil in great quantities.

Another patent was issued in 1716 to the Messrs. Betton
of Shrewsbury, for a process for extracting oil from the
black, pitchy rock found overlying the coal beds, which
consisted in grinding them to powder and subjecting them
to destructive distillation. The oil thus obtained was
used in medicine, and we find it mentioned in 1761 in
Lewis' Materia Medica under the name of British or petroleum oil. Any adequate knowledge of the use and value of this class of hydrocarbonates was, however, first
arrived at and given to the world by Reichenback of Mo-
ravia, who made extended investigations into the character and properties of the numerous products obtained
from the destructive distillation of organic bodies. He
applied the name *eupione* to a mixture of hydrocarbons
such as constitutes the modern kerosene and called
attention to its superior illuminating qualities, and to the
fact that it might be brought into entensive use for domestic purposes if some cheap method could be found for
separating it from the other products of distillation. His
researches attracted much attention and were extensively
published, appearing in several scientific journals in
1830-31. At about the same time we find the extraction

of oil from bituminous substances being entered upon to a considerable extent in France. In 1832, Blum and Monense took out a patent for the application of these oils to illuminating purposes. Sellique seems to have been the first to have manufactured them in large quantities for illuminating purposes, he having commenced operations in 1834, and in the six years from 1838 to 1843 manufactured 15,000 barrels (40 gallons each) of shale oil. Abraham Gesuer, in Prince Edward's Island, made oil from coal in 1846 and was the first to give it the name kerosene. In 1850 James Young, of Glasgow, Scotland, introduced paraffine oil which he made from the Torbane Hill mineral, or boghead coal. This manufacture proved very profitable and Mr. Young rapidly extended his operations and in 1854 his productions amounted to 8,000 gallons a week and his yearly sales to £100,000. His success soon led others to embark in the manufacture, and coal oil factories rapidly sprang up in England and were also introduced into the United States.

The first factory in this country was that of the Kerosene Oil Co., built upon Newtown Creek opposite New York City in the year 1854. This factory, and others which were soon after built, used principally the boghead coal of Scotland imported for the purpose, although cannel-coal from Nova Scotia and from western coal mines as also Trinidad pitch, candle tar, and numerous other substances were employed. Albertite from Nova Scotia was found to yield the oil very abundantly but its use was monopolized by a single company. The cannel-coal found along the Ohio river was found to yield oil in remunerative quantities and factories were built in Perry,

Licking, Mahoning, and Coshocton counties and others in Kentucky. The manufacture was increasing rapidly and becoming of great importance when in 1859 the Pennsylvania Rock Oil Co. " struck oil" in Venango Co., and the manufacture of coal oil was doomed to a speedy death. On the first of January, 1860, there were on the Atlantic border 40 coal oil factories, which were producing oil at the rate of 200,000 barrels per annum and at least 25 factories in Ohio besides others in Kentucky, and West Virginia.

These factories were soon after that date all converted into refineries for extracting kerosene from the crude petroleum obtained from wells. As has been already mentioned the existence of petroleum had long been known and it had been collected and used to some extent in various parts of the world. The earliest evidence of its use is in the ruins of Nineveh and Babylon in the construction of both which cities an asphalt mortar (the *slime* of the Old Testament) was used, the asphalt for which was a partially evaporated petroleum. The oil from Arigentum was burned in lamps as long ago as the time of Pliny, under the name of Sicilian oil. In this country petroleum was used by the Indians for various purposes under the name of Seneca oil, and was formerly collected by the white people, to some extent, and used as medicine. When, however, it was first obtained in boring salt wells on the Muskingum River, Ohio, it was regarded as an unmixed evil, as it interfered seriously with the manufacture of a good quality of salt, and was thought to be entirely worthless. It was not until kerosene obtained from coal and shale had become of importance, and lamps

suitable for burning it had been invented, that attention
was called to petroleum as a source of supply of this illuminant.

The Pennsylvania Rock Oil Co. was formed in 1854 for
the purpose of collecting petroleum as it was found floating
upon the surface of the water in ditches and pools along
Oil Creek in Venango Co., Penn. This method of obtaining the oil, however, proved too slow and expensive,
and in 1858 Col. Drake, the superintendent of the company, commenced to bore in the same locality an artesian
well for oil. On the 28th of August, 1859, oil was found
at a depth of 71 feet, in this well, which immediately began to yield at the rate of 400 gallons per day, the product selling at 55 cents a gallon. There was at once
great excitement. Crowds rushed to the oil region.
Every one was anxious to invest his money in companies
which were at once formed to bore for oil. Wells in great
numbers were bored, many of them proving wonderfully
productive. No mines ever afforded fortunes so rapidly.
Some wells yielded $ 20,000 worth of oil per day, and at
almost no expense, the oil flowing from the mouth of the
well so that pumping was unnecessary. The poor farmers
of the vicinity at once found themselves wealthy, single
farms sold for $ 500,000 to $ 1,000,000. The production
in 1860 was 650,000 barrels of crude oil and in 1861 it
reached 2,000,000 barrels, since which time it has steadily
increased until now it exceeds 10,000,000 barrels per annum. Of course the price rapidly declined until the production has grown into a steady and thriving industry,
furnishing the world with an illuminating material entirely
eclipsing in cheapness, convenience and adaptability to

universal use any and all materials previously used for this purpose. More than three fourths of all the petroleum of commerce is obtained from the limited " oil region" in the north-west corner of Pennsylvania. Other deposits are found in West Virginia, Kentucky, Ohio, Canada and Southern California, as also upon the banks of the Caspian Sea, in Burmah, in Italy and especially in the Dutch East Indies.

In some places it is found flowing from the earth in the form of springs, but in most cases, as in Pennsylvania, it is obtained by boring artesian wells, from some of which it flows freely, even rising to a considerable height above the mouth of the well ; and from others it is pumped by steam power. Petroleum is found in rocks of nearly all geological formations, from the Lower Silurian to the present epoch. The Devonian rocks furnish the oils of Pennsylvania, Ohio and Canada. It is usually found associated with shales, though often permeating sand and lime stones and accumulating in cavities of other rocks. It is generally believed to have originated from the decomposition of vegetable and mineral remains, diffused in a finely divided condition through fine mud and clay. The theory that it originated from the natural distillation of coal is no longer held by scientific men, as there is no evidence of heat to be found in the oil-bearing strata. Crude petroleum as obtained from the wells varies somewhat in character in different localities but is usually of a dark greenish brown color, thin liquid consistency, and offensive odor. Chemically it consists of a mixture of a great number of hydrocarbons most of which belong to two groups, whose general formulae are C_nH_{2n+2} and C_nH_{2n}.

The average proportion of these two elements in the mixture is Carbon 85 pr. ct., Hydrogen 15 pr. ct. The hydrocarbons of which the mixture is composed differ from each other physically chiefly in volatility, specific gravity and inflammability. Some are so volatile as to very rapidly evaporate, even at very low temperatures, and so inflammable as to render it dangerous to approach an open tank of petroleum with a flame ; others require a temperature of 800° or 900° F. to vaporize them and can be ignited only when raised to a high temperature. The volatility and inflammability vary with the specific gravity, the light oils being volatile whilst the heavier, denser oils have high boiling points. The two series to which these compounds belong have not been fully studied as yet and the composition of the heavier compounds especially is not at the present time fully known.

The two following tables give, so far as have been studied, the composition of the compounds found in the two groups, together with their boiling points and specific gravities.

The Paraffines, or Marsh-gas Series of Hydrocarbons.

NAMES.	Formulae C_nH_{2n+2}	Carbon.	Hydrogen.	Boiling point.	Specific gravity.	Density Baumé.
Methane Marsh-gas	C H_4	75.00	25.00	Gas		
Ethane,	C_2 H_6	80.00	20.00	Gas		
Propane,	C_3 H_8	81.81	18.19	Gas		
Butane,	C_4 H_{10}	82.80	17.20	34° F.	0.600	106°
Quintane,	C_5 H_{12}	83.33	16.67	86°	0.628	98°
Hexane,	C_6 H_{14}	83.72	16.28	154°	0.669	86.5°
Heptane,	C_7 H_{16}	84.00	16.00	200°	0.699	72.0°
Octane,	C_8 H_{18}	84.21	15.79	242°	0.726	64.5°
Nonane,	C_9 H_{20}	84.38	15.62	278°	0.741	60.5°

Decane,	$C_{10} H_{22}$	84.51	15.49	321°	0.757	56.5°
Endecane,	$C_{11} H_{24}$	84.61	15.39	360°	0.765	54.5°
Dodecane,	$C_{12} H_{26}$	84.70	15.30	388°	0.776	52.5°
Tridecane,	$C_{13} H_{28}$	84.78	15.22	422°	0.792	48.0°
Tetradecane,	$C_{14} H_{30}$	84.85	15.15	460°		
Pentadecane.	$C_{15} H_{32}$	84.90	15.10	490°		

The Olefines, or Ethyline Series of Hydrocarbons.

NAMES.	Formulae $C_n H_{2n}$	Boiling points.	Specific gravity.	Density Baumè.
Ethylene,..............	$C_2 H_4$	Gas.		
Propylene,.............	$C_3 H_6$	0° F.		
Butylene,.............	$C_4 H_8$	37.4°		
Annylene, ...	$C_5 H_{10}$	95.0°		
Hexylene,.............	$C_6 H_{12}$	156°		
Heptylene, ...	$C_7 H_{14}$	203°		
Octylene,.............	$C_8 H_{16}$	240°		
Nonylene, ...	$C_9 H_{18}$	284°		
Dicatylene, ...	$C_{10} H_{20}$	343°		
Endecatylene, ...	$C_{11} H_{22}$	384°	.782	50°
Dodecatylene, ...	$C_{12} H_{24}$	421°		
Decatriylene, ...	$C_{13} H_{26}$	455°	.791	48°
Cetene, ...	$C_{15} H_{32}$	527°		
Cerotine, ...	$C_{27} H_{54}$	......	Solid.	Solid.
Meline.	$C_{30} H_{60}$	707°	Solid.	Solid.

Besides the members of these two groups there are several other hydrocarbons of very similar nature and composition which are sometimes found in petroleum, but not in sufficient quantities to render them of much importance.

Only the members of the middle portion of these two groups are fitted for burning in lamps for illuminating purposes, the lighter oils or napthas as they are called being inflammable to a dangerous degree, and so extremely volatile as whenever exposed to the atmosphere to give off vapors which form, with the air, explosive mixtures, thus often leading when used in any way to the most serious accidents. The heavy oils forming the higher members of the series, on the other hand do not burn readily in lamps, partly from their lesser degeee of inflammability, but more especially from the presence of solid paraffine and tarry matters which gum up, and obstruct the action of the wicks. To effect the separation of these valuable members of the series from the lighter napthas and heavier paraffines, the crude petroleum is subjected to the processes of refining which consist essentially of three parts : I, Fractional distillation, II, Agitation with sulphuric acid, III, Agitation with hydrate of soda or ammonia.

For distillation the crude petroleum is placed in large iron stills, made of boiler plate and resembling steam boilers. These stills are heated in the same manner as steam boilers, and as the temperature of the petroleum rises the more volatile compounds are converted into vapor which passes off into condensers made of gas pipe, placed in long wooden boxes filled with cold water. These boxes are usually 4 by 4 feet in cross section, and 200 to 250 feet long and in the bottoms of them are placed the condensing pipes running their entire length. A stream of cold water enters at one end of the box and is discharged after having become heated at the end nearest the still. The condensing pipes all end in a receiving house, where the products of distillation which have become condensed are received in troughs from which they are run into cisterns for storage, different cisterns being employed to contain different qualities, which are determined principally by specific gravity.

The compounds which are first vaporized are not condensed in the condensers, and are not saved but allowed to escape into the air in the form of gas. Sometimes aside from the cold water condenser a mixture of ice and salt is used by which means a very volatile oil called Rhigolene is condensed and saved in the liquid form. It is, however, usually allowed to escape with the other gases. It boils at 65° F. and evaporates so rapidly as to produce intense cold, and is from this property used by dentists and surgeons as an anæsthetic, destroying the sensibility of the part to which it is applied by freezing it. It is exceedingly dangerous being one of the most volatile and inflammable liquids known, whilst its vapor forms an explosive mixture with air.

The first products of distillation which are condensed by cold water have a specific gravity of about 95° Baumè and as the distillation proceeds, the product becomes heavier and heavier. It is usually all received into one tank until the density reaches about 63° Baumè. The material thus obtained is known as crude naptha, and is afterward redistilled and separated into I; *Gasoline*, the lightest, used in air gas machines for producing burning gas. II; Naptha, used for oil cloths, etc. III; Benzine, used for cleaning, for paints, varnishes, etc.

When the density of the liquid which comes over from the still reaches 60° to 65° B. it is turned into the kerosene tank, where it is stored until the density reaches a point varying with the quality of oil to be obtained from 38° to 51° B. The heavy oils which are then coming over contain a large amount of paraffine, and the stream is turned into the paraffine oil tank, where it is allowed to flow until the process of distillation is complete, when nothing remains in the still but coke.

The paraffine oil is chilled to solidify the paraffine, and then pressed in cloths through which the oil is expelled, which is used for lubricating and other purposes, and the solid crude paraffine is left folded in the cloths from which it is removed and purified. Frequently the last part of this process is varied by removing the tarry residue from the still when oil fit for the kerosene tank ceases to come over, and transferring it to other retorts where by slow distillation the heavy oils are " cracked" or converted into the lighter oils, and the product is mixed with the crude petroleum used for charging another still. When this is done, as is the case at many of the refineries of Cleveland and Pittsburgh, no lubricating oil or paraffine is produced.

The product obtained in the kerosene tank is removed and treated with sulphuric acid, to destroy the offensive odor and also to remove the small amount of coloring matter which it still contains. About two per cent., by measure, of acid is used which after being thoroughly shaken up with the oil, causes a tarry sediment to separate upon standing. The clear oil is then carefully decanted off and a quantity of hydrate of soda or ammonia is added to it, to remove the last traces of acid, after which the oil is ready to be barrelled and marketed.

The following table given by Prof. Chandler gives a clear idea of fractional distillation and its various products, together with the yield of each.

Products of Distillation of the Crude Petroleum.

PRODUCTS.	Limits of density, Baumé.	Limits of Average Baumé.	Specific gravity.	Boiling point.	Yield per cent.
1. Gases, uncondensed,					
2. Cymogene,	115° to 105°	110°	.600	32° F.	
3. Rhigolene,	105 to 95	100°	.625	65°	
4. Gasolene,	95 to 80	87	.664	120	1½
5. Naptha, refined,	80 to 65	73	.700	175	10
6. Benzine,	65 to 60	63	.750	250	4
7. Kerosene,	60 to 38	46	.807	340	55
8. Lubricating oil,	38 to 25	30	.885	425	17½
9. Paraffine,					2
10. Cake, gases, & loss.					10

When the process of cracking is resorted to, Professor
Chandler says that the above oil would yield

     Crude Naptha,   20 per cent.

     Kerosene,   66   "

     Coke and loss,   14   "

                       100

but the Cleveland refiners claim considerably better results—that they get 70 to 75 barrels of kerosene from 100
barrels of crude petroleum. From the character of the
process of refining it is evident that the quality of the oil
obtained will depend very much upon the point at which
the oil flowing from the condenser is turned into the kerosene tank, and the point at which it is again turned away
and directed to the paraffine oil tank. If in the first
place the oil be run into the kerosene tank at too early a
stage of the process of distillation, the kerosene will contain a quantity of the lighter volatile oils which will form
vapor in the lamp when burning, and, mixing with the air
in the upper portion of the partially filled lamp, will form
an explosive mixture liable to cause the explosion of the
lamp and produce most serious results. The oil will also

be rendered very much more inflammable, and in case of the accidental breaking of the lamp, or the oil becoming spilled in any other way, it is much more likely to take fire, and when burning is much more difficult to subdue. It was thus from the presence of the more volatile oils that the kerosene formerly in use, and still used in many parts of the country, was the cause of so many lamentable accidents resulting in the loss of great numbers of lives and the destruction of untold millions of property. Upon the other hand if the oil from the condenser be conducted into the kerosene tank until the process has reached too late a stage, the oil will contain a large amount of paraffine, which greatly injures its illuminating power, principally by gumming up the wick and destroying its capillarity. The refiners are tempted to go to both of these extremes by the fact that there is but small demand for naptha and paraffine oils compared with the amount produced and they consequently bring but a very low price, whilst kerosene, being used in great quantity, brings a much higher price. Paraffine oil is worth about ten cents per gallon, and naptha but about three or four cents, when kerosene is selling at twenty-five cents or upward.

In view of the dangerous character of much of the oil in use, many of the States of this country, as also Great Britain, have passed laws requiring that all oil sold or used within their boundaries should be submitted to certain tests to determine its quality. These tests were formerly two, a *flash test* and a *fire test* or *burning test.*

The flash test is employed to determine the lowest temperature at which it gives off inflammable vapor, and the fire test, or more properly termed burning test, to determine the lowest temperature at which the oil will take fire. Both are very simple of application. To apply the flash test the oil is placed in a small vessel which is placed in a water bath and slowly heated. A thermometer whose bulb is just covered by the oil serves to show its temperature. A small flame is then at frequent intervals passed somewhat quickly over the surface of the oil and the temperature at which a flash of burning vapor is first produced is termed the flashing point of this oil. To avoid variations in the result, which may be caused by draughts of air carrying away the vapor as it is formed, and by the different distances from the surface and difference in speed at which the flame may be moved, the vessel holding the oil should have a chamber attached above the oil to retain the vapor, when, if the flame is passed into it, if the oil is giving off inflammable vapor in sensible quantities, its presence will be revealed by a flash. Particular forms of testers are required to be used by some States. To apply the burning test it is only necessary to slowly heat the oil and to note the lowest temperature at which a burning splinter plunged into the oil will, instead of being extinguished, set the oil on fire. The burning test is not now generally considered as valuable as the flash test, and has been abolished from the statutes in England and in some of the American States.

There is a considerable difference of opinion as to what is a safe oil to use as determined by the flash test, many holding that as the air in our rooms rarely if ever reaches a temperature of 100° F. that an oil which will not flash below this point is safe to use; but by numerous experiments published in the American Chemist for August, 1872, it is shown that the oil in lamps frequently rises much above this point. But even this does not determine the limit of danger, for it is well known that the brass top of the lamp becomes much more highly heated, and the oil is liable to be splashed against this top and raised much above the temperature of the mass of oil in the lamp, in which case vapor will be produced though it were not when the lamp was at rest. It is also necessary to take into this consideration the fact that accidents of various kinds, like the breaking of lamps, will happen, and it is unquestionably true that *the higher the flashing point, the safer is the oil;* 100° is evidently too low, 120° is certainly not too low, and 140° is unquestionably better than either. The flashing point fixed upon by the various states as a test below which oils are not allowed to be sold, varies from 100° to 140°, most of them fixing the test at 100° or 110°, whilst a few have adopted 120° and one only, (Michigan), 140°. These laws have very greatly decreased the danger from the use of kerosene, and where the higher tests have been enforced accidents from its use have almost if not entirely disappeared.

Where the higher tests have been required, as especially in Michigan, the refiners have endeavored to create a prejudice against the high test oils and at the same time largely increase their profits by, instead of running less of the light oils into their kerosene, keeping the quantity of light oils equal to that in the low test kerosenes, and bringing up the test to the point required by law by adding the dense paraffine oils. They have thus added largely to their profits both upon the light and heavy oils, and at the same time, by furnishing a standard test oil which upon account of the paraffine present burns but very poorly, have induced many people to believe that a high test oil is necessarily a poor burning oil, which is not by any means the case.

To remedy this evil the Legislature of Michigan, at its last session, amended the law by adding a paraffine test which requires that the oil shall remain colorless and transparent when cooled for ten minutes to a temperature of 20° F. The effect of the present law is to furnish the people of Michigan with an entirely safe oil of excellent illuminating quality, at a price but little above that of the old death-dealing article.

The following table, prepared by Professor Chandler, gives the production and export in Pennsylvania from the year 1859 to 1875, inclusive.

Year.	Product'on in barrels.	Average price for year at wells.	Total value at wells.	Exported, crude or its equivalent, in barrels.	Value of exported at wells.
1859	3,200	$ 13.00	$ 41,664		
1860	650,000	6.72	4,368,000		
1861	2,113,600	2.73	5.770,128	27,812	75,926
1862	3,056,606	1.68	1,135,098	272,192	457,282
1863	2,611,359	3.99	10,419,322	706,268	2,818,009
1864	2,116,184	9.66	20,442.318	796,824	7,697,319
1865	3,497,712	6.57	22,979,967	745,113	4,895,556
1866	3,597,527	3.73	13,418,775	1,685,761	6,287,888
1867	3,347,306	3.18	10,644,443	1,676,300	5,330,634
1868	3,715,741	4.15	15,420,325	2,429,498	10,082,416
1869	4,215,010	5.85	24,657,750	2,568,713	15,026,971
1870	5,659,000	3.80	21,504,200	3,530,068	13,414,258
1871	5,795,000	4.35	25,208,250	3,890,326	16,922,918
1872	6,539,103	3.75	24,521,636	4,276,660	16,037,475
1873	9,879,455	1.84	18,178,197	4,981,441	9,165,851
1874	10,910,303	1.17	12,765,054	4,903,970	5,737,644
1875	8,619,639	1.21	10,429,763	5,200,000	6,292,000
Total.	76,326,733		245,704,880	37,690,971	20,242,147

Lard. The oily part of hog's fat separated from the

tissue by means of heat, at the temperature of boiling water, and commonly with the addition of a little water. The process of extracting the lard is known as rendering. The best lard is obtained from the fat surrounding the kidneys, but the lard of commerce is derived from the entire fat of the animal. To render the lard more firm, various adulterating substances are added, as mutton suet, potato flour, starch and lime. Alum is also added to increase its whiteness. Water is also used to adulterate lard, often as high as twelve per cent. The presence of water and its quantity may be determined by submitting a weighed portion to a moderate heat when the water will escape in bubbles. The loss of weight will determine the amount of water that was added. If starch is present, it may be detected by putting a small piece of lard in a solution of iodine, and if starch is present it will turn the solution a deep blue, or even black. The amount of adulterating material is often as high as twenty-five per cent. and consists mostly of some starchy material. Lard as generally prepared is run into kegs, barrels or tierces, but in England the best qualities are collected in bladders. In this country it is also put up in small caddies of several pounds weight.

Pure lard should be firm and white, and free from taste or smell. It should melt at 212° F. without bubbling, and the melted lard should be nearly as clear as water, and should deposit no sediment. The melting point of lard varies from 78° to 87° F. The composition of lard is 62 parts oleine to 38 of stearine and palmatine, the former, called *lard oil*, being used for lubricating machinery and illumination, and the latter for the manufacture of candles. The manufacture of lard oil is carried on to an immense extent in Chicago and Cincinnati. A large part of this oil is sent to France where it is used to adulterate olive oil, to the amount of 60 or 70 per cent. and is then returned as pure olive oil. Lard is extensively used in culinary operations as an article of food, and is the chief material used in pharmacy for forming ointments and cerates, for the latter purpose only the best lard is used and is difficult to obtain. When lard is mixed with rosin in certain proportions, it forms an excellent application for leather and for lubricating pistons of a pump, as it is found to protect the brass from corrosion. The rosin seems to prevent the formation of an acid in the lard, and is thus enabled to protect the surface of metals from rust. When used in making soap the presence of the rosin keeps the material from getting rancid when kept damp. The production of lard in this country has reached about 250,000,000 lbs. annually. In 1875 there were exported from the United States to Europe, 166,869,393 lbs. of lard, valued at $22,900,522. The amount of lard oil exported for the same year was 146,594 gallons valued at $147,384. (See Pork and Pork Packing.)

Laurel Leaves, the leaves of the tree *Laurus nobilis*. They are also known as Bay leaves and are used in cookery for the purposes of flavoring; the better qualities of figs always come packed with a few bay leaves placed at the top of each box to repel an insect which is very destructive to the fruit. The leaves are of a dark, shining green color, wavy on the margin and pleasantly aromatic.

Lead Pencils are made of a small stick of graphite

enclosed in a wooden holder and used for writing upon paper. Graphite is rarely found sufficiently pure that it can be used for pencils in the condition in which it is taken from the mines. That taken from the famous Barrowdale mine in England and the Alibert mine in Siberia is however sometimes used by simply being sawed into sheets and these again into rods which are enclosed in the wooden holders for use. A. W. Faber of Stein, Germany, has long held the monopoly of the Alibert mine the product of which has been brought by this house, by long and expensive overland journeys, from the frontiers of China.

Graphite is usually prepared for pencils by grinding to a fine powder, washing to free from impurities, after which the powder is compressed, sometimes with the addition of cement, by hydraulic pressure into solid cakes which are then sawed up in the same manner as native blocks. Recently pencils have been made from the graphite produced in the gas retorts in making illuminating gas.

Lemon, (*Citrus lemonum*), a tree closely related to the orange, citron, and lime; some botanists have considered all these as simply varieties of one species, the citron (C. medica). The lemon grows wild in the north of India, and has been long in cultivation among the Arabs who carried its culture into Europe and Africa; it is now naturalized in the West Indies and other parts of tropical America. Over thirty varieties of lemons are in cultivation, but in common they are generally classified according to the port from which they are shipped. The principal supplies of lemons received in this country are from

Sicily and are known as Messina lemons; they are generally of an oval shape, with a thick rind, smooth or rough and an abundant, sour juice. The Lustrata lemon is of large size, and with a thin, smooth, shining, and fragrant rind, under which it is difficult to discern any white. The pulp is very delicate, and abounds in an agreeable acid juice which has a delightful aroma.

It is grown in the neighborhood of Rome. The *citron* lemon is a large, oblong, warty fruit, with a rough rind which is thick and eatable. It is the least delicate of all the lemons. Lemons of good quality are also exported from Valentia. The lemon can be successfully grown in Florida and California and is receiving considerable attention.

The lemon is valued for its aromatic rind and its acid juice, and is used for cooling drinks and for flavoring in cooking. The oil of lemon is obtained by rasping the rinds and subjecting them to pressure; after resting to deposit its coarse impurities it is filtered and put into copper cans of about six gallons capacity, in which shape it is exported; the supply comes from the south of Europe. The oil has the same composition as the oil of turpentine. The oil is largly used in cookery and confectionery; the *Extract of Lemon* sold for domestic use is simply a dilute solution of the oil in alcohol, and may be made of any desired strength. When mixed with alcohol the oil retains the purity of its flavor and is preserved by the addition of alcohol, which is added as soon as received. Concentrated lemon juice is largely employed on shipboard for the prevention of scurvy on long voyages; drinking the pure juice is also said to be efficacious in attacks of acute rheumatism. *Lemon peel* is the rind of the Lemon preserved in sugar, and is preserved in the same manner as the citron (which see).

Lentil, the seed of *Ervum lens*, a plant closely related to the pea, and has been used as an article for food from the earliest times. It is a native of Europe being extensively cultivated in the southern part, also in Asia and Egypt where the seeds form an important article of food. They are largely used by the Roman Catholics during the Lenten season. The plant is slender and branching, and grows only twelve or eighteen inches high. The small flowers resemble those of the pea, and are succeeded by pods which contain from one to four round, flattened, doubly concave seeds. Lentils are imported into this country to some extent, but their use is mainly confined to Europeans. The Germans use the lentils in the preparation of soup. Lentils contain a large amount of nutriment, and lentil meal, flavored with sugar and salt, is sold under high sounding names as a food for children.

Lettuce, (*Latuca Sativa*) a well known garden vegetable used in the form of a salad. It has been cultivated in England for over 200 years and has been used from the earliest times. Lettuce is an annual plant and is largely raised by our market gardeners and finds a ready sale. For early spring use, the plants are raised in frames, or may be wintered over as in some of the hardier varieties, and transplanted in the spring. The varieties of lettuce in cultivation are very numerous and are generally divided into the cabbage lettuce, in which the leaves form a compact cluster like a cabbage, and the cos lettuce which has firm and oblong leaves, forming a long, erect head, largest above and tapering below. Among the best varieties are the Silesian, Tennis ball, Curled India, Hanson and Drumhead. Lettuce as a food contains but little nutriment, but it is said to have a cooling and soothing effect on the system. During the period of flowering the plants abound in a milky juice which is collected and evaporated, and has the properties of opium but in a much milder degree.

Liquorice, the extract obtained from the root of the plant, *Glycyrrhiza glabra*, and *G. echinata*, natives of the south of Europe and now largely cultivated all over the world. The plant belongs to the same family as the bean and the pea; it grows to the height of four or five feet with few branches. The root which is perennial grows to the length of several feet and attains an inch in diameter. After a plantation is made it is allowed to remain three years before it is disturbed; the roots are then dug and when cleansed and dry are ready for the market, and are known as liquorice root or stick liquorice. The extract of liquorice, called Spanish Juice in commerce and popularly known as ball liquorice, is prepared by boiling the root with water; the decoction is then drawn off and evaporated to a proper consistence for forming it into cylinders five or six inches long and one inch in diameter. These, packed in cases with bay leaves, are the extracts of liquorice of commerce. It is dry and brittle, of shining fracture, and if pure and genuine wholly soluble in water. It is, however, rarely found in a pure state, for it is much adulterated. The Spanish liquorice is frequently nothing else but a mixture of the juice with the poorest quality of gum arabic; starch and flour sometimes constitute nearly one half the material. Liquorice may be easily refined by dissolving it in water, and removing the foreign material which is not soluble, and it may be reformed into cylinders of any convenient size. But in place of the substances removed, others are commonly introduced, as sugar, flour, starch and gelatine. Much of our best liquorice is made in Catalonia and that made in Calabria is also of excellent quality. Liquorice is used in medicine, especially in diseases of the bronchial tubes, and also to cover the taste of disagreeable substances. Liquorice is cultivated to some extent in this country, and enters into the manufacture of chewing tobacco and into some branded liquors.

Pontefract cakes, are round lozenges of refined liquorice made at the town of that name and impressed with a rude figure of the castle.

Liquid Rennet, prepared from the dried rennet of the calf. It may be prepared by steeping the rennets in whey or brine. The steeping occupies about a week, during which time the rennet is squeezed and rubbed to extract the active principle. The liquor is then strained off and bottled for use. The English method is to steep the rennets in brine strong enough to bear an egg, adding six rennets, one sliced lemon and an ounce of saltpetre to two gallons of brine. This brine liquor is generally prepared some time before using as it is thought age improves its coagulating properties.

Lobsters a well known shell fish of the genus Homarus. The common lobster of the United States (H. Americanus), has the general appearance of the crawfish but is of larger size and lives in salt water. The shell,

which is olive or blackish geeen, with dark spots and
blotches, becomes rèd by boiling. This shell or external skeleton is changed periodically as the animal grows.
It splits in two on the head and body, the new shell forming underneath ; the old shell is cast off, and the animal
is now in a defenseless condition and hides in crevices in
the rocks until the new shell hardens. The eggs of the
lobster are glued together by a viscid matter and attached
in clusters to the hairy feet, where they remain until the
embryos are fully developed. The young differ but little
from the adults, and take shelter under the mother's tail.
They are often seen surrounded by the young six inches
in length, which retire when warned of danger by the
mother. The lobster comes to shore from deep water,
from March to May, according to locality, and departs as
irregularly in the autumn. They vary in length, as caught
for market, from one to two feet, and in weight from two
pounds upward. They are common in the markets, especially in spring and summer, and are considered a
great delicacy though the meat is rather indigestible.
There is only one American species found from the
coasts of New York northward. The best are taken on
the rocky shores of New England, north of Cape Cod.
Their food is wholly animal. The capture of the lobster
employs a large number of men both in this country and
Europe. They are caught in baskets or nets, built on
the principle of some rat traps, having funnel shaped
ends with a hole in the centre which admits the animal,
but prevents its egress by the extension of his claws.
These traps being baited are sunk in deep water and
raised every few days and the contents removed. The

number of lobsters annually consumed must be very large. It is estimated that Boston alone consumes 1,100,000 annually. In Boston the male lobster is preferred, while in New York the female has the preference. In winter the supply is principally derived from Maine, and they are there found in comparatively deep water. In Europe the great supply of lobsters is derived from Norway, and the time of catching them is regulated by law. In this country the yield is decreasing, and similar precautions should be observed. The limit of salable size in Massachusetts, is ten and a half inches. During cold weather lobsters are shipped to the interior cities, and large quantities are canned, and sold in all parts of the country.

Logwood, a name applied to a dyewood obtained from the Hæmatoxylon Campeachianum, a medium sized tree growing in Campeachy, Honduras, and other parts of tropical America. It has also become naturalized on the island of Jamaica. The tree grows to a height of from twenty to forty feet, and not over twenty inches in diameter. The trunk is crooked and covered with a rough bark, and the branches are provided with thorns. The wood is hard, compact and heavy, and susceptible of a fine polish. The outer or sap wood is yellow, but the interior or heart wood is of a deep red, and is the part exported for dyeing purposes. The wood furnishes red, blue, and black dyes, mostly the latter. To prepare the imported wood for use it was formerly cut in small chips by means of machinery; but the practice is now to grind the wood to a powder, as in this form the infusion is more easily obtained than from the chips. Logwood was used in England as a dye, soon after the discovery of America, but met much opposition and in the reign' of Elizabeth an act was passed prohibiting its use. In 1661 the act was repealed and the use of logwood rapidly increased. It was obtained from the Spanish possessions in America, and by a special treaty the English were allowed to cut and ship wood in the Bay of Campeachy, from which it is sometimes known as Campeachy wood.

Lye, (See Potash).

Macaroni, a name applied to a paste or dough worked and formed into tubes, ribbons or threads. It is an Italian invention and though of very simple process has never been made elsewhere equal to it in quality. This may be owing to the fact of the wheat having more gluten. The hardest and flintiest varieties of wheat are selected, worked, and thoroughly dried in the sun. It is then coarsely ground and run through an immense revolving sieve where the bran and flinty portion is separated from the starch. It is then successively passed through a series of sieves, six in number, each one finer than the preceding, the last being the finest quality made. The bran being all removed nothing remains but the clean flinty farina known as *seminola*. This is then mixed with warm water into a stiff dough and this dough is thoroughly mixed by means of a lever fastened on one end and the pole is then raised and depressed kneading and squeezing the dough till it is of the required consistency : this process is continued for about an hour. Another way of kneading the dough, is by piling in masses and treading down with the naked feet after, which it is rolled with a heavy roller. The dough being prepared it is then put into presses with perforated bottoms, and pressure being applied it is forced through these holes and assumes their shape. Workmen cut them of the required length as they come out. To have the pieces hollow, wire is suspended from above into the perforations and the dough forced through. During this process it is partially baked by a fire under the vessel. It is necessary to have the larger pieces hollow as they would not dry if solid. *Vermicelli* is made in the same way, only smaller and without perforations. Macaroni and vermicelli enter largely into the preparation of soups.

Mace, (see nutmeg.)

Machine Oils, Lubricating Oils, may be of either animal, vegetable, or mineral origin. Sperm oil obtained from the head of the sperm whale where it is found in a semifluid condition mixed with spermaceti; and whale oil obtained from the blubber of the right whale are the best of the animal oils for lubricating purposes, after them coming lard oil which is also excellent. Neats-foot oil is used to some extent as a machine oil. Vegetable oils found ready formed in the seeds, nuts, and other parts of various plants and obtained by pressure are of very great variety and are naturally divided into two classes: I, drying oils, of which linseed oil is an example, II, Fatty or non-drying oils. The drying oils cannot be employed as lubricants, but any of the second class may be used for this purpose.

The best mineral lubricating oils are such as have been subjected to fractional distillation and the more volatile compounds expelled. Of these the best example is the

heavy lubricating oil obtained from the paraffine oil of
the petroleum refineries. (See Kerosene). It is produced in great quantities and is of excellent quality.
Crude petroleum is considerably used and is tolerably
good under light pressures.

Most of the machine oils in market are mixtures of a
variety of different oils, usually consisting of one which
will give good body mixed with other less valuable ones.
Mineral oil with lard oil is a common mixture.

Mackerel, a well known food fish belonging to the
genus Scomber. The most important species are the
S. vernalis of North American Atlantic waters, and
S. vulgaris of European seas. The mackerel is said to
perform migrations as extensive as the herring. The fish
is taken on the shores of Great Britain from March to
June, when they retire to deeper waters. The mackerel
is a very voracious fish, feeding principally on the fry
of other fish; it is a rapid grower and attains an average of fifteen inches and a weight of two pounds. It is
considered best in May and June; the flesh rapidly becomes soft and must be eaten soon after taken from the
water; the flavor is retained in the salt fish. The fish
are taken on the British coast by means of drift nets,
which extend about two feet below the surface and are a
mile in length; they are set in the evening and the fish
are caught during their journeys at night by getting in the
meshes of the net and retained by the pectoral fins. A
single boat's crew will sometimes take £ 100 worth in a
single night. Mackerel of different species are found in
all the northern seas from Greenland to the Mediterranean, in the Black sea and that of Azov, in the waters of

Australia, East Indies and the Cape of Good Hope. The common mackerel of our coast is found in all the north Atlantic waters. Mackerel fishing is extensively carried on in Massachusetts and Maine, Gloucester and Yarmouth being the great center of fishery in this country. The fishery is carried on in vessels ranging from 45 to 90 tons, and carrying crews on an average of 15 men. The seine which is now most used did not come into general use till 1873. It weighs about 2000 pounds and is about 1000 feet in length, 150 feet wide or deep in the middle, and narrower at each end. The seine is carried by the means of a large boat and two smaller to assist. When a shoal of mackerel is observed the boats tow the seines so as to head off the shoal, when one end is carried round so as to enclose the fish in the circle. The vessel is then drawn alongside and the fish taken from the seine by dip nets. Sometimes the fish escape by diving and going under the seine. About two hours time is required to make a cast of the net: sometimes 250 or 300 barrels are taken at a single cast. In the Gulf of St. Lawrence the fish are taken by hook and line, their habits being unfavorable to seining. The process of dressing mackerel consists of four operations, splitting, gipping, ploughing and salting. The splitter splits the fish at the rate of 1500 an hour, the knife passing along the back from the head to the tail, leaving the back bone on the right side, and throws them into a tub. Two gippers stand at each tub, remove the gills and entrails and pass the fish into a barrel called the wash barrel, where they are allowed to soak. They are afterward taken out singly, laid on a board, skin down and a light stroke of the plough, which consists of a piece of a knife blade or similar instrument, is given on each side of the fish from the head two thirds down to the tail. This operation is sometimes postponed till they are landed. Salting is performed by laying the fish singly in a barrel and sprinkling a small handful of salt on each. They are then allowed to remain over night, when some of the pickle is drained off and the barrels are filled, headed up, and stowed below. A little less than a bushel of salt is used for a barrel, and it takes five wash barrels to make four barrels of salted fish. After being landed the fish are assorted, inspected, and branded by a state officer, appointed for the purpose, and repacked for market. The size and quality are denoted by numbers, 1, 2, 3, 4. No. 1 mackerel should not be less than 13 inches in length from the extremity of the head to the tail, fat, free from rust, taint or damage: No. 2 must not be less than 11 inches in length, fat, free from rust etc: No. 3 should not be less than 10 inches in length; No. 3 large, must be 13 inches in length, and are those left after the selection of No. 1: No. 4 mackerel comprise all others, and must be free from taint or damage. Mess mackerel are the finest fish with the head and tail removed. Mackerel are packed in barrels, half barrels, quarter barrels, and kits, and should contain when of full weight, 200, 100, 50, 20 and 15 pounds but the kits are often short weight. Mackerel are also preserved by canning. For the custom year ending June 30, 1875, there were received in the United States 527,633 cwt. of cured mackerel valued at $ 2,655,623. Spain, Spanish America, and the south and west of the United States are the great markets for salt mackerel.

Madder, (*Rubia tinctorium.*) The roots of this plant are used as a red dye ; it is a native of southern Europe and is largely cultivated in France, Asia Minor, and Holland. Its cultivation in the United States has not been very successful. The roots are perennial and throw up annually slender, four sided, pointed stems with the leaves arranged in whorls. The stems are furnished with prickles so as to enable it to climb on other plants. The roots proceeding from a central head are long succulent fibres, and those used for dyeing are from the size of a goose quill to that of the little finger. They are dug the third summer after sowing, deprived of the dark bark which covers them, and dried by artificial heat, and thrashed by a flail to remove the cuticle. They are then carefully sieved and the dirt removed. Being again dried in a stove till quite crisp, they are cut up by a machine furnished with knives, and then ground between mill stones and the powder bolted. In commerce the powdered roots are called madder, the whole roots being known as *lizaria.* The best qualities are from Asia Minor and Cyprus. The European madders are known as Dutch, Alsatian, and Avignon. The quality is very variable, that prepared without removing the epidermis being darker and is known as stripped. Madder as a dye is largely used in the printing of calico, on account of the great variety of tints it gives with different mordants. Madder is often adulterated with saw dust of pine barks, mahogany, logwood etc., which seriously impair its quality as a dye, and they can only be detected by actual tri-

al in dyeing the goods.   Madder has the peculiar property
when fed to animals of tinging the milk, urine and bones
red.

Malt, barley or other grain allowed to partly germi-
nate, and then kiln dried, thus preventing further germ-
ination and preserving the saccharine principle developed
during the process.   It is used in brewing.

Mandioca, Cassava, Manioc names applied to the *Manihot Utilissima* and *Manhiot sept* half shrubby, euphorbi-
aceous plants of South America.   The plant reaches a
height of six or eight feet and has a white, fleshy, tuberous
root of immense size, sometimes weighing thirty pounds.
A poisonous principle is found in all parts of the plant. in
the form of a milky, acrid juice, and the root, if eaten in
a fresh state, is highly poisonous.   The plant is of rapid
growth and the roots come to perfection in about six
months.   When the roots are taken up they are washed
and scraped, and are then grated or ground into a pulp,
and the pulp submitted to pressure, by which the poisonous juice is expressed and preserved.   The meal or pulp
that remains in the press is then dried and made into
meal and is used in making a coarse kind of bread, called
cassava bread ; the poisonous principle is so volatile that
it escapes with the heat.   The expressed juice being allowed to stand, a white, starchy deposit is found which
forms the tapioca of commerce (see tapioca).

Manna, a patent preparation used for food, similar to
semolina (which see).

Maple Sugar, a sugar made in large quantities in the
Northern United States from the sap of the sugar maple
(*Acer saccharinum.*)   This sap rises in the tree as the

frost is leaving the ground in early spring and any wound made in the tree at such time bleeds freely. As soon accordingly as thawing weather begins and while the nights are still cold and freezing, the trees are "tapped" by boring one or more holes about three fourths of an inch in diameter, usually to a depth of about two inches, into the side of each tree, a height of, three or four feet from the ground. Hollow "spikes" or spouts are then driven into these holes, or trough like spikes are set into the bark just below the holes, and buckets are placed below to catch the sap as it flows. In good weather trees will yield from three to five gallons of sap each during the day; five to seven gallons of sap being required to produce a pound of sugar. Once or twice a day the sap is collected from the buckets and drawn to the sugar camp where it is evaporated in shallow pans or sometimes in large kettles until it reaches the consistency of thin syrup. It is then removed from the pans, strained through thick flannel cloth to remove gummy matter and impurities and set aside in deep vessels and allowed to stand twenty-four hours to deposit suspended impurities. The clear syrup is then decanted off, placed in smaller pans or kettles, and egg, milk or other substance added to clarify it, and as it is brought to the boiling point is carefully skimmed. It is then boiled a short time longer until having attained the proper consistency it is removed and canned or put up in cakes and sold as maple syrup, or if sugar is to be made it is boiled until it becomes somewhat viscid whilst hot, when it is removed from the fire and allowed to cool slowly that a good "grain" may be developed, after which it is placed in moulds and allowed to solidfy, Maple syrup and sugar are much prized upon account of their peculiar pleasant flavor, and as this would be destroyed by the process the sugar is never refined.

The production of maple sugar in the United States, in 1870, according to the census statistics, amounted to 28,443,645 pounds, of which Vermont produced nearly 9,000,000 pounds, and together with six other states, namely, New York, Ohio, New Hampshire, Michigan, Pennsylvania and Indiana, produced upward of 25,000,000 pounds. The yield of *Maple syrup* for the same year was 921,057 pounds, of which Ohio and Indiana produced nearly 600,000 pounds.

Marmalade, a conserve made of the harder fruits, such as apple, pear, quince and orange, and with a large proportion of sugar. It is evaporated enough to assume form in a mould. A conserve made of softer fruits such as berries, etc., of a soft or pasty consistence is known as *jam*.

Martynias, a name given to the fruit of *Martynia proboscoides*, a plant native to the valley of the Mississippie and the plains of Mexico. The whole plant has a clammy appearance, viscid pubescent and fetid odor. The long beaked fruit when in a young state is used for making pickles.

Match, a name now applied to a small stick of wood dipped in some preparation of sulphur, phosporus etc., and producing fire by friction. It is also known as the " lucifer match," or " lucifer". The earliest form of the match was that of a stick of wood dipped in sulphur; this was ignited by applying it to the flame produced by rubbing phosphorus between folds of brown paper. This was in 1650 a few years after the discovery of phosphorus. Another form in common use was known as chemical matches, which were ignited by dipping the end which was coated with a composition of chlorate of potash, sulphur, rosin and gum and sugar, into a vial containing sulphuric acid when it was ignited by chemical action. But it was not till 1829 that the lucifer match was invented, and was introduced to the public by Faraday. Their use rapidly spread, until the manufacture became an important article of industry in Europe and the United States. The wood employed in the manufacture of matches, is the best, clear, white pine, and the quantity consumed is enormous. The wood is first sawed into blocks of equal size and of two matches in length. Then by machinery they are divided into splints of the proper size. These are dipped into melted sulphur and afterward into the phosporus composition, consisting of phosporus, 4 parts, nitre 10, fine glue 6, red ochre 5, smalt, two parts. In this country the wood is divided into splints by being forced through tubes, with numerous perforations made as near together as possible, leaving just enough of the match to give the requisite strength for cutting. These perforations may be either round or square. Matches are often made without dipping into sulphur, paraffine oil being used as a substitute. Safety matches are those in which the phosphorus is on sand paper, and the other material on the end of the match. Neither can be ignited without the use of the other. The making of matches is now almost entirely conducted by machinery. They are sawed, cut into proper sizes, carried on a double chain to the sulphur vat, then to the phosphorus vat, back again to near the cutting machine, when they are taken off and carried to the packing room. Matches are sold by the gross, and packed in boxes of various sizes. The parlor match is manufactured without sulphur, and phosphorus is replaced by the chlorate of potash and antimony; the wood is prepared with paraffine or stearine. No correct statistics of match making are given, but it is estimated that in Europe and North America, each individual uses six matches a day. Thus some idea of the immense number consumed may be formed. The workmen employed in match factories are liable to a terrible disease of the teeth and jaw, and only the utmost cleanliness can prevent it. Wisconsin and Michigan furnish a large share of the matches consumed in this country. Matches are exported to the East and West Indies, Australia, China, Mexico, South America etc.

Melon, the large edible fruit of a running vine belonging to the gourd family. The watermelon (Citrullus vulgaris) is found wild in Africa and is also a native of Asia. It is extensively cultivated in all warm countries and requires a rich soil to reach perfection. Many varieties are cultivated, and the fruit is of various sizes and colors; the seed may be white, brown or black; while the edible part may be yellow or red. The first variety seen in the northern markets is the Mountain sprout or Carolina, which is brought in large quantities from the southern states each season. It is of the largest size, longish oval; skin dark green, marbled with lighter shades; red fleshed and of excellent quality. The Black Spanish is an excellent variety; fruit medium, almost round; flesh

red, sweet and delicious. The Ice Cream, with white
flesh, and the Orange are varieties also extensively cultivated. The *Muskmelon* is *cucumus melo* and is said to
be a native of Persia. The fruit, which is very variable
in size, has a thick and fleshy pericarp ribbed externally,
while the seed and stringy placenta occupy the centre and
are separated when the fruit is eaten. This melon reaches its greatest perfection in the South but is also successfully cultivated in the North. In England they are raised
with certainty only under glass. The different varieties
mix very readily and great care is required to keep them
pure. Those most fixed in the character and the sort in
general use, are the Green Citron, a variety with medium fruit deeply netted, green flesh, delicious flavor, and
in shape almost round. The Nutmeg; fruit nutmeg
shape, skin deep green, thickly netted; flesh greenish
yellow, sugary and of excellent flavor. Other varieties
are White Japan, Skillman's Netted, Persian Ispahan and
Christiana. Muskmelons for shipping are commonly
packed in crates containing from one to two dozen.

The *Citron Watermelon*, is small, nearly round, with a
handsome variegated shell, with a white, solid, tough and
seedy flesh which is unpalatable, but is used for making
sweetmeats. The flesh is cut into convenient pieces or
fancy shapes, and cooked in syrups, becoming semitrans-
parent, and it has a distinct and peculiar flavor. The
green, thick shell of the watermelon may be preserved in
a similar manner.

Milk, condensed, a name applied to a preparation of
preserved milk. The process of condensing milk is sub-
stantially as follows; as soon as the milk is received at

the factory it is passed through the strainer into the receiving vat; from here it is conducted through another strainer into the heating cans, each containing about twenty gallons. These cans are then set in hot water and the milk is held in them till it reaches the temperature of 150° to 175° F. It is then passed through another strainer into a large vat at the bottom of which is a coil of copper pipe through which steam is conducted and here the steam is then heated up to the boiling point. The best quality of granulated sugar is then added, in the proportion of one and a quarter pounds to a gallon of milk, when it is drawn into the vacuum pan, having a capacity of condensing 3000 quarts or more at a time.

Here it remains subjected to steam for about three hours during which time 75 per cent. of the bulk of the water is removed, when it is drawn off into cans containing about forty quarts each, which are placed in cold water and allowed to cool to a little below 70° F. It is then poured into large drawing cans furnished with faucets from which it is drawn into the small cans holding about a pound each, which are taken to the tables and immediately soldered up to exclude the air. Milk prepared in this manner can be kept any length of time, and is used for all the purposes of ordinary milk. It is generally of excellent quality as only the best and sweetest milk is used, for if tainted or adulterated it would not keep.

Preserved milk thus prepared contains about one third of its weight of sugar. Numerous factories are employed in its preparation and it is destined to become an important article of food.

Molasses, the thick, viscid, dark colored syrup which drains from sugar in the process of manufacturing and when cooling. It consists essentially of water, coloring matter, uncrystallizable sugar and various 'impurities. West India and New Orleans molasses are the products that come from the sugar plantations, while " sugar house" molasses is the syrup which remains in the conversion of brown into refined sugar, and contains too little cane sugar for farther treatment. Molasses is also the term applied to the evaporated juice of the sugar maple and the sorghum plant (see sugar). Molasses is used as a substitute for sugar and is also imported for the manufacture of *rum.* The total amount of molasses produced in the United States for 1870, according to the census, was over 23,000,000 gallons, of which over 16,000,000 was sorghum, 6,000,000 cane, and nearly 1,000,000 maple. During the year ending June 30, 1875, there were imported into the United States 49,112,225 gallons of molasses, valued at $ 11,635,224 of which the larger proportion came from Cuba.

Mushroom, a species of edible fungus *Agaricus campestris.* This is the species cultivated, though other species commonly called toadstools are also edible. From the difficulty of distinguishing the poisonous from the edible species, great care should be taken in the gathering. The common and successful method of raising mushrooms is to mix fresh horse dung with bran in such proportions as to prevent too violent heating, when it is placed into long narrow beds of a foot or eighteen inches in height and the spawn or mycelium is placed in the center and covered slightly with loam. They should be covered to protect them from the sun and to retain the moisture. Mushrooms find a ready sale and are considered as excellent food.

Mustard. Two kinds of mustard are found in commerce, black and white, so named from the color of the seed. *Sinapis nigra* is the black mustard, and *S. alba* the white mustard, both natives of Europe but now cultivated and naturalized in this country. The seeds of the black mustard are small, globular, of a deep brown without and yellow within. The white is somewhat larger, and light externally. It is from the ground seed of these two mustards that *flour of mustard* so much used as a condiment is obtained. The original *Durham mustard* was made from *S. arvensis* the common wild *charlock* of England, which grew very plentifully near the city of Durham and hence its name. Mustard seed is ground by being crushed between rollers, powdered and sifted. As commonly prepared mustard is largely adulterated. Rape seed, turnip seed too old to vegetate, and wild radish are often ground with it. After being ground it is adulterated with wheat flour and turmeric; as mustard contains no starch grains, the presence of wheat flour may easily be found by the use of the microscope. Turmeric may be known by its being colored brown by a weak solution of ammonia. Mustard is largely used as a condiment and also in medicine; swallowed in any quantity with water it acts as a prompt emetic and is useful in cases of poisoning; mixed with water it is applied to the skin in the form of a plaster.

From the seed an oil is extracted by expression and is called *oil of mustard;* which is a fixed oil with little smell and not unpleasant taste. After the fixed oil is extracted from the seed, there is obtained from the residue a volatile oil which is of an exceedingly pungent odor and having sulphur among its constituents; sulphur is also present in flour of mustard and is the element that causes silver to turn black, when the mustard is mixed with water or vinegar.

Nutmeg, the kernel of the seed of Myrista, a small tree, a native of the East Indian Islands, but also cultivated in India and Central America. The tree attains the height of thirty feet with a straight stem and a branching head. The flowers are male and female situated on different trees, small and of a yellow color. The fruit is round or oval, about the size of a small peach, with a smooth surface, green at first, but becoming yellow when ripe. The external covering, which may be called a husk, is thick and fleshy; becoming dry at maturity this husk splits open in two halves, and discloses the nut covered with its aril, or mace, which is of a beautiful blood red color. Beneath the mace is a brown, shining shell containing the kernel or nutmeg. There are two varieties of the nutmeg, the royal nutmeg which produces the long nuts and has the aril or mace much larger than the nut; and the queen nutmeg which yields the more valuable round nuts and has its mace extending only half way down the nut. A plantation of nutmeg trees is raised from seed and it is not till the eighth or ninth year that the tree produces flowers. The sexes being on different trees, after the plants are two years old they are all headed down, and grafted with scions taken from the female tree, reserving only male stock for fecundation.

The natives of the East gather the fruit by hand, take off and reject the outer shell or husk; the mace is then carefully taken off and exposed to the sun's rays for one day, when the beautiful red color changes to a light brown; it is then removed from the direct rays of the sun and allowed to remain for eight days more, when it is moistened with sea water to prevent it from drying too much, or losing its oil. It is then put in bags and firmly pressed. The nuts which are still covered with their wood shell are exposed to the sun for three days, and afterward dried before a fire till they rattle when shaken; they are then beaten with small sticks in order to remove their shell which flies off in pieces; the nuts are then distributed in parcels; the fruit which contain the largest and most beautiful are intended for exportation; the second are those reserved for the use of the inhabitants; and the third contains the smallest which are damaged or unripe; these latter are burnt. Oil is obtained from the nutmeg by pressure, which has the consistence of tallow and preserves the flavor of the nutmegs. The nutmegs after having been thus selected, are pickled in lime water made from calcined shell fish and mixed with water until of a semifluid consistency. Into this mixture they plunge the nutmegs contained in small baskets, two or three times, till they are completely covered over with the liquor. They are then laid in heaps and allowed to sweat, after which they are packed in barrels or bales for exportation. The best nutmegs are those from Penang, which are about an inch in length, shaped like a damson plum, pale brown in color, furrowed on the exterior and gray inside, with veins of red running through them. Penang mace is also highly valued, and is usually of a pale cinnamon color when dry. Various ingenious methods have been resorted to for concealing defective nutmegs, and it is said they are perforated and boiled in order to extract the essential oil, and the orifice carefully closed to avoid detection ; but they may easily be told by their light weight. Mace and nutmegs are used as condiments, and to some extent in medicinal preparations. For the year ending June 30, 1875, there were consumed in the United States, nutmegs to the value of $ 650,675.

Nasturtium, (*Tropœlum Majus,*) an ornamental plant native of South America ; root annual ; stem three to eight feet long, fleshy, smooth. The fruit fleshy, becoming coriaceous. The plant is cultivated for its young fruit, which is prepared as a condiment and affords a substitute for capers.

Oat Meal, the ground grain of the common oats, *Avena sativa.* The grain of oats was formerly largely consumed in the north of England, Wales and Scotland, but is now giving way largely to wheat. The oat is peculiarly adapted for human food and is said to conduce to healthy and vigorous constitution. The husk of the oat is peculiarly hard and is indigestible and must be broken or the gastric juice cannot act upon the kernel. It is also furnished with long, sharp spike, which are apt to accumulate and irritate the intestines. Hence it is desirable that the husk should be removed entire, when it is used as an article of food for man. Only the best quality of oats should be used to form meal. The meal is generally ground in two forms in somewhat large grains as in

Scotch oat meal and in fine powder. There is also a meal intermediate between these and it is known as medium. Oat meal is generally used as a porridge although it may be made into cakes. It requires much boiling to break its starch cells, the coarse kinds requiring the most boiling. Oat meal, from being the main food of the lower classes in England and Scotland, has now become a luxury on account of its increase of price. Although a very nutritious food, its use in the United States is comparatively limited, but is undoubtedly destined to increase. *Groats* are the whole kernel of the oat when freed from its husk; it is boiled in milk or water for the preparation of gruel, and requires a long time to thoroughly cook it.

Olive, (*Olea Europa*), is supposed to have come originally from Asia. It grows well in Syria, and is now naturalized in the south of France, Italy and Spain. The culture of the olive is one of the principle commercial resources of the countries of southern Europe and the Northern States of Africa. The olive has been cultivated from the earliest times, and is of common mention in the Scriptures. The olive tree is from fifteen to twenty feet or more in height, having the growth of a bushy tree, and is very long lived, some specimens being considered a thousand years old. The flowers are small and white, and the fruit is an oval drupe or plum, of a greenish, whitish or violet color, with a stone in the center, the flesh on the exterior containing the oil. There are many varieties of the olive in cultivation; the long leaved is that which is generally grown in the south of France and Italy, and the broad leaved is that which is mostly grown in Spain. The long leaved variety produces the finest oil, that of the latter being of a strong, rank flavor. The oil is obtained by pressure; when the fruit begins to ripen, it becomes of a wine color and is fit for making the oil. The fruit is gathered, carried to a mill and bruised, the stones being set at such a distance that they do not crush the stone of the olive. The flesh covering the nut and containing the oil in its cells being thus prepared, is put into bags made of rushes, and moderately pressed; and thus is obtained in considerable quantity a greenish, semi-transparent oil of superior excellence which is known as *Virgin's oil.*

The pulp after the first pressure is moistened with water, and again pressed; this oil though inferior to the first, is still used for table oil. The pulp is again broken in pieces, soaked in water, left to ferment in large cisterns and again pressed. The oil thus obtained is of inferior quality, and is used in making soap and for manufacturing purposes. Olive oil may be said to form the butter and cream of Spain and Italy. It is very nutritious and is extensively used as an article of food. The fruit is prepared as a pickle, by repeatedly steeping them in water to which quick lime has been added, or any alkaline substance, to shorten the operation. They are afterward soaked in pure water, and then taken out and boiled in salt and water, with or without an aromatic. They are preserved by being kept in strong brine, and excluded from the air; they are also preserved in oil. For the year ending June 30, 1875, there were imported into the United States, 173,688 gallons of olive oil, valued at $ 127,240.

Salad Oil or Sweet oil is the name applied to olive oil after being purified by settling, filtering, washing, and by various chemical means. Of this salad oil, there were imported for the same year, 176,119 gallons valued at $ 335,918. Much of the table oil imported from France is adulterated with lard oil obtained from the United States, and reshipped as oil of Lucca or Provence. It is also largely adulterated by the oil from the common peanut, which is grown in Northern Africa for that particular purpose.

Onion, (*Allium Cepa.*) A well known garden vegetable belonging to the Lily family. The onion is cultivated for its bulb like root which is simply the bases of the leaves, thickened and overlapping each other. The onion is a native of Asia and Egyyt where it has been cultivated from time immemorial, and from there distributed all over the world. The bulb of the onion is highly nutritious and is eaten raw or cooked in various ways. As grown by market gardeners they are grown from sets and nearly all sold in bunches in the green or unripened state. Grown from seed they are mostly raised on farms, and are sold in the dry or ripened state, and form an important article of commerce. The best varieties in common use are Red Wethersfield, Yellow Danvers and White or Silver skinned onion.

Potato onions or Multipliers as they are sometimes called, are the mildest of all onions, but are little grown for market. They are raised from the bulbs, planted early in spring, and the increase is formed by the bulb as it grows splitting up and dividing into six or eight bulbs, these forming the crop when at maturity. *Top or*

Tree onions are the bulbs formed at the top of the plant in place of the flowers. They resemble a cluster of hazel-nuts, and are planted to produce early crops of green onions for the market. The field onions are dug in August, and allowed to remain on the ground for two or three weeks till they are thoroughly dried, and then packed away in a cool, dry place. Our early markets are supplied with ripe onions from the Bermuda Islands, and they are of excellent quality.

Orange, the fruit of several varieties of the genus *Citrus,* but mostly referred to *Citrus Aurantium.* It is a small, evergreen tree, with beautiful leaves and most fragrant flowers. It is supposed the orange originally came from the East Indies or China ; it is now cultivated in every region of the earth where the temperature is sufficiently warm to permit it to thrive. The oranges of commerce are mostly derived from Spain, Sicily, Malta, Portugal and Cuba. Florida also exports fine fruit and its cultivation is profitably conducted in California. The young plants are raised from seed in nurseries and after cultivation for about six or eight years, they are grafted with a scion of a cultivated tree, and in two years more are transplanted to the orchards. They begin to bear fruit at the age of thirteen or fourteen years, and if well cultivated will produce 28 or 30 oranges for the first crop. In about six years more it reaches maturity, and will bear from 1000 to 10,000 oranges and even as high as 20,000. The orange tree in Italy yields but one crop a year. It flowers in May and is not fit for gathering until in December. In some places it is gathered in September, and allowed to ripen afterwards. This is the method generally pursued when shipped to America. The fruit is gathered in September while yet green, wrapped separately in light paper, and carefully packed in wooden boxes or cases, and shipped on a voyage lasting some weeks, and when opened are found fresh, sweet, and quite ripe. The blood orange is largely cultivated in Sorrento, but is not considered a distinct species. Our supply comes largely from Spain, Portugal, Italy, the Islands of the Mediterranean and Cuba. Among the varieties of oranges imported is the Portugal or Lisbon. This is the most common of all, and is generally of a round shape sometimes flattened, and sometimes a little elongated or oblong. The rind is thick and of a reddish yellow or deep orange color. The China orange is the most delicious of all oranges, and has a smooth, shining rind, so thin it can scarcely be separated from the pulp. The St. Michæl's is probably a variety of this, is small and flattened at the end, with a very smooth rind, a light colored pulp, and sugary flavor. When the tree of this orange is young and vigorous, the skin of the fruit is thick and contains many seeds. But when the tree becomes old, the rind of the fruit is thin and the seeds are absent. The oranges from Valentia are also of excellent quality. Oranges shipped from Messina and known as Messina oranges are very common in our markets. From the flowers of the orange is distilled the well known perfume, *Orange Flower Water*. They also furnish by distillation, the oil of *neroli* much used in making *eau de cologne*. The rind of the orange is also candied and preserved in the same manner as the Citron, and is known as *Orange Peel*. It is used by confectioners and in domestic economy. The young, unripe fruit of the orange is preserved whole in sugar, crystallized and eaten as a sweetmeat.

Oysters, the common name applied to numerous species of bivalves, mollusks belonging to the genus Ostrea, of the family Ostreidæ. The genus is very widely distributed, members of it being found in nearly all seas except in polar latitudes. The best known species are two, the *Ostrea edulis* of Europe, and *Ostrea Virginiana* of the Eastern United States. The American species is larger and better flavored than the European. It is found all along the eastern coast of the United States, but is especially abundant in Chesapeake Bay. It is found naturally in beds, the shells being attached to each other, and to any rough objects upon the bottom, in moderately deep water ; water usually from seven to thirty feet, but varying with climate and other conditions. They are more frequently found in semi-fresh waters, at the mouths of rivers and in bays, and necessarily in somewhat sheltered positions, for where the water at the bottom is agitated, they become covered with sand and mud and are thus killed. There are very many different varieties, their character and especially quality seeming to depend very much upon the locality and conditions under which they are grown. Considerable quantities of fresh water mixed with the water of the ocean, is especially necessary to produce oysters of large size and good quality. Chesapeake Bay furnishes the required conditions in a high degree, and the oysters grown there are universally regarded as superior.

In recent years the cultivation of the oyster has become of very considerable importance. In France and England the natural beds have become almost entirely exhausted, which has led the French government to make extended investigations into the feasibility of artificial culture, and to adopt measures to encourage the production of this valuable and easily grown food supply. Through government encouragement and aid, large quantities of American oysters have been obtained and planted, and the industry has grown to large proportions. The French system of oyster farming differs from that of England and America, in one important particular, namely: in breeding from their artificial beds, thus growing their own young instead of obtaining plants from natural beds.

Artificial beds for the growth and fattening of oysters are abundant in this country, but artificial breeding is scarcely at all practiced. Plants are gathered from August to October generally along the coast of the Carolinas, where are prolific natural beds, in which the oysters are too salt and small for use, being but from one to two inches in length when taken. These are taken immediately to the planting grounds, where they are shoveled overboard in sufficient quantity to cover the bottom, where they are allowed to remain for from six months to a year to grow and fatten. At the end of this time, they will have become four or five inches in length and fit for market. The best and most largely used planting grounds are in Chesapeake Bay, sheltered localities where the water is from two to seven feet deep being preferred. The implements used in oyster fishing are the dredge, the tongs and the fork. The dredge is used upon natural beds in deep water. It consists of an iron net set in an iron frame, furnished with teeth so arranged as to tear the oysters from their beds, and gather them into the net as it is dragged over the bottom by a small vessel, to which it is attached by a rope. The dredge weighs about 150 pounds, and will hold about three bushels. When filled it is drawn on board its vessel by means of a windlass. The tongs consist of two iron rakes jointed together near their heads, and furnished with long, wooden handles. They are used where the water is from two to eight feet deep. The fisher uses them from a small boat, over the side of which he leans and gathers the oysters from the bottom. The fork is but little used, and only where the water is shallow and the oysters entangled in sea moss.

The oysters after being taken are for the most part carried to large oyster houses, where several hundred hands are frequently employed in opening and packing them for the market. They are put up either in cans or in bulk, and are of several grades the best being known as *selects* ; following which come *standards* and various lower grades.

The oyster beds of the Chesapeake Bay cover an area of over three thousand square miles, and the annual yield of oysters from them is estimated at upwards of thirty millions of bushels. Large quantities of oysters are hermetically sealed in cans and are known as *cove oysters*.

Oyster Plant, (see Salsify.)

Paper. The earliest form of paper of which we have any mention was the papyrus of the ancient Egyptians, used by them 2500 years B. C., and manufactured from the papyrus-plant. About 450 B. C. parchment was introduced into use for the purpose of making books. The Chinese have also long made paper from silk and cotton. The Moors introduced the manufacture of paper into Spain, from whence it gradually spread over Europe. Paper making at the present time is an extensive industry, in the United States, about $ 40.000,000 being invested, in the manufacture. Paper is made from cotton and linen rags, various kinds of straw, wood, some species of grass, old books, paper and all sorts of waste material containing vegetable fibre. Wood used in making paper is reduced by mechanical or chemical means to the condition of pulp and is generally mixed with rags in the manufacture. In making paper from rags, the rags are first carefully sorted and all foreign material removed; cut fine by the workmen or by a cutting machine, thoroughly dusted over wire screens, and then subjected to boiling in large vats under a steam pressure of twenty to sixty pounds per square inch. They are usually boiled in a solution of lime, and for some grades soda-ash is added, which dissolves all the grease and loosens the dirt. From the boiler the rags are placed in the washing engine with plenty of water, where they are thoroughly washed by means of machinery. After being thoroughly washed the mass is bleached by the addition of chloride of lime and a small quantity of sulphuric acid. From the bleaching vats the material is taken to the beating engine, where the chloride liquor is washed out, and the pulp thoroughly beaten. This half stuff, as it is now called, is ready for the paper machine, where the pulp is made into sheets of paper.

Before the introduction of the Fourdrinier machine the pulp was made into sheets of paper by hand. When the sheets come from the machine they are of course wet, and are then hung up to dry. When dry the operation of sizing follows. For writing paper this is performed by dipping the dry sheets in animal sizing, a weak solution of glue. The sheets are again hung up to dry, after which they are pressed, calendered, and otherwise worked as their quality may require. Wrapping paper is generally made from straw, flax, hemp, manilla and also rags. It is packed for market in bundles and sold either by the ream, or by the pound. Paper sacks are manufactured by machinery and immense quantities are used by the retail trade. A waterproof paper has lately appeared in the market and is very useful in the handling of butter, lard, or any greasy or wet material. It is made of thin, transparent paper, dipped in a solution of some kinds of wax, or paraffine.

Paraffine, a white, waxy solid resembling spermaceti, found native in petroleum as obtained from the oil wells, in the mineral wax azocerite which is found in great quantities in Spain and Austria, also in coal and shale oil, and is a product of the destructive distillation of many organic substances. It may be obtained from any of these substances, by first freeing them from their more volatile components by the process of fractional distillation, and then cooling and pressing the residue, after which it is purified by treatment with sulphuric acid and caustic soda. When pure, paraffine is colorless, tasteless, and odorless. Its specific gravity is 0.870, it melts at from 113° to 149° F. and boils at 600° F. It is insoluble in water but readily soluble in boiling alcohol from which it crystallizes out almost entirely upon cooling. It is very little affected by any of the acids or alkalies. Paraffine is rapidly becoming of much importance in the arts and is already applied to many economic uses, although it was discovered so recently as 1830 and not produced in any quantitiy until since 1860. Its most important application is perhaps in the manufacture of candles (which see). It is also largely used for waterproofing fabrics and leather for shoes. Dress silks are frequently treated with it, being thus protected from stains if liquids chance to be spilled upon them. It is employed to a considerable extent in the manufacture of electrical apparatus, being valuable from its high resistance to the passage of the current. Chewing gum in large quantities is now made from paraffine (See *Kerosene.*)

Paris Green, the popular name in America of the Aceto-Arsenite of Copper $\left. \begin{array}{c} (C_2H_3O)^2 \\ Cu \end{array} \right\} O_2 + 3\ CuOAs_2O_3.$ It is more properly known as Schweinfurt green, the name Paris green being applied in Europe to an entirely different pigment.

It is a powder of a rich green color and has been long in use as a pigment for which purpose it would be very valuable if it were not for its intensely poisonous character. In paint it produces one of the finest green colors possible to obtain. It is much used for coloring paper, especially wall paper, but this practice cannot be too strongly condemned, as children are often poisoned by chewing such paper, and all who live in houses whose walls are covered with paper colored with this material are liable to be seriously and even fatally poisoned by minute particles which become separated from the paper and float in the air of the room. Numerous cases of wholesale poisoning from this source are to be found in medical statistics.

Since the appearance of the Colorado potato beetle, Paris green has become familiarly known and very generally used throughout the entire country, for the destruction of this insect pest. For this purpose it is first mixed in the proportion, of one part to twenty or thirty, or even more, of some dry substance as gypsum or flour; or two or three spoonsful are stirred into a pail of water and the vines are then sprinkled with this dry or wet mixture. As thus employed it is very effective in destroying the beetle and is the only effective remedy which has been found available where the insect appears in great numbers. Strong fears were entertained when it was first used in this way, that ill effects would result from the poison being absorbed by the potato or that wells in the vicinity would become poisoned by it. It has however been conclusively shown that it is soon rendered insoluble and harmless by combining with other elements found in the soil. Its long continued use throughout the western United States, without a single evil result being recorded is a sufficient answer from experience to any fears that may be entertained. It is of course necessary that great care be exercised in handling the material and many accidents have resulted from carelessness in leaving it where it might be gotten at by children or animals.

Parsley (Petroselinum sativum) a biennial umbellife-
rous herb cultivated in gardens.   It is in more general
use for garnishing meats than any other vegetable of our
gardens.   It is also extensively used in soups, stews,
etc.   It comes into use during the fall and winter and
spring.

Parsnip, (Pastinaca sativa) a plant of the Parsley family ; root biennial, fusiform, large and fleshy ; stem 3-5
feet high, rather stout, furrowed and branching.   It is a
native of Europe but now of universal cultivation, for its
fine, esculent root, which in the best varieties are remarkably rich and marrow like.   A number of varieties are in
cultivation but they closely resemble each other, and
their peculiarities are probably determined by the soil on
which they are raised.

Pea (Pisum sativum) a well known plant of the order
Leguminoseæ, and largely cultivated in the market gardens.   It matures at widely different dates in the northern
and southern sections of the country.

The pea is used as an article of food for both man and
beast, and one species *P. Arvemse* in some regions is largely cultivated as a forage plant.   Peas are eaten both in
the green and dry state.   In the dry state large quantities are shipped to England where the dry pea is much
more used than in this country.   The canning of green
peas is quite an industry and it is aways found on grocers shelves.   The native country of the pea is unknown ;
but it is cultivated largely in Europe as well as in this
country.

Peaches, the fruit of the *Prunus Persica*, a small tree
belonging to the Rose family, and native of Central

Asia. Peaches are grown in nearly all warm, temperate climates, the northern limit at which they are hardy in ordinary situations in the United States being about 42° north latitude, or about the isothermal line of 50° F. The more noted peach growing sections of this country are portions of New Jersey, Delaware, Maryland and Illinois, and a narrow belt along the lake shore in western Michigan.

Peaches are of two principal varieties, clingstones and freestones and of each of these there are numerous subvarieties some of the best of which are Hale's early, Crawford's early, early York, Red Rareripe, Old Mixon Free, Smock Free, and Crawford's Late. Fresh peaches are sold very extensively in the larger markets but from their tendency to decay require to be handled rapidly. They are put up in baskets varying in size from a half peck to a bushel and sold by the basket but rarely measured. It is very desirable that some uniformity or regulation in regard to baskets should be adopted in order to avoid the present uncertainty in regard to quantity in handling this fruit. Great quantites of peaches are now put up in cans and form the most staple of the canned fruits. Very many are also dried but from the great loss of flavor this method of preserving them is much less common than before the process of canning was resorted to. Peach brandy is made in considerable quantities by distilling ripe peaches.

Peach trees and fruit are subject to a very serious disease known as the *yellows*, which in many sections of the country threatens to entirely prevent the growing of this fruit. The disease also renders unfit for use many of the peaches which are now sold in our markets. The symptoms of this disease are, in the tree, a production of numerous wire like shoots from the sides of the limbs and a yellow color of the leaves; in the fruit, 1st premature ripening; the fruit being ripe from two to four weeks before its proper time; 2nd the presence of patches and spots of a deep purple color upon the peach, no matter what is its proper tint; 3d a deeper color, watery condition, and insipid taste of the flesh.

The cause of the disease is not well understood. Many have been led to believe that it was caused by an attack of fungoid parasites, whilst others have supposed that it was due to overbearing and poor cultivation. It is undoubtedly true that trees which have become weakened by such means are more liable to the attacks of the disease than strong and vigorous ones.

It is also a question of dispute whether the disease is contagious or not, although it is well known that if the disease makes appearance in an orchard the whole will soon be destroyed unless the diseased trees be at once removed.

The yellows are known only in the northern United States; the southern United States and Europe having never been troubled by the disease. No effective remedy is known.

Pea Nuts, Ground Nuts, the fruit of the *Arachis hypogeæ*, an annual plant of the order Liguminoseæ, native of South America. It is cultivated in the southern United States, in southern Europe, in Africa and Asia. The plant is of a trailing, straggling habit, growing to a height of about two feet. It has a remarkably interesting peculiarity in the manner of producing its fruit. After the flowers have fallen off, the young pods are, by a natural motion of the stems, forced into the ground to a depth of three or four inches, where they remain to develope and ripen, and from whence they are obtained by pulling the vines to which they adhere. This peculiarity has led to the quite prevalent but false idea that the pods grow upon the roots of the plant. Peanuts furnish a very important article of food among many of the negro tribes of Africa, and they are also extensively grown in that country for the manufacture of oil, which is entensively used to adulterate olive oil, and great quantities of which are also sold as olive oil without the admixture of any of the genuine article. By many it is claimed to be fully equal in value to olive oil. In this country since the war the crop has become of much importance in Virginia and some other southern states. There are two well marked varieties, the *Virginia* and *Carolina* or *African*, the former having a much larger pod, and the bean is sold for eating while the latter is used principally for the manufacture of oil. An average crop of peanuts is 50 or 60 bushels to the acre.

Pears, the fruit of *Pyrus communis*, a small tree belonging to the order Rosaceæ, native of Europe but now cultivated in all temperate climates. Pears have been cultivated from the earliest historic time, but all of the varieties now considered at all valuable are of quite recent origin, greater improvement having probably been made in the quality of this fruit within a comparatively few years than in any other. Many varieties of the pear are nearly as hardy and as easily grown as apples, whilst some of the best varieties are quite tender and liable to be destroyed by the cold winters of the northern United States. The Pear is grown both as a standard, budded or grafted upon pear seedlings, and as a dwarf by grafting it upon quince stock. The thorn and mountain ash are sometimes used as dwarf stocks. Dwarf trees come into bearing much younger than standards and in some varieties the quality is improved by the quince stock. There are now upward of one thousand varieties of pears in cultivation, a few of the best of which are Bartlett, Doyenné d'Eté, Flemish Beauty, Belle Lucrative, Sickel, Beurré d'Anjou, Duchesse d'Angoulême, Jarganelle, Lawrence and Winter Nelis. Most varieties are much improved in quality by being picked from the trees some days before ripening and placed in a cool, dark place to ripen. Some are almost entirely worthless if allowed to ripen on the tree. Pears are sold in market either fresh or put up in hermetically sealed cans.

Pecan, (*Carya olivæformis*) a species of hickory growing on river banks from Indiana southward to Texas. The tree is tall and straight, reaching to a height of 60 to 70 feet. It has annually an abundance of sweet   flavored nuts, their husks being thin and the shells soft and easily broken, and of a yellowish brown or olive color. In gardens where it is well sheltered it will bear the winters as far north as the Hudson River. Its culture was introduced into France many years ago. Pecan nuts form quite an article of commerce, and are sold by the pound.

Pepper. BLACK PEPPER and WHITE PEPPER are both the fruit of *Piper Nigrum*. The plant is a native of India and is cultivated throughout the whole of the tropics and particularly in Java, Sumatra, Borneo and Molucca; it is also largely raised in the the tropical regions of America. It is a shrubby plant, eight or ten feet in length and when cultivated, requires support by trellises or by planting against some rough-barked tree. The plant is propagated by cutting and comes into bearing in three or four years after planting, and furnishes two crops a year for eleven or twelve years. The fruit is a berry, small, produced in spikes, green at first, then changing to red, and black when fully ripe. When ripe they are gathered and spread on mats to dry, and trodden under foot to separate them from their spikes. White pepper is the ripe berry, deprived of its skin by soaking it in water, rubbing it off and drying it in the sun. It is of less value than the black pepper and is not so generally employed. Pepper is used as a condiment, and is a warm, carminative stimulant; it strengthens the stomach and assists digestion. In the tropics the inhabitants use it with all their food, drink it in decoction and make fermented liquors from it. The ground pepper of our shops is largely adulterated with mustard, ground rice, wheat etc. Pepper dust, the refuse and sweepings of ware rooms, is used to mix with the ground article. For the year ending June 30, 1875, there was consumed in the United States pepper to the value of $ 922,941.

Africa, the East and West Indies furnish the .largest part of the spices consumed in this country.

Pickerel or **Pike,** a name applied to the many species of fish of one genus, *Esox*. All the species bear a general resemblance to each other, and most people are familiar with some of the many species. They differ in the length of the snout, the number of rays in the dorsal and anal fins and in the color. The pike is a very strong, active and fierce fish: it darts from its cover with extreme velocity, swallowing small fish, water-rats and even small aquatic birds. It is called the shark of fresh waters, and is very destructive to other fish. The common lake pike reaches a length of three feet; the back is of a deep greenish-brown color, the sides with numerous rounded, oblong and pale yellow spots. The common pike or pickerel abounds in all the rivers and lakes of the northern United States, and is excellent for eating. Large numbers are taken through the ice in winter, by means of a hook, and sent to market in a frozen condition. The lake pickerel is also salted and packed in barrels, but its flesh is not very good in this condition.

Pickles, vegetables of various sorts, as cucumbers, onions, green beans, cabbage, mushrooms; also fruits, as melons, pears, peaches, unripe nuts, etc., preserved in vinegar, and to be eaten as a condiment. They are generally prepared by being allowed to steep some time in salt water and then parboiled and transferred into vinegar, along with salt and various spices, such as ginger, pepper, allspice, mustard, pepper pods, etc. East India pickles are flavored with currie powder mixed with mustard and garlic. The vinegar is sometimes put on the pickles in a cold state, or it may be boiling. Immense quantities of pickles are used, especially on shipboard, and they form an almost necessary article of diet. In order to render them more attractive they are often colored by the addition of sulphate of copper, or by boiling the vinegar in copper vessels. Most of the vinegar used in pickling contains sulphuric acid, and this acting on the copper of the kettle forms sulphate of copper, a deadly poison. Pickles are now put up colored and uncolored, so that there is no necessity of using the colored article. The presence of copper may easily be detected by its giving a blue color to a solution of ammonia. For the acid in the vinegar, see *Vinegar*.

Pie Plant (see Rhubarb).

Pine Apple, (*Ananassa sativa*) a native of South America but now cultivated in Florida and the West Indies and to some extent in the East. In England they are cultivated in hot houses erected for the purpose and consequently are very costly. The fruit called the pine-apple is not in reality one fruit, but a collection of many, what are called the pips being the true fruit, so that the pine-apple is a head formed of many fruits closely united together. Before maturity the fruit of the pine-apple is almost caustic and its use is then attended with danger. The plant is propagated by suckers and crowns, the fruit maturing in from three to four months after planting the suckers. The fruit varies in size from one to nine or ten pounds.

Pine Apples should be cut before fully ripe, leaving on a stem several inches in length, and with the crown adhering to the tip. The leaves of the plant yield an excellent fibre and in the East the natives manufacture from it a cloth known as Pina Muslin. Pine-apples are also canned for the market.

Pipe, an implement for the smoking of tobacco. It consists of a bowl of wood, stone, clay or meerschaum, and a tube either stiff or flexible, long or short, and connected with a mouthpiece, through which the smoke is drawn. Pipes of clay are largely manufactured in England and imported into this country. *

Plums. The old cultivated varieties are generally referred to *Prunus domestica*, a native of the Old World. It grows to a height of twelve or fifteen feet and branching. The flower precedes the leaves ; the fruit is a drupe, oval, of various colors from black to pale greenish-yellow, covered with bloom, and the flesh rather fine. Numerous forms of this have been in cultivation, but the ravages of the plum curculio have been so bad that the culture is comparatively abandoned. Among the best varieties of the cultivated plums are the Washington, Duane's Purple, Yellow Egg and Green Gage. The American wild plum, *Prunus Americana*, grows wild in thickets, along fence rows and banks of streams, from Canada to Texas. The fruit is red and in its wild state is rather small and unpleasant, but it is much improved by cultivation and although of a pleasant flavor when fully mature, is not adapted to culinary purposes. The foreign or garden plums when fully ripened are among the most delicious of our fruits.

Pollock, a name applied to several species of fish of the genus *Merlangus*, and members of the cod family. They have a general resemblance to the cod, being generally of a greenish or darkish color above, and white or whitish on the belly. They range in length from one to three feet. They are valuable as food, and some of the species are cured similar to the cod but are less valuable than the latter fish.

Pork and Pork Packing. The importance of the

trade in pork and lard is so great that an extensive description of its production will be given. The great pork packing points in this country are the cities of Chicago and Cincinnati. The method pursued in both places is very similar. The buildings are of large size and strongly constructed. In those of three stories, the lower floor is used for curing and storing the material, the second floor for packing and shipping, and the third for cooling and cutting up the hogs. The roof is constructed flat and very heavy and tight, and divided off into yards and pens, and will in some cases hold as high as 4,000 heads at once. The animals are driven up an inclined plane to the roof, where they are allowed to remain for a few days before being killed. When all is ready for killing, the hogs are driven, some twenty at once, into a small pen with a fine-grated floor. A man then enters, and, with a long-handled hammer, deals each hog a heavy blow on the forehead, between the eyes, which instantly drops him to the floor. After he has lain a few moments another man enters the pen, and with a sharp knife sticks each hog, the blood flowing through the grating and being conducted by spouts to large tanks out-side the building. While this is done another lot is driven into an adjoining pen and served in the same manner.

The first lot, by this time having sufficiently bled, is slid down an inclined plane directly into the scalding tub or vat, made of wood, some six feet wide, twenty feet long and three feet deep, the water in which is heated by steam pipes and kept at a regular temperature ; here they are floated along and turned by men at the sides until they are taken out by a simple contrivance, operated by a single man, and deposited upon the end of a long inclined table. Two men stand ready and take from the back in an instant all the bristles that are suitable for the brush maker and cobbler, depositing them in boxes and barrels for removal. Another pair of men standing on opposite sides of the table divest another part of the hog of its coat, and so on through some eight or ten pairs of men, who each have a different part to perform in the cleansing of the hog, until it reaches the last pair, who put in the gambrel sticks and swing it on a track on an overhead railway, where it receives a shower bath of clean, cold water, washing it clean from any particles of dirt, and giving it a final scrape with the knives. It then passes along to a man who opens it and removes the large intestines. It then passes to a second man who takes out the small intestines, heart, lights, etc. ; the hog then receives a thorough drench of clean water and passes to another man, who splits the backbone down. They are then taken from the hooks and borne away by overhead railways and hung up to cool, one man being sufficient to handle the largest hog with ease. At this point a man loosens up the leaf-lard, ready to be removed when cooled, which, together with the splitting of the back-bone, helps much to cool the meat. The hogs are allowed to hang for about two days before being cut up. The fat on the small intestines is removed by men and boys, and after being washed is ready to be placed in the lard tank.

After cooling, the hog is ready to be cut up, and is carried from the cooling room to the cutting room, each hog being weighed as he is brought up, and a record kept of the weight. Having been rolled on the block one blow from an immense cleaver severs the head from the body ; another blow severs the saddle, or hind parts containing the hams ; another lays it open on the back ; another one for each leg. The leaf lard being already loosened is now stripped from the carcass. The remainder of the hog is then cut up into the various kinds of meat it is most suited for, the whole operation taking but a few moments of time, two good men having cut over 2,000 in less than eight hours. A day's work is ordinarily from 1,100 to 1,200 head.

The building for the extraction of lard adjoins the main building, separated by a heavy wall, and is also three stories in height. In the second story are arranged several iron tanks, made of heavy boiler iron, twelve feet high, and six feet in diameter, capable of sustaining a high pressure. These extend up through the floor above into the third story, where each one is provided with a large manhole, into which the leaf lard, head, gut lard, and pork trimmings are emptied, until the tank is full, when it is closed and the whole subjected to a jet of steam from the boilers, of a pressure of fifteen pounds per inch ; each tank is supplied with a safety valve, so that on reaching the maximum pressure allowed, it passes off, forcing a continual flow of steam through the whole mass. By this process every particle of lard is set free. One of the tanks is reserved for making *white grease*, in which the paunches, intestines, etc., and the refuse from the slaughter houses are placed and subjected to the same steam process. Another tank is used for trying out dead hogs which have been killed by accident, into which they are dumped whole. The product of this is known as *yellow grease.* After the mass in the lard tanks has had steam on for a proper time, a faucet is opened about the middle of the tank where the lard and water meet, and the lard is drawn off into an immense open iron tank, called a clarifier, with a concave bottom, provided with a steam jacket at the bottom; here it is heated up to 300° F., sending all foul matters in a thick scum to the top, where it is skimmed off, all heavier matters settling to the bottom. A faucet is then opened at the bottom, and the sediment withdrawn. The remaining lard is then run into coolers, and thence into barrels where it is weighed and branded pure lard. After the lard has been drawn from the tanks, a large manhole is opened at the bottom and the whole mass is drawn out in large wooden tanks set even with the floor.

The mass is again subjected to a boiling heat, and all the remaining lard is set free and runs to the top. The water is then drawn off and the solid residue is used in the preparation of manure. In this residue you will find the bones and even the teeth so soft as to be readily crushed by the fingers. The bristles and hair are purchased and but little of the original hog is wasted. The curing room occupies the lower floor. The first process is to dress all the meats except the shoulders, with a solution of saltpetre, which is applied with a swab to the green meat, and while wet with it is covered and rubbed with salt, and then packed in tiers to cure. In three weeks it is all handled over and treated to a second dressing of salt, and again in seven days more when it is pronounced cured. After a few days the English meats are carefully scraped and smoothed off preparatory to packing. These meats are usually packed in square boxes containing 500 pounds. The barrel meat is packed in the second story. Enough pieces of the various kinds are weighed out for a barrel; it should be 200 pounds, but 190 to 196 pounds is generally put in as it is found the pork increases in weight by the absorption of brine. It is then packed, a layer of meat, then salt, until filled, the whole are then headed and branded. Each barrel is then filled with brine and allowed to stand with a small bung open a short time. More brine is added if necessary and the bung closed. Most of the hams are cured and smoked. The curing process varies with different houses, some applying the saltpeter and salt and packing in bulk to cure; while others prepare a pickle (sweet pickle) by the use of three ounces of saltpetre and one to two quarts of molasses for a brine, the brine being made to show 30° of saltness by the meter After the meat has lain a sufficient time in the pickle it is taken out and packed in bulk for curing, or hung up and allowed to remain for several weeks; after this the hams may be smoked if so desired. For summer shipment the hams are wrapped in paper and canvassed; the canvass being generally covered with a preparation of chrome yellow; and in its use great care should be taken as it is a deadly poison. Hams shipped to England are seldom smoked but are shipped in pickle.

The various terms applied to packed pork are generally as follows:

CLEAR PORK, is pork put up of ribs with the sides out.

MESS PORK is made of the sides of the thickest and

fattest hogs, cut into strips six to seven inches wide running from back to belly.

ORDINARY MESS PORK is cut as above but made from lighter hogs ranging from 170 to 200 pounds.

PRIME MESS is cut from a still lighter class ranging from 100 to 150 pounds, the shoulder being included. It is generally cut into four pound pieces so that fifty should make a barrel.

In the cutting of meats for the English markets the following are the terms and description:

SHORT RIBBED MIDDLES. This is the side of the medium weight hog (shoulder and ham off) the bone removed, and the ribs cracked through the middle.

SHORT CLEAR is the same part cut from the best hogs with back bone and all the ribs taken out.

LONG CLEAR is the side including the shoulder with all bones removed.

LONG RIB is the same as above with the shoulder and back bone out; ribs left in.

CUMBERLANDS is the shoulder and side together, with back bone out; the shank cut short.

STRETFORDS sides and shoulders together; the shoulder and bone taken out, shank left in; back bone and upper half of rib removed.

LONG ENGLISH HAMS is the whole hip bone being left in and the ham left the full size.

BACON, made from the shoulders and ribs and known as *rib, clear rib* having the back bone sawed out; and *clear* being free from both back bone and ribs.

LARD OIL is made by placing the lard in heavy duck bagging, and subjecting it to heavy pressure; the residuum being stearine largely used in the manufacture of candles.

To recapitulate the products derived from the hog we have; No. 1. Lard, Common lard or grease, Inferior grease, Lard oil, Red oil, Oleine oil, Glycerine and Stearine.

Port Wine, a wine supposed to be shipped from Oporto, Portugal. (See Wine.)

Potash, the name applied to a commercial article consisting of carbonate of potassium, and caustic potassa together with various impurities. It is obtained by the lixiviation of wood ashes, in connection with lime. The lye obtained by this means is evaporated, and the solid residue is sold as crude potash. It contains 40 per cent of impurities, chiefly sulphur and carbonaceous matter. For purification it is calcined in a reverberatory furnace by which means sulphur and carbon are expelled, but the potash is nearly all converted into the form of carbonate. For the preparation of pearlash this is again dissolved and filtered, and the solution evaporated with frequent stirring. Commercial potash is used in the preparation of the various potassium salts which are extensively used in the arts, and was formerly much used in the manufacture of soap, but is now replaced to a very great degree by the cheaper caustic soda.

Potato, (*Solanum tuberosum*) this valuable food producing plant is a member of the night shade family, a family of plants having the most varied characteristics; to this family belong tobacco, belladonna and henbane, as well as the egg plant, tomato and capsicum. The potato is an annual plant, with stem two or three feet high, thick and fleshy, dissected leaves, and flowers in terminal corymbs, with bluish white corolla and yellow anthers. Berries globose, about half an inch in diameter. The potato is cultivated for its *tubers*, which are simply the thickened underground stem, composed mostly of starch, and furnished with eyes or buds, from which start the new plant. The potato is a native of the tablelands of Mexico, Peru and Chili, where it is yet found growing in its wild state. Its culture is said to have been carried from Florida to Virginia by the Spanish explorers, and from Virginia to England in 1565, by Sir John Hawkins; it was cultivated in Ireland in 1610, where they furnish three-fifths to four-fifths of the entire food of the people. In the eighteenth century it was cultivated in the New England States; it is now of almost universal cultivation in Europe and America and is the most productive of our food bearing plants; the same amount of ground yielding thirty times greater weight of potatoes than of wheat.

Potatoes, besides water, consist almost wholly of starch, with small proportions of sugar and nitrogen. As a sole article of food they are not well adapted, and are eaten in connection with other foods. Potatoes are of easy cultivation and will yield well in soils of even moderate richness. They are planted in hills or drilled in rows, and are dug both by hand and by machinery. They should be well protected from the light, as this acts on the bitter principle found in the potato, and causes them to turn green. Potatoes are propagated by their tubers, as their characters are not well enough fixed to be raised from seed. A large number of varieties are in cultivation and new ones are constantly being added. The best varieties seem to deteriorate by long cultivation and new ones must take their place. Among the best varieties now in cultivation are the Early Rose, Peachblows, Snowflake, Extra Early Vermont and Compton's Surprise. In 1870 the production of potatoes in the United States was 143,337,473 bushels. Of late years the Colorado Potato Beetle has done serious damage to the potato crop, but its ravages are now stayed by artificial means and no great alarm is now manifested. Potatoes yield by distillation a brandy known as potato spirit, and largely used in the adulteration of wine brandy.

Prunes are the dried fruit of certain kinds of plums, such as the Green Gage and St. Catherine. Prunes are largely produced in France, Germany, Spain and Turkey. The French process of drying plums is as follows ; when the fruit is so ripe that it falls by slightly shaking the tree, they are gathered and spread out separately on frames, or sieves made of lath or wicker work, for several days exposed to the sun till they become quite soft. They are afterward put into a spent oven, shut up quite close for twenty-four hours and then taken out. The oven is reheated rather warmer than it was before, and the plums are put in again. The next day they are taken out and turned by slightly shaking the sieve. The oven is again heated, but one fourth hotter than before, and they are put in a third time and after remaining in for twenty-four hours, are taken out and allowed to get cold. They are then rounded, an operation which is performed by turning the stone in the plum without breaking the skin, and pressing the two ends together between the thumb and finger. They are again put on the sieves, which are placed in an oven from which the bread has been just drawn. The oven is then tightly closed; an hour afterwards the plums are taken out and a cup of water placed in the oven; when the water is so warm as to just be able to bear the finger in it, the prunes are placed again in the oven and allowed to remain for twenty-four hours when the operation is finished. They are then packed loosely into small, long and rather deep boxes for sale.

The common sorts are gathered by shaking the trees, but the finer kind for making the French prunes are gathered in the morning by taking hold of the stem and picking them so as not to touch the fruit. They are placed in baskets containing vine leaves and are not allowed to touch each other. When the baskets are filled they are removed to the fruit room, where they are allowed to remain for two or three days exposed to the sun and the air, after which they are cured by the process above described. These are the fine, fleshy plums used for dessert. The most of the French prunes are made from the St. Julia plum and are of secondary quality. All the prunes received in this country are comparatively of poor quality as the best are retained for home use. In commerce prunes are distinguished as Turkey and French. The former being supposed to come from Turkey, but are largely obtained from Spian and Ger many. The value of the prunes and plums consumed in the United States for 1874–5 was a little over $1,600, 000. Prunelles are the finest sort of prunes. Prunes are extensively employed in cookery and to some extent in medicine.

Pumpkins, (Cucurbita Pepo) a coarse running vine belonging to the Gourd family. The vine reaches a length of ten to thirty feet, sparingly branched. Fruit is of various forms, sizes and colors, the flesh of the rind usually yellow, the cavity loosely filled with a yellow stringy pulp. It is generally raised with Indian Corn.· It is a native of the East. Pumpkins are largely offered for sale in all our markets, and are used in soups and the making of pies; the "pumpkin pie" of New England has passed into history. The pumpkin is of great value as food for cattle; but as a garden vegetable it is inferior to the squash which must ultimately take its place. Pumpkins are also dried, and ground pumpkin in the form of "flour" or "meal" is also an article of commerce.

Quince (Cydonia vulgaris) a shrub, native of the south of Europe, but largely cultivated in England and in this country. It belongs to the Rose family of plants, along with the apple, pear, etc. Its fruit, of which there are several varieties, is seldom eaten raw, but is stewed and used in making pies and puddings. It makes an excellent marmalade and is also largely made into preserves. The best varieties of the quince are the Orange and Portugal.

Radish, (Raphanus Sativus) a plant of the mustard family, a native of China and cultivated for its fleshy root. There are numerous sub species and varieties in cultivation. The root varies in shape from globose to fusiform, and may be white, red or black in color. Radishes are used in immense quantities as a table relish, though not containing much nutriment. Early radishes are largely raised in the southern markets and shipped to the north where they bring good prices and find a ready sale. Among the best varieties for summer cultivation are the Long scarlet, Short Top, Scarlet Turnip, Scarlet Olive shaped and white Turnip and Long White. For fall and winter use we have the Yellow and Grey Turnip rooted, Rose colored Chinese and Black Spanish.

Raisins, the dried fruit of certain species of grapes. There are several varieties of grapes in market, but the best are obtained from Spain. The finest raisins are all made near Malaga, and are known as Malaga or Muscatel. The country in the region of Malaga is very rocky but every spot that will hold a plant is utilized and the whole product is converted into raisins. The grape which produces them is the large white Muscatel. These grapes are dried on the vine in the sun; the leaves are removed, and the stem partly severed and they are allowed to remain until cured. These have a fine flavor, retain their freshness, and are less liable to have a saccharine deposit on the surface. The other species of raisins are dried, after being picked from the vine, either in the sun or in heated rooms. During the drying they are sprinkled several times with lye water, which causes them to deposit a saccharine matter on the outside. The best qualities of Valentias and Denias are hung on lines to dry and dipped in lye once or twice during the operation.

The Turkish raisins are the Sultanas and Black Smyrna. The Sultanas are without seed and small, and commonly known as seedless raisins. We have in market three kinds of raisins. The true Muscatel which are the finest, should be packed in boxes of twenty-five pounds, and in half and quarter boxes. Sun oɪ Bloom raisins are prepared in the same manner as the Muscatel but from a large grape, the Uva Larga. These are generally packed in boxes but sometimes in casks. Those in boxes are called bunch or layer raisins, and the others which are generally of an inferior quality, are separated from their stems. The Lexias raisins are packed in casks or grass mats called "frails." These raisins are of an inferior kind and require to be dipped in lye of wood ashes, with a little oil before drying. The raisins in boxes are partly Bloom or Sun, but mostly Muscatels. The barrels and frails are chiefly Lexias. The raisins of commerce are derived from Spain, Turkey and Sicily. Raisins of a superior quality are also in market from California. Raisins are bought and sold by the box, and there is no uniform weight in the packages. They should be bought and sold by the pound, and a reform is much needed in this direction.

The value of the raisins consumed in the United States for the year ending June 30, 1875, was $ 2,433,155.

Rape Seed. The seed of *Brassica napus*, a plant closely related to the turnip and belonging to the same family. The plant is cultivated for its herbage and for its seeds. From the seeds are obtained *rape oil*, so extensively used for machinery, and the residue after the oil is expressed is known as *rape cake*. The seeds are also used as food for cage birds.

Rhubarb or **Pie Plant,** *Rheum Rhaponticum*, a plant of the buckwheat family, and a native of Scythia,

is now largely cultivated for market purposes in the vicinity of all large cities, and few private gardens are
without it. The plant is cultivated for its fleshy, acid
petioles or leaf stalks, which are used in early spring as a
substitute for fruit in making pies and sauces. The root
of other species furnishes the medicinal rhubarb. Among
the varieties of rhubarb cultivated by the gardeners, are,
the Linnæus, Victoria and Cahoon; from the latter wine
is manufactured, but it is of inferior quality.

Rice, (*Oryza Sativa*) a food producing plant, a member of the grass family. Rice has been cultivated from
the remotest antiquity, and, like many plants of long cultivation, its native country is unknown, but it is a native
of the East. It is of the first importance as furnishing
food to the human race, as nearly three fourths of the
population of the world subsist on this grain, and even
wheat is not more valuable. Rice is cultivated all over
the tropical and sub-tropical regions of both hemispheres.
The vast populations of Eastern Asia subsist almost entirely on this grain. It is also cultivated in Southern
Europe and Northern Africa. The plant is an annual
and varies in height from one to six feet according to the
variety, of which the number is almost unlimited; in
Ceylon alone there being enumerated over 160 varieties.
The plant delights in wet, marshy situations, and the rice
grounds are therefore in low, flat lying regions of country, where water is abundant and irrigation can be practiced if necessary. The upland rice (O. Mutica) is
raised in Ceylon and Java and to some extent in the
United States. This species has very long awns and
grows to the height of three feet, having a slender culm

or stalk. It is cultivated much as other small grain and is sown on high and dry uplands. The quality of the rice is good, but the yield is much less than that of the rice grown on bottom lands. In the East the Bengal rice is a favorite, while that preferred in the European markets is the "Patna rice", small grained and very white. But the best of all rice is the large, white and sweet grain known as the "Carolina rice" and superior to all others in the market. It is of the variety known as gold seed rice, the most widely cultivated of all the varieties in this country. The grain is three eighths of an inch long, slightly flattened on two sides, of a deep yellow or golden color. When the husk and inner coat is removed, it is of a pearly white and somewhat translucent.

Rice was introduced into this country in 1694. In that year a vessel from Madagascar took refuge in Charleston harbor, and the Captain presented a bag of rough rice or paddy to one of the citizens, who planted it, and, the crop being a success, its cultivation rapidly spread, not only over South Carolina but over all the Southern States. The rice cultivated in South Carolina is the lowland variety. The plantations are made from the swamps and rush lands lying adjacent to tide water rivers, and a little above the junction of salt and fresh water. The plantations are made perfectly level and the rice is subjected to extreme irrigation. The inland swamps are also utilized in the culture of rice, but are being abandoned for the lands nearer the coast. Louisiana rice is also of excellent quality and is of the lowland variety. The plantations are along the rivers, by means of which they can be irrigated when necessary. Louisi-

ana rice is inferior to that of South Carolina, probably
from deficiency in cultivation. When the grain reaches
maturity it is cut with the sickle or cradle, and spread
evenly on the stubble, where it is allowed to remain for
a day till it is thoroughly dry. It is then bound into
sheaves and put into shocks similar to wheat. It is then
thrashed in the field, or taken to the barn yard and
stacked in ricks. The operation of thrashing rice only
removes the outer husk, the inner one being still attached
to the grain. The grain is then winnowed and is fit to
be taken to the mill. In this state it is known as "paddy." To separate this inner husk from the rice requires
expensive machinery and the planters take the rough rice
to the pounding mills to have it cleaned. The rough rice
is first ground between very heavy stones running at a
high speed, which partially removes the hull chaff. This
chaff is conveyed out of the building by means of spouts,
and the grain conveyed by similar means into mortars
where it is beat or pounded for a certain length of time
by the alternate rising and falling of very heavy pestles
shod with iron. From these mortars, elevators carry the
rice to the fans which separate the grain from the remains of the husks. From here it goes through other
fans which divide it into three qualities, " whole", " mid-
dling" and " small." The whole rice is then passed
through a polishing screen, lined with gauze wire and
sheep skins, which revolving vertically at the greatest
possible speed gives it that pearly whiteness, with which
it appears in commerce. From the screen the rice falls
directly into a tierce which is slowly revolving and struck
on two sides with heavy hammers, so it can be filled to

its greatest capacity. It is then coopered and sent to market; these tierces average about 600 pounds of rice, net. The broken rice if freed from grit is equally as good food as the whole. The small rice is sometimes ground into flour, and is used to some extent to adulterate wheat flour to give it whiteness. Although rice constitutes so large a portion of the food of the human family, with us it is used more as a luxury in the form of puddings, cakes, jellies and soups. It is easy of digestion and an excellent food for invalids. The composition of Carolina rice, according to Bracannot, is 85.07 per cent. of starch ; 3.60 of gluten ; 0.71 of gum ; 0.29 of crystallizable sugar ; 0.13 of fixed oil ; 4.80 of vegetable fibre ; 5.00 of water and 0.40 of saline substances. In the East, wines and fermented liquors are made from rice. In the year 1875 there were imported into this country 59,414, 749 pounds of rice, valued at $ 1,547,697. For the same period there were exported 12,352,330 pounds, valued at $ 342,894.

Rosin, the residue remaining after distilling crude turpentine, obtained from the pine tree. The water and volatile oil pass over and the rosin remains as a pale yellow and transparent or brownish yellow, and translucent, according to the purity of the crude turpentine and the care taken in its manufacture. Rosin softens at 160° F. and melts at 275° F. Rosin enters largely into use in the manufactures and arts. It is used in varnish and cements, in plasters and ointments, in calking of ships, in the manufacture of soap, and in covering the bows of violins, to produce vibrations. It was formerly employed in the production of rosin oil, and used for illumination.

Rosin of commerce is mostly furnished by North Carolina and Virginia.

Rum, a spirituous liquor distilled from molasses. It is almost exclusively a West Indian product. It is made from fresh cane juice and the scum which rises in the manufacture of sugar ; also from a mixture of the scums and molasses, or from molasses alone. The rum prepared from the above mixtures differs considerably in the volatile oils and ethers, and therefore in the flavor of the rum. The most is prepared by taking equal quantities of the skimmings of the sugar pans, of lees or returns, as they are commonly called, and of water, and to 100 gallons of this wash are added 10 gallons of molasses. After ten or fifteen days of fermentation and distillation it yields about 10 per cent. of rum, or one gallon from ten of wort. Every plantation produces sugar, molasses and rum. The rum thus distilled is colorless and is sometimes sold as white rum, but it is generally colored by the addition of caramel or burnt sugar. Pineapples and guavas are also added during distillation, to produce new flavors. The quality of rum improves very much by age. Rum and water is largely used as a drink on shipboard. Great quantities of rum are produced from rectified proof spirit, by the addition of coloring and flavoring matter.

Sago, a kind of starch prepared from various species of palms of the genus Sagus, S. Rumphii generally producing the true sago of commerce. It is a small tree, not over thirty feet in height. It is a native of the East India Archipelago and grows in the lowlands of all the islands of that region. Before the tree has arrived at maturity the stem consists of a mere shell about two inches thick, while the interior is filled with a great mass of spongy pith, becoming gradually absorbed, and ultimately the stem remains hollow. At the time when the pith is fully developed and before it has begun to diminish, the tree is felled and the trunk cut into lengths six or seven feet long, which are split to admit of the pith being more easily removed. This pith is in a state of coarse powder, and is mixed with water in a trough having a sieve at one end, the water, loaded with farina, passes through the sieve into vessels and is allowed to stand until the insoluble matter has subsided. The water is then strained off and the farina which is left may be dried into a meal or moulded into any form desired. Sago as it comes to this country is prepared by making it into a paste with water and then rubbing it into grains. It is said that a single tree will yield from 500 to 600 pounds of sago.

Common sago is insoluble in cold water, but swells and forms a jelly when boiled. The Chinese of Malaca purify it so as to give it a pearly lustre, and this is somewhat soluble even in cold water. Sago is adulterated by adding potato starch, but this may be detected by the microscope. Sago forms the principal food of the natives of the Moluccas, and from it they distil alcohol. *S. laevis* and *S. farinefera* are natives of the same island and also furnish the sago of commerce.

Saleratus (see Soda).

Salmon, a name applied to several species of fish of the genus *Salmo*, and also to the species of the genus *Oncorhynchus*. The salt water is the natural habitat of all these species, where they obtain their food and rap-

idly increase in size. It is only towards fall that they
ascend fresh water streams and do so for the purpose of
depositing their spawns. *Salmo salar*, or salmon of our
eastern coast, is found in the Arctic sea, whence it enters
the streams of both continents. In the United States it
is found only in some rivers in Maine. It is found in the
streams of Eastern Canada from Quebec to the coast of
Labrador, and the streams are leased by the government
to private individuals, but so few salmon are taken in this
region that they scarcely become an article of commerce.
Only on our Pacific coast is the capture of salmon followed as a commercial pursuit. On the Columbia River,
Oregon, large numbers of men are engaged in the salmon
fishery, and it is a source of great profit. The fish are
taken only in gillnets, and at night, when the water is
clear, two men with a boat and net will average twelve
hundred pounds in one night.

The fish are taken to the factories, where they are either salted or put up in hermetically sealed cans. These
canned salmon will keep for many years in any climate,
and find a ready sale at high prices. Many hundred
thousand cans are put up annually, a large portion of
which go to England. Salmon are found in great abundance in the waters of Alaska and considerable quantities
are packed in barrels and shipped to the Eastern market.
The salmon of the Pacific coast is *Salmo quininat*. The
artificial production of salmon is now being carried on by
the United States Fish Commission, and numerous streams
have been stocked with the young fish. The salmon
ranges in length from two to four feet, and sometimes attains a weight of a hundred pounds; from twenty to fifty

pounds are the ordinary sizes. The flesh of salmon is of a reddish hue and is highly esteemed as an article of food.

Salsify or **Oyster Plant.** (*Tragopogon porrifolius*) a perennial or biennial plant belonging to the order compositæ and cultivated for its fleshy roots which are long and tapering, and when properly cooked have something the flavor of fried oysters, whence one of its common names; it is also boiled or stewed like parsnips or carrots, and is sometimes eaten as a salad, sliced and dressed with vinegar, salt and pepper. The plant is cultivated in our gardens, and is used in the fall and spring. It is a native of Europe.

Sal Soda, (see Soda.)

Salt. The salt of commerce is a slightly impure chloride of sodium, (Na Cl). The impurities differ in the salt obtained from different sources both in kind and amount, those most commonly found being the chlorides and sulphates of lime, magnesia and soda. Salt has been known and used from the earliest times; long before the beginning of the Christian era it seems to have been in almost as common use as at present. Salt is found very widely and abundantly distributed in nature, the world's supply being drawn from three sources, namely, seawater, rock salt and natural brines. Sea water contains about three per cent. of common salt in connection with about one per cent. of other mineral matters the most important of which are chloride and sulphate of magnesia and the sulphates of soda and lime. So weak and impure a brine cannot be profitably evaporated by artificial heat, but by allowing it to flow into shallow reservoirs which are then shut off from the sea, it may be and is largely evaporated by the sun's heat and large amounts of salt are thus obtained.

This is the chief source of supply in France, Spain, Portugal, Italy, Central and South America. In the United States but comparatively very little salt is obtained from sea water. Deposits of salt in beds in connection with other geologic formations are quite common throughout various portions of the Earth. Salt found in this condition is known as *rock salt* and is the source of a large portion of the salt used in England, Russia and many other countries of the world. These beds were undoubtedly formed by portions of the sea having become cut off from the main body and the water thereof having become evaporated has left its entire saline constituents deposited, and where the conditions have been such as to preserve them we have the rock-salt beds of the present time. Rock-salt usually exists in large cubical crystals, and in some cases in such a state of purity as to be fitted for use by no further labor than simply removing it from the beds. More commonly however, it is contaminated with impurities, various coloring matters frequently being present which make it of a blue, red or yellow color. In such cases it is usual to dissolve the salt in the mine by flowing in water which is afterward pumped out and treated in the same manner as natural brines for the production of salt. In this country there are large deposits of rock salt in Louisiana which served for the almost entire supply of the Southern States during the Rebellion.

Natural brines furnish nearly all of the salt manufactured in the United States. They are found abundantly at Syracuse and Onondaga, New York, in the Saginaw Valley, Michigan, at Saltville, Virginia, in Ohio, Nebraska, and other localities. These brines are undoubtedly produced by solution in the earth of deposits of rock-salt, the position and extent of the deposit being sometimes known, but in other cases only indicated by the presence of brines. In some localities the brine flows from the earth in the form of natural springs, whilst in others it is only obtained by boring artesian wells and pumping from them the brine. These brines are treated in somewhat different manners, according to the quality of the salt which the manufacturer desires to produce. For the production of coarse salt artificial heat is not employed, the entire evaporation being conducted by solar heat alone, upon account of the well-known fact that in a solution of any crystallizable substance the more slowly the crystals are formed, and the more entirely at rest is the solution, the larger will be the crystals formed. In this country the evaporation is conducted in wooden vats supplied with wooden covers for excluding rain and to lessen the cooling of the brine during the night. In order the more effectually to remove the impurities of the brine, which consist principally of sulphate of lime (gypsum), chlorides of calcium and magnesium and carbonate of iron, several different vats are used to complete the evaporation, the brine being drawn successively from one into the other. It is allowed to stand in the first until the carbonate of iron becomes decomposed, the carbonic acid escaping and the iron becoming converted into hydrated sesquioxide, in which form it settles to the bottom of the vat as a bulky, brown semi-solid.

The brine is then drawn off into another vat, where it remains until crystals of salt begin to form. During this time a considerable amount of the sulphate of lime will have become separated out and is left behind as the brine is now drawn off into still another vat. Here, as the process of evaporation goes on, the salt separates out in large crystals, which are removed from time to time until the mother liquor reaches a density of about 30° Baumè, when it is discharged. The crystals, when taken from the brine, are washed and placed in the perforated top of the vat to drain.

For the production of common fine salt, large iron pans or iron kettles, heated by steam or over a furnace, are made use of. In this country cast-iron kettles holding about 140 gallons are in most common use. Fifty or sixty of these are set in a double row along two flues, placed six or eight feet apart and furnished with separate fire-places but a single chimney. The kettles nearest the fire are protected from receiving too much heat, whilst, by a high chimney, assisted by blowers, a strong draught is created, to carry the heat to the kettles farthest away. To remove impurities a sheet-iron false bottom provided with a bail is placed in each kettle before the brine is introduced. As soon as the evaporation has proceeded so far that salt crystals begin to form, these false bottoms are carefully lifted out of the kettles together with the gypsum and other impurities which have settled upon them. When, as the boiling continues, a sufficient quantity of salt has become crystallized out, it is well stirred for the purpose of washing it in the remaining liquid and it is then removed and placed in baskets which are suspended over the kettles to drain. After some hours draining the salt is removed to the stove rooms where it is dried for two or three weeks, when it is fit to be barrelled and sent into market.

The quality of both coarse and fine salt depends upon the amount and kind of impurities present in the brine, and the care exercised in removing them in the process of manufacture. Sulphate of calcium, which is usually present in the largest quantity, is much less objectionable than the chlorides of calcium and magnesium and the sulphate of magnesium. These latter are present in considerably larger proportions in the brines of Michigan and Ohio than in those of New York, which accounts for the difficulty of obtaining a good dairy salt from the works in the former states. Dairy salt should be entirely free from the last named and bitter salts. It is usually obtained by selecting an extra pure quality of coarse or fine salt and subjecting it to a carefully conducted process of washing, after which it is ground to facilitate its solution. Ordinary coarse salt is principally used in salting pork and beef, whilst common fine salt answers well for ordinary table use, and great quantities are converted into " soda" to be used in the manufacture of soap and glass and by the house-keeper in cooking. In England more than one half of the salt produced is converted into soda-ash. Hydrochloric or muriatic acid, so extensively used in the arts, and also chlorine, now used almost exclusively in the large bleacheries for bleaching cloths, are made by decomposing common salt. Salt is put up for market in different ways, Ashton's, Marshall's and other Liverpool brands come in bags, 224 pounds; New York

State in barrels and bags, 240 and 280 pounds ; Saginaw in barrels, 240 pounds ; cases table salt contain 60 boxes, about two pounds each.   Salt also comes in small packets, put up in sacks, three sizes ; 25 10 pound packets, 40 6 pounds and 80 3 pounds.   The production of salt in the United States amounts to about 20,000,000 bushels annually, whilst 10,000,000 bushels are annually consumed.

Saltpetre, Nitre, the common names of the nitrate of potassium (K N O_3) an anhydrous, crystallizable salt found native in beds in Peru, and mixed with the soil, and as an efflorescence upon its surface in the East Indies and in lesser quantities in many other parts of the world.   The principal supply is however obtained from Peru and the East Indies.   That obtained from Peru is sold extensively in the crude state in which it is taken from the bed and is known by the misnomer of Chili saltpetre.   The East Indian article is obtained by leaching the soil and evaporating the solution thus obtained from which, upon cooling, the saltpetre crystallizes out.   The crystals are six sided prisms, soluble in less than one half their weight of hot water but requiring four times their weight of water to produce solution.

Nitre is one of the essential constituents of gun powder in the manufacture of which large quantities are consumed.   It is used to some extent as an antiseptic, for preserving meats, butter, etc.

Sardines, (*Clupea pilchardus*), a small fish caught in the Mediterranean sea near Sardinia whence the name sardine.   It is from three to five inches in length and large quantities are caught and preserved in oil in small tin cans, and used as a luxury. It is prepared by being dressed, salted, partly dried, and then scalded in hot oil and hermetically sealed in tin boxes, with hot salted oil, or oil and butter. They are sometimes preserved in red wine. The menhaden, a fish abundantly caught near Long Island, and formerly used for manure and its oil, is now preserved in oil as sardines. Several factories are now in operation in New Jersey and also in Norway in Europe. The fish are prepared by softening the bones by steam and trimming the body to the proper size.

Sauce. A mixture or composition of vegetables, meats and spices, along with vinegar or wine, and used as a relish to other food. The English sauces have a fine reputation and are perhaps unequaled.

Sauerkraut, an article of food prepared from the cabbage. The cabbages are finely sliced and pounded into a cask or barrel along with salt, pepper corns, caraway or anise seed, and subjected to a heavy pressure. It is then allowed to stand in a warm place for several days when fermentation takes place and during this process it gives off a very disagreeable, fetid, acid odor. Strong brine is then added, and it is then set away for use. It is freshened before using and may be boiled, fried or eaten cold. It requires about two hours to complete its cooking. The dish is of German origin.

Sealing Wax. Red sealing wax is made by carefully forming a mixture of shellac, Venice turpentine, Peru balsam, vermilion and sulphate of lime. In the cheaper kinds of sealing wax red lead is substituted for vermilion, and there is a large addition of common rosin, which

causes the wax to run into thin drops when fused. Black
sealing wax is made of shellac, Venice turpentine, and
colored with ivory black. The ancient sealing wax was
a mixture of beeswax and turpentine, with the addition
of some coloring matter.

Sea-moss Farine, Iceland Moss, Lichenine, a substance very closely resembling starch and having the
same chemical composition. It is obtained from several
varieties of lichens especially the reindeer moss, Iceland
moss, and one or two others found growing in the extreme northern portions of both continents. Iceland
moss and reindeer moss consist almost entirely of lichenine, which is prepared from them by simply soaking
and washing repeatedly in cold water until all taste is
removed, the washed moss being then dissolved in boiling water, strained and evaporated; the lichenine is obtained as a hard, brittle moss which is sold in our markets under a variety of names and used in making puddings and pastry.

Semolina, a name applied to the central part of the
grain of wheat which is not reduced to powder in the process of grinding by stones, and is produced from the
grains of wheat of very sunny climes, as Spain, Odessa
and the south of Italy, where the grain becomes very dry
and hard. It is used for the making of puddings and is
very nutritious. A similar preparation is made from
maize and millet but the flavor is inferior.

Shad a name applied to fish belonging to the family
Clupeidæ. The shad are inhabitants of the northern
hemisphere, and live in the sea during the greater portion of the year, but ascend the rivers in the spring for

the purpose of depositing their spawn. The European species of shad are not considered as good for food as those
of America and Asia. The capture of this fish forms a
large industry, and in the early spring they are taken by
fixed seines or nets. While in fresh water the fish eat
little or nothing; in the sea their food consists of small
crustaceans. Through the exertions of the United States
Fish Commission the rivers connected with the gulf, and
on the Pacific slopes have been stocked with young shad
artificially hatched.

Shadine, (*Alosa sadina*) a small spotted shad not over a foot in length, caught to some extent off the New
York and New Jersey coasts. It appears in our markets put up in oil as a substitute for sardines.

Shot, are small globular masses of lead used for killing
birds and other small game. Lead shot are manfactured
from a compound of lead and arsenic. The arsenic is
added to the lead to render it more soft and ductile, by
which it more readily assumes the globular form when
subjected to the process of shot-making. When a quantity of lead is melted in the pot, a circle of ashes or powdered charcoal is laid around the edge of the metal, and
the arsenical compound, wrapped in coarse paper, is introduced into the centre by means of a wire basket, and
stirred in. The pot is then closely covered and left for
several hours, during which time the arsenic is decomposed, the greater part uniting with the lead. The mixture
is then tested by dropping some through a colander into
water; if the lead assumes a lenticular form the arsenic
is in excess; if they are flattened on one side, hollowed
or elongated, too little arsenic was used.

After the mixture has been experimented upon until it is of the required consistence, it is run into bars, which are taken to the top of the shot tower, where it is again melted and poured through the colander. These colanders are either hollow, hemispherical iron dishes or rectangular iron sheets, perforated with holes of a uniform size, made perfectly smooth and exact. Each size of shot requires a special temperature of the lead when poured. The holes vary in size from one fiftieth to one three hundred and sixtieth of an inch, but the shot are of larger dimensions than the holes. When the lead is poured through the colanders, the particles are allowed to fall to the base of the tower, and in this falling they assume the globular form, the same as does falling rain. By the time they reach the bottom they are sufficiently hardened to fall into the baisin of water placed to receive them, without thus being injured. Large sized shot require a greater height than small, one hundred feet being sufficient for the latter while the former require one hundred and fifty.

After the shot are taken from the water they are dried and assorted, according to size, by means of a revolving copper cylinder slightly inclined, perforated with holes, which increase in size to the lower end. The imperfect shot are separated by being allowed to run down an inclined plane so arranged that the truly spherical run down the middle, while the imperfect work off to one side. The shot are polished by being left in a rotating cylinder with powdered graphite. Shot are made without the use of a tower by having the lead placed on a swiftly revolving table, which throws the particles through a perforated cylinder of copper against a linen screen so placed as to intercept them. Another method is with a low elevator, and forcing upward a powerful current of air, which has the same effect as a long continued fall. The different sized shot are distinguished by names and letters. The Chicago Shot Tower Co. have the following grades : the smallest size is No. 12 ; as the size increases they are known as Nos. 11, 10, 9, 8, 7, 6, 5, 4, 3, 2, 1, B, BB, BBB, 0, 00, 000. Of buckshot the largest is

No. 1.— 50 to the pound.

" 2.— 70 " "

" 3.— 90 " "

" 4.—110 " "

" 5.—125 " "

" 6.—140 " "

" 7.—215 " "

" 8.—260 " "

Shrimp, a name applied to a large number of small crustaceans, properly should mean *Crangon vulgaris*, of Europe, which is extensively caught for food. The common shrimp of the United States is principally used for fish bait.

Snuff. (See tobacco.)

Soap, a combination of the fatty acids with some metallic base usually with soda or potassa. Fats and true oils consist of a union of several organic acids, chiefly palmitic, oleic, and stearic, with a peculiar base called glycerine. When treated with alkaline hydrates, or lye, the fats are decomposed, the potash or soda of the lye uniting with the fat acids forming soap, whilst glycerine is at the same time set free.

Various metallic oxids such as lime, magnesia, zinc

and lead oxides will in the same manner decompose fats with the formation of soap but not of a kind valuable for cleansing purposes, upon account of being insoluble in water. The curdy solid which forms when toilet soap is used in hard water is an insoluble lime soap formed by the decomposition of the toilet soap by lime in the water. Commercial soaps are now made almost entirely with a soda base upon account of the great cheapness of soda as compared with potassa. Soda soaps are in general hard soaps, whilst potash soaps are soft soaps. The latter are still made to a considerable extent in the household economy, the refuse fats from the kitchen being employed, while the lye is furnished by the leaching of wood ashes. The grease and lye are simply boiled together until complete saponification takes place. The soft soap thus formed is by no means a pure soap but contains all of the glycerine produced by the decomposition of the fats together with a considerable excess of lye and a large amount of water, usually from 40 to 50 per cent. It forms a thick yellow like mass possessing very strong detergent properties owing to the presence of free alkali and is very useful for many of the coarser uses to which soap is applied such as scouring wool and yarn, or the cleansing of any article in which is a large amount of oil or grease.

For the production of a good quality of hard soap a more extended operation is required together with more care and skill. The lye employed in the commercial manufacture is prepared by adding slacked lime to *soda-ash*, which is the carbonate of soda; the lime uniting with the carbonic acid forms carbonate of lime and there is left a solution of caustic soda or lye. The fats or oils made use of may be of any kind either animal or vegetable but should be clean and sweet. The process of saponification is conducted in large iron pans capable of holding twenty or thirty tons of soap and which are heated either by steam or by being set over furnaces.

A quantity of fat is first placed in the pan and to it is added a quantity of decidedly weak lye, these being boiled together form, after a little time, a uniform milky emulsion in which no oil globules can be detected and which has no alkaline reaction, when a quantity of stronger lye is added and the boiling is continued until a strong alkaline reaction is obtained, when more fat is added and the process continued with the addition of continually stronger lye and more fat with frequently a quantity of rosin until the pan is filled, care being taken that in the end a sufficient quantity of alkali shall be added to saponify all of the fat and yet not be in excess.

Rosin is added simply as an adulterant, it becoming in a manner saponified and adding cheaply to the quantity of soap produced. When the pan has become filled and the saponification is complete, salt is added to induce the separation of the soap from the spent lye and glycerine which has been set free and the whole is allowed to stand and cool when the soap will float as a curdy mass upon the mother liquor which is then drawn off and usually thrown away, it not being profitable to extract from it the glycerine which it contains, that article being more cheaply obtained from other processes.

The soap after removal from the mother liquor is frequently again subjected to a continuation of the boiling process with the addition of more lye and fats and once more separated by the use of salt from the spent lye, after which it is removed and allowed to become thoroughly cold and solid when it is ready to be cut up and boxed for market. This is in a general way the method employed in the manufacture of the cheaper varieties of hard soap in large establishments. For the preparation of particular varieties of soap the process is modified and for choice soaps particularly pure oils are employed.

Ordinary hard soap contains its materials in about the following proportions.

Fat acids 61.0 per cent.
Soda   6.2 per cent.
Water   32.8 per cent.
_____
100.0

Castile soap is made in southern Europe from a mixture of olive and rape seed oils. It is of well known excellent quality, but an imitation of much poorer quality, made in England, is very largely sold as Castile. The spurious may generally be detected by the coloring matter being in streaks instead of giving the peculiar mottled appearance of the genuine. Genuine Castile soap has been found to contain of fat acids 76.5 per cent. of soda 9 per cent. and of water 14.5 per cent. Soap made from cocoanut oil is remarkably hard and may contain a great amount of water, even as much as 75 per cent. without becoming soft.

It is not readily decomposed by weak salt water and is consequently used for washing in sea water and is known as *marine soap*. Toilet soaps are made from very pure and sweet oils the saponification being conducted without the aid of heat and the soap perfumed by the addition of essential oils. Silicated soap is made by the addition of sand or finely powdered pumice stone to ordinary hard soap.

The most important test of the quality of soap is to determine the amount of water it contains not in chemical combination. This is easily learned by cutting the soap in shavings and drying for some time at a temperature of 212° F. The loss of weight in good, white hard soap should not exceed 20 per cent.

Soap is readily soluble in alcohol and the solution mixed with camphor and oil of rosemary is known as opodeldoc.

Soda, a name applied somewhat indiscriminately to *Sodic hydrate* or *caustic soda* ($Na_2 H_2 O_2$) ; to *Neutral carbonate* of *soda* ($Na_2 C O_3$ 10 $H_2 O$) also called *Sal soda* and *washing soda* ; and also to Bicarbonate of soda ($Na_2 H_2 C_2 O_6$) known as cooking soda. These are all obtained commercially from common salt by the process invented by M. Leblanc. By this process common salt (chloride of sodium) is converted into the neutral carbonate and from this are prepared caustic soda and sodium bicarbonate. Previous to Leblanc's discovery soda was obtained entirely from the ash of sea weeds or kelp. During the French revolution this supply was cut off from that country and as a result the government was induced to offer a large sum as a reward for a practical method of obtaining the much needed material from some other source. This led to Leblanc's famous discovery

which has been denominated the greatest of the appli-
cations of chemistry to the useful arts.

The discovery was made public in 1794 and in the
more than three quarters of a century, which has since
elapsed, no important modification has been made in the
process. Common salt is first decomposed by sulphuric acid, the products of the decomposition being sulphate
of soda and chlorhydric acid. The acid escapes from the
retorts as a gas, and is condensed in towers filled with
coke over which water is kept flowing. The sulphate of
soda is removed and 100 parts of it is mixed with 100
parts of chloride of calcium and 55 parts of charcoal,
and the mixture is roasted in a reverberatory furnace, by
which means it is converted chiefly into carbonate of soda and sulphide of calcium, but also contains in greater
or less proportions sulphate of calcium, carbonate of calcium, undecomposed salt and sulphate of soda together
with a quantity of charcoal. In this condition it is known
as *black ash* or *ball soda*, and is used in the manufacture
of soap.

To obtain the carbonate in a purer form the black ash
is thoroughly lixiviated with water and the solution, or
lye, thus obtained is evaporated to dryness leaving a solid residue consisting of carbonate of soda, caustic soda,
and small quantities of sulphate of soda. This is then
calcined at a moderate heat in connection with sawdust
or fine coal, by which means all traces of sulphur are expelled and caustic soda is converted into carbonate of soda. The material as now removed from the furnace is
known as *Soda Ash*, and is used in the manufacture of
glass, and for the preparation of caustic soda and bicar-

bonate of soda. By being still further purified it is obtained in transparent crystals and sold as *Sal-soda*. Bicarbonate of soda is manufactured by forcing a stream of carbonic acid gas through a saturated solution of neutral carbonate. It readily gives up a half or all of its carbonic acid when treated with other acids, and is upon this account used for aërating biscuits, cake, etc. In this case the carbonic acid is set free in the dough, when heated, by the lactic acid of the sour milk, or by the cream of tartar or other acid substance which may be employed. The articles now sold as *saleratus* and *soda* are practically the same thing, both consisting of a somewhat impure bicarbonate of soda. *Concentrated lye* is a strong solution of caustic soda and carbonate of soda.

Sorrel, (*Rumex acetosa*) a well known perennial plant cultivated to some extent in this country. It is cultivated for its acid leaves, and used in soups and sauces, mostly by the Germans and French. In the French markets it is nearly as abundant as the spinach is in ours, and is commended as a wholesome vegetable.

Spinach, (*Spinacia oleracea*), an old world plant, largely cultivated in our gardens as a pot herb. It is of easy culture and may be had fit for use the entire season. For spring use it is sown in the fall and slightly covered to protect it during the winter. The root is annual, stem eighteen inches to two feet high and the leaves two to four inches long tapering to a petiole one, three and four inches in length. The varieties in use are the Round, Prickly and New Zealand Spinach.

Sprat, (*Harengulus sprattus*) a small herring of the European Seas. The sprat is about six inches in length and its habits are similar to those of the herrings. It is eaten fresh, salted, dried or spiced, but is generally used by the poorer classes. The French preserve great quantities of small sprats and sell them for sardines.

Squash, (*Cucurbita pepo and C. maxima*) vegetables belonging to the gourd family and of great importance as an article of food. They are of various sizes, forms, colors and qualities. Being of tropical origin their growth is consummated in the summer months, and yet the winter varieties may be kept till May. They are rapid growers and are raised with little trouble; care should be taken to keep them away from the pumpkin as they readily mix and form a worthless hybrid. Squash are used either stewed or baked, and the winter squash makes excellent pies. Baked, it is but little inferior to the sweet potato. Among the summer varieties in cultivation are Yellow and White Bush Scalloped, Summer Crook Neck and Boston Marrow. For winter the Hubbard and Marblehead are both excellent varieties. The native country of the squash is unknown.

Starch, a white, granular substance obtained from the vegetable world in which it is found very widely distributed, occurring in some part of nearly every known plant, whilst in many it occurs in abundant deposits, in stalks, thickened fleshy leaves, seeds, roots, tubers, etc. Most of the grains as wheat, rice, and corn contain about 60 per cent. of starch, and 15 per cent. of water the remaining 25 per cent. consisting of gum, gluten, fibrine, etc. Peas and beans contain about 40 per cent. of starch and 15 per cent. of water. Potatoes, starch, 21 per cent. water, 75 per cent.

Starch for domestic use has for many years been man-ufactured in large quantities from the potato. When used for this purpose the potatoes are first thoroughly washed, and when clean are passed through a grating machine by which they are reduced to a fine pulp and de-livered upon an endless belt which distributes the pulp evenly over fine wire or hair sieves where it is constantly washed by having numerous fine streams of water direct-ed upon it. The starch is thus washed out, and passes through the sieve with the water, giving it a milk like col-or and consistency whilst the fibrous portion of the pota-to amounting to only about three or four per cent. is left upon the sieves. The milky liquid is left to stand sev-eral hours, when the starch will have all settled to the bottom and the clear supernatant water is drawn off by means of a siphon. The starch is then removed and re-peatedly washed with clear, cold water, and passed through very fine hair or silk sieves until the last traces of fibrous matter are removed, when, being again allowed to settle and the clear water drawn off, the semi-liquid mass remaining is removed and dried in dessicating chambers.

Wheat starch has been prepared and used in large quantities in European countries. The wheat for the purpose is first softened by wetting and is then submitted to crushing, rolling and pressing with a continual supply of water until the water ceases to be milky as it flows from it. The milky water contains the starch together with the gluten of the wheat. A part of the gluten re-mains in solution in the water after the starch has settled to the bottom and being allowed to stand becomes sour, when the acid liquid will dissolve considerably more of the gluten. By repeatedly washing with water and allowing to sour and settle, and then drawing off the clear liquid the gluten is at length completely removed: after which the further treatment of the starch is the same as that from the potato.

Corn starch prepared from Indian corn has in quite recent years come into quite common use in this country both for laundry use and for the preparation of articles of food for the table. The manufacture was first undertaken in this country in 1842 by Thos. Kingsford for whom a large factory was built at Oswego, N. Y., by a stock company, in 1848. The manufacture has proved so successful that large additions to the factory have from time to time been made until it now has a capacity for consuming nearly 1,000,000 bushels of corn, and producing upward of 20,000,000 pounds of starch annually. Another factory established in 1858 at Glen Cove, Long Island, by Messrs. Duryea has nearly equal capacity. This starch from its excellent quality and cheap price has nearly replaced all other kinds, has entirely stopped the importation of foreign brands and is itself now largely exported. It is manufactured by first treating the corn with water in which is a quantity of caustic soda or hydrochloric acid until the gluten has become dissolved, after which it is crushed, washed upon sieves, and dried much as in the preceding processes.

The method of dissolving out the gluten by acid or alkalies before crushing the grain, instead of separating it out by the process of souring as before described is known as the *new* or *chemical* process of manufacture. A decidedly better quality of starch is obtained in this way.

Rice starch is manufactured in considerable quantities in Europe. The process does not differ in any important particular from those already described.

Starch for food is prepared from the Sago-palm, Arrow root, and Manioc, which will be found described under their respective names.

Starch Polish, an article used in the laundry for giving a polish to starched goods. Starch polish is made from the following ingredients : starch, white castile soap, paraffine, borax and white wax. Another patented polish is made from white wax, spermaceti, castor oil, mutton tallow, borax, salt, gum arabic and isinglass.

Stove Polish. A preparation used for the blacking of stoves. It is generally prepared from graphite or black lead. It is put up in the form of cakes or of a fine powder.

Strawberry, the fruit of plants of the genus *Fragaria* of the Rose family. The whole plant is hairy, with perennial root, leaves often green through the winter : the stem is short, but the crown of the root sends out several prostrate radicating runners from one to two feet long. The flowers are in cymes, 3 to 8 or 9 to 15 flowered ; petals are white. The receptacle in the strawberry becomes much enlarged and fleshy and is generally called the fruit, but the true fruit is the seeds which adhere to this receptacle. The species are very numerous and improve or deteriorate very rapidly under cultivation. The most widely known species are the *F. Vesca* or Alpine, known in England as the wood-strawberry, and the *F. Virginiana,* or common wild strawberry of the United States. The best market varieties grown in the United

States are the "Wilson's Albany," "Hovey's Seedling," Agriculturist and "Monarch of the West." New Jersey and Delaware largely supply the eastern markets, while Central Illinois and the Lake Shore region of Western Michigan supply the markets of the west.

Sturgeon, the common name applied to the fish of the genus *Acipenser*. They are a singular looking fish and have large bony plates arranged in longitudinal rows, the mouth under the snout, without teeth and very protractile and the lobes of the tail unequal. They inhabit lakes and the sea, and ascend the rivers of many countries. The sharp nosed sturgeon of the Atlantic coast of North America is from four to eight feet long. The Lake sturgeon of the Great Lakes is from three to six feet long and of a ruddy hue. The Great sturgeon of Europe reaches a length of sixteen feet, and a weight of from 1500 to 2000 pounds. Sturgeon are largely caught in the Hudson river and the streams flowing into the Great Lakes. The flesh is of a reddish tinge and is highly esteemed by some people ; it is said large quantities are cured and smoked and sold for the genuine halibut. A large industry in connection with the sturgeon is the manufacture of their roe into caviare which is sent to the Russian markets. Isinglass is made from their air bladders and an oil may also be manufactured from the fish.

Succotash, a name given to green maize and beans boiled together. The name and dish are of Indian origin. Succotash is largely canned and in this form is quite an article of commerce.

Sugar, is a name applied to a great number of substances somewhat closely resembling each other in physical properties and chemical composition, but also differing in many particulars. Chemically all are compounds of carbon, oxygen, and hydrogen in but slightly varying proportions. Physically they all agree in possessing a sweet taste, are soluble in water, forming more or less viscid liquids, and most are crystallizable. Sugars exist in a great variety of vegetable juices and in a few animal secretions, as in milk. The sugars of commerce are but of two kinds. (1) *Sucrose* ($C_{12}H_{22}O_{11}$) usually known from its most abundant source as *cane sugar* although including the principal part of the sugar made from the cane, the beet, the maple, and the palm. (2) *Dextrose* or *ordinary glucose* ($C_6H_{12}O_6$) called also grape sugar, starch sugar, and fruit sugar which is found in most kinds of fruits, and is readily formed by the action of dilute acids upon starch, of strong sulphuric or muriatic acid upon cellulose or woody fibre, or by dilute acids, yeast or other ferments upon cane sugar. It thus appears that it may be made from almost anything of vegetable origin, for all contain either starch or woody fibre; thus any kind of grain, roots, wood, paper, cotton rags, etc, may serve as a source from which to obtain this sugar. It is manufactured in large quantities from potatoes and corn and used as an adulterant for sugar house syrups, also for confectionery and to mix with grape juice to be made into wine. There were in 1873 fifty-one factories in Germany engaged in the manufacture of grape sugar from the potato, producing nearly 60,000,000 pounds of sugar and syrup annually. The process consists in simply boiling the potato starch in dilute acids. A quantity of water is first brought to boiling when a small quantity of acid is added to it and starch diluted with water to about the consistency of milk is run into it, and the boiling continued until the conversion of starch is complete when the excess of acid is neutralized by the addition of carbonate of lime and the clear liquid is drawn off from the sulphate of lime formed, after which it is evaporated to form syrup or sugar. Grape sugar is much less soluble in water than cane sugar and possesses much less sweetening power, it requiring two and a half to three pounds of grape sugar to produce as great sweetening effect as one pound of cane sugar. It is much less readily crystallizable than cane sugar, and as it is almost always associated with and is easily converted into *levulose* which is entirely uncrystallizable, and which interferes with the crystallization of other sugars with which it is mixed, it is commonly met with in an uncrystallized form, as in sorghum syrup, in molasses from sugar refineries, etc.

Cane sugar is produced in quantity from the juice of the sugar cane (*Saccharum officinarum,*) from the juice of the sugar beet (*Beta vulgaris*), from the sap of the sugar maple (*Acer saccharinum*), and from the juice of several species of palm trees. Sugar was first introduced into England in the fourteenth century and was then imported from the Indies and was consequently so expensive as to be used only as a luxury by the wealthy.

It seems however to have been known to the ancients before the beginning of the Christian era, but never to have been made or used by them in any considerable quantities, and until quite modern times honey has served the people of the world their only saccharine food. Previous to the discovery of America most of the sugar consumed in Europe was produced in the Canaries, Madeira, and Sicily, but the amount was exceedingly small as compared with the present consumption of the article.

The cultivation of sugar cane was introduced into the West India islands and the adjacent main land soon after their discovery, and so early as 1520 the industry had attained to a very considerable degree of importance. The common sugar cane is probably a native of South Eastern Asia but it is not known to now exist anywhere in a wild state.

It belongs to the grass family being somewhat closely related to Indian corn; it has a solid jointed stem one and a half to two and a half inches in diameter, and growing to a height of from sixteen to eighteen feet; leaves are borne along the stem at the joints, and flowers are borne in a long panicle at the top, though it is not usually allowed to flower when cultivated for its juice. It is cultivated very generally throughout the world in tropical and sub tropical climates, being found to flourish best where the average temperature is from 75° to 78° F. but is grown in much cooler climates even where the average temperature is as low as 60 or 65° F. It is extensively grown in Louisiana, the West Indies, Central America and along the entire coast of northern South America; it is scarcely at all grown in Southern Europe but throughout large portions of Asia and the East Indies it is grown extensively. As the seed rarely matures the plant is propagated by cuttings which are made from the tops of smaller and shorter stems cut into lengths of 15 to 20 inches, which are set in the ground in rows about five feet apart, usually in September or October, and the stems growing from them reach sufficient maturity to be gathered in the early part of the second season, when they are cut as close to the ground as possible, the sugar being more abundant in the lower part of the stem than the upper.

The root which is left will again sprout and produce a second crop of stems at the end of about two years, and will thus continue to sprout after being cut and will furnish good crops for a considerable number of years sometimes as many as twenty, the length of time during which the roots will prove prolific depending upon the favorableness of the climate and soil. The stems after being cut are trimmed of their leaves and tops and carried to the mill. The mill now in almost universal use for the extraction of the juice consists of three horizontal iron rollers one being placed above the other two ; the cane is fed to the mill between the upper roll and one of the lower ones, and from these passes between the upper and the other lower roll.

The mill is usually turned by steam power and extracts by pressure the juice from the canes which runs down from the rolls into a sort of pan from which it is conveyed by spouts to reservoirs. The stems contain about 18 per cent of sugar, of which nearly one half is left in them after pressure. The pressed stems are known as bagasse and are dried and used as fuel. The juice as obtained from the mill is a yellowish green liquid having a specific gravity of from 1.07 to 1.09 and usually contains from 18 to 20 per cent. of sugar, together with a small quantity of albumen and fragments of cane and other impurities. Owing to the presence of these last the juice is very liable to ferment if allowed to stand, sometimes even for a few minutes.

To remove these matters and prevent fermentation the juice is at once passed from the mill through strainers and into iron or copper kettles holding several hundred gallons, where it is raised to a temperature of from 100° to 150°, when there is added to it a quantity of slacked lime after which it is brought nearly to the boiling point. The albumen is coagulated by the heat, and rises, with other impurities, to the surface, as a dense scum, which is carefully removed, after which the juice is ready for evaporation.

The evaporation is conducted in various ways, sometimes entirely in open vessels with the use of either steam or direct furnace heat, sometimes partly in open vessels and the process finished in vacuum pans, sometimes entirely in vacuum pans, and at others various ingenious evaporaters are used, by some of which a current of heated air is blown through the juice, and by others an especially large surface of the liquid is exposed to the heat. One of the more common methods is to first boil the juice in large iron or copper vessels, which allows of the juice being frequently skimmed, which cannot be done if the juice is at once placed in the vacuum pan. The evaporation here is not usually carried to a great degree of condensation before the juice is removed to the vacuum pan. This consists of a large, closed copper or iron boiler furnished with an air pump, by which a partial vacuum is produced inside and with a condenser to condense the steam which escapes from the boiling liquid. The advantage in the use of the vacuum pan is that the boiling can be conducted at a much lower temperature, and thus the conversion of cane into grape sugar, which takes place at high temperatures, is prevented, and, besides, the quality of the cane sugar itself is better when it has not been over heated.

The syrup in open pans, before becoming evaporated to sugar, boils at a temperature of between 230° and 240° F., whilst the evaporation can be completed in the vacuum pan at as low a temperature as 130°, although to obtain a coarse grain a temperature of 170° to 180° is usually employed. The syrup, when sufficiently concentrated, was formerly and is still on many plantations run out into coolers, where it was allowed to become cold and hard, when it was dug out and filled into hogsheads having holes bored in their bottoms through which the molasses drained off, and the sugar, when thoroughly drained, was sent into market as *muscovado*, and the drainage from the hogsheads was sold as West India or New Orleans molasses. Another class of sugar known as *clayed sugar* was also largely produced in former times. The partially solidified sugar was removed from the coolers and placed in conical moulds, having an opening at the smaller end through which the molasses was allowed to drain away. After the molasses ceased to run from the moulds, a quantity of wet clay was placed upon the top of the sugar, from which the water would slowly trickle down, and remove by a process of slow washing more of the uncrystallizable molasses together with coloring matter and impurities, leaving the sugar much purer and whiter than muscovado.

The uncrystallizable molasses is now however removed entirely by centrifugal force. · The machine for the purpose consists essentially of a cylindrical box having its sides perforated with small holes, and being supported upon a horizontal shaft about which it is made to revolve at a speed of from 1200 to 1500 revolutions per minute. The sugar from the coolers being placed in the box is thrown by its revolution against its sides, and the molasses by the centrifugal action is rapidly forced through the perforated sides and accumulates in a second cylinder which encloses the revolving one. In this way the drying of the sugar which used to take days or even weeks is now more effectually accomplished in a very few minutes. The molasses from the centrifugal machine contains but little cane sugar and is sent into market without further treatment.

The raw sugar after the molasses is extracted is not as formerly sent into market as muscovado, clayed sugar, etc., but is instead sent to the large sugar refineries. These with the introduction of the new processes require the combination of large amounts of capital involving as they do the use of very expensive machinery and extensive buildings. Their number is consequently small, there being less than three hundred in the world but some of them have a capacity of 1,000,000 pounds of raw sugar daily.

The raw sugar as received from the plantations is first mixed with about 30 per cent. of water, and melted in iron vessels heated by steam, and is then pumped into cisterns situated upon the upper floor of the refining house. From these cisterns it is drawn off into large iron vessels furnished with steam coils and known as "blow ups." In these it is diluted and heated to about 180° F. Lime and blood are generally added to clarify the solution. The albumen of the blood coagulates and rises as a dense scum entangling with it much of other impurities. The scum is carefully removed and the solution brought as nearly as possible to a density of 28° Baumè when it is run hot into bag filters, which consist of a number of bags of cotton cloth about two feet in length, wound with twine, and supported in iron boxes containing two or three hundred bags each. After having filtered through these bags, the solution is next conveyed to the bone black filters.

The use of bone black in the refining of sugar is one of the most important discoveries in the whole process of sugar manufacture, and, together with vacuum pans and centrifugal machines, has revolutionized the entire industry, and made the production of refined sugar possible. Bone black is the charcoal obtained by burning bones in retorts ; it consists chiefly (75 to 80 per cent.) of phosphate of lime, together with 6 to 12 per cent. of carbon and about the same amount of carbonate of lime, with several others salts in small proportion. Its action was first supposed to be valuable only in removing coloring matters from the sugar solution, but it has since been found that the removal of other impurities which the bone black effects is of even greater importance.

It removes besides coloring matters a variety of nitrogenous bodies, such as albumen, gluten, legumine and also dextrine and gummy substances and salts of soda, potassa and lime. These impurities when present tend to convert cane sugar into grape sugar and to a still greater degree prevent the crystallization of the sugar ; thus largely decreasing the product of crystallizable sugar and adding to the less valuable molasses.

Bone black filters consist of large, upright, iron cylinders furnished with perforated false bottoms, covered with cloth, placed near the lower end, and above which they are filled with coarse bone black to near the top, where is a pipe for the introduction of the sugar solution. They usually have closed tops so that the filtration may be conducted under pressure. The filter is frequently thirty feet in height and from five to ten feet in diameter. After the filter is charged with fresh bone black the solution first passed through is sufficiently purified, but the black soon becomes contaminated and removes the impurities much less completely. The solution running from the filter after a short time is consequently raised and passed through a second one for complete purification. When the bone black becomes so much contaminated as no longer to effectually perform its work it is removed from the filter, carefully washed and again heated to redness in retorts, when it may again be used as at first.

The solution, after being purified by filtration, is next conveyed to vacuum pans where, at a temperature of from 130° to 150° F., it is evaporated until becoming sufficiently concentrated that when removed and cooled it will at once set into solid sugar. It is then drawn from the vacuum pan into *agitators* and from these into *moulds.*

The moulds are cone shaped and have a small opening at the small end, which is closed by a plug when the hot semi-solid sugar is run into them, but the sugar soon becoming cold and hard, the plugs are removed and the cones are set in iron pots to drain. When the mother liquor, called *first greens*, has ceased to run from the moulds, the top of the loaf is cut smooth and a quantity of pure solution of sugar, *white liquor*, is poured over it, which washes out the last traces of mother liquor and leaves the loaves perfectly white. When it has entirely ceased to drain, the loaf is removed from the mould and the damp tip is broken off. The subsequent treatment depends upon the condition in which it is to be marketed ; if in loaves, they are first placed in rubber sockets connected with an air pump and by exhaustion the last particles of liquid are drawn out. The loaf is then placed in a lathe and turned smooth, when it is ready to be sent into market as *loaf sugar*. For the production of " *A* " *sugar* the loaves whilst still quite moist are placed in a cutting machine and shaved fine. This shaved sugar is sometimes carefully dried and the powdered portions separated by sifting, when the remainder is sold as *granulated sugar*. The loaves are at other times dried in hot air chambers and then broken in a crushing machine and the product separated by sieves into coarse *crushed sugar* and *powdered sugar*.

The dried loaves are also sometimes cut into cubes and sold as *cube sugar*.

The mother liquor, or first greens, which has drained from the moulds is diluted, blown up, filtered through the bag and bone-black filters and again concentrated in the vacuum pan, from which it is drawn off into the agitators, from which it may either be placed in moulds to drain or introduced into the centrifugal machine by which the mother liquor, known as *second greens*, is removed. The sugar thus obtained is of a light buff color and is sent into market as " *C*" *sugar*. The several greens are again subjected to purification by the filters, evaporated in the vacuum pans, transferred to the centrifugal machine which extracts the mother liquor, known as *green syrup*, and leaves a quite dark colored sugar, which is sold as " *X*" or *yellow sugar*. The green syrup is still again diluted, blown up and filtered, and concentrated to a proper consistency and sold as *golden syrup*.

The loaf, " *A*", and other white sugars contain, when dry, 100 per cent. of cane sugar. C sugar contains usually 85 to 87 per cent of cane sugar, and yellow sugar from 80 to 83 per cent. The details of the process of refining sugar vary considerably in different refineries, and the quality of the above grades of sugar produced will vary much with the quality of the raw sugar from which they are obtained, and a further gradation of commercial sugar is consequently used. In this country the grades usually named are Standard A, Off A, White Extra C, Yellow C, Yellow and Brown. The Dutch standards are simply an arbitrary series of numbered raw sugars selectted in Holland and in general use as standards.

Sugar and syrup are made in the northern United States to a considerable extent from sorghum or northern sugar cane. These are names given to several varieties of the *Sorghum saccharatum*, a species of duna millet, native of the East Indies and recently assuming importance as a sugar producing plant. It seems to have attracted no attention until since 1850 but is now cultivated to a considerable extent. The cane from Chinese seed is called sorgo and 'that from African seed imphee. There are numerous varieties of each. Sorghum will in general grow where corn will and should receive much the same kind of cultivation. The seed is planted in early spring in rows or drills about four feet apart. It is in condition for cutting when the seeds begin to harden in the fall. It is then cut near the ground, the leaves and top are removed and serve as forage for cattle, and the stems, which contain about nine per cent., or only one half as much as those of the true sugar cane, are taken to the mill. This and the process of extracting the juice differ in no important particular from those used for the sugar cane.

The fresh juice is greenish yellow and contains about ten per cent. of sugar. It is usually evaporated in open vessels with the addition of slacked lime to purify it, whilst the albuminous matters it contains cause the production of a large amount of scum, which has to be frequently removed. Owing to the large amount of impurities present in the juice, the crude processes employed, and the lack of sufficient knowledge on the part of the average manufacturer a very large part of the cane sugar present in the juice becomes converted into grape sugar in the process of evaporation, and it becomes consequently impossible, or nearly so, to make sugar from the solution, which is accordingly boiled only to syrup and sold and used as such. The juice as obtained from the stems contains only cane sugar, whilst the syrup as sold in market usually contains about 50 per cent. of cane sugar and 30 per cent. of grape sugar. The yield of syrup is from 125 to 180 gallons per acre of sorghum.

Sugar from the maple. (See Maple Sugar.) Sugar from the beet. More than one third of the sugar made in the world is obtained from the sugar beet, (*Beta vulgaris*) of which there are several varieties cultivated, the more important being the Silesian, the French vilmorin, the Siberian and Imperial. The beet first began to be used for the production of sugar about the beginning of the present century. Now nearly all the sugar made and consumed in continental Europe is from this plant.

The method of manufacture does not differ very greatly from that used in making cane sugar. The roots are first washed in a revolving, open cylinder, placed beneath water, and the juice is then extracted, several different processes being in use for the purpose, the more common being to rasp the beets to a fine pulp in a machine, consisting essentially of a large, rapidly rotating drum, having its surface thickly set with iron teeth, the rasped pulp being then placed in sacks, is pressed between iron plates in a hydraulic press. By this process from 80 to 85 per cent. of the weight of beets used is extracted as juice. Good beets contain 96 per cent. of juice, of which about 12 per cent. is cane sugar. The juice is sometimes extracted from the pulp, by centrifugal machines and sometimes by repeated washings, and maceration in cold water. A process by diffusion, in which the beet roots sliced into thin shavings, are exposed to the action of water for several hours is sometimes also employed. The juice after extraction is purified by boiling with lime, is filtered through bag and bone-black filters, and concentrated to the crystallizing point in vacuum pans. The processes of refining the raw beet sugar are practically the same as for raw cane sugar and the refined product cannot be distinguished from the refined cane sugar. The introduction of beet sugar manufacture into the United States, has been tried to some extent but without great success. It is apparently reasonable to suppose that where beets can be produced so cheaply as in the Western States, with capital, experience and skill, the manufacture might be conducted with great profit.

Sugar from Palm.   In the East large quantities of sugar are made from the juice of various species of palm tree.   The tree is usually tapped, a spout inserted, and the sap collected much as in making maple sugar in this country.   The sap is evaporated in open kettles, and a crude sugar of dark color, but tolerably agreeable taste is obtained, which is common in Eastern markets under the name of *Jaggery.*

The total amount of sugar produced in the United States, in 1870, as given by the census reports, was, of cane sugar, 87,043 hogsheads, sorghum, 24 hogsheads, maple, 28,443,645 pounds, of cane molasses, 6,593,323 gallons, sorghum molasses, 16,050,089 gallons, of maple, 921,057 gallons.   The total production of sugar in the world in 1867 as given in one of the Jury reports of the Paris Exposition, was, of

Cane sugar, 3,420,467,930 pounds
Beet sugar, 1,433,000,000   "
Palm sugar,   220,462,000   "
Maple sugar,   66,138,600   "
—————————————————
Total 5,140,071,530 pounds.

The island of Cuba produces annually about 700,000 tons of sugar, or more than one fourth of the entire production of the world. The importation of foreign sugar into the United States in 1875, amounted to about 850, 000 tons, very nearly all being raw sugar. The exportation of refined sugar for the same year amounted to about 25,000 tons. The consumption for the same year amounted to about 850,000 tons.

The following interesting table giving the consumption of sugar in different countries of the world is from the *Journal des Fabricants de Sucre*, Paris 1875.

Countries.	Consumption in pounds.	Pounds per head.
England,	1,826,000,000	50.6
United States,	1,694,000,000	44.0
Germany,	673,000,000	16.5
Sweden,	121,000,000	15.6
France,	550,000,000	15.5
Austria and Hungary,	374,000,000	10.5
Italy,	220,000,000	5.9
Spain,	110,000,000	6.6
Russia,	330,000,000	6.0
Turkey,	55,000,000	3.3

Sulphur, Brimstone, is found very widely and abundantly distributed throughout the earth in various forms of combination with other elements, and is also found native in many volcanic districts, the chief sources of supply being the Island of Sicily and the Solfatara, near Naples. The sulphur, together with other mineral matter with which it is found adherent, is broken up and submitted to distillation in fire-clay pots, when, at a comparatively low temperature, the sulphur is distilled over in a nearly pure condition, and a second distillation serves to remove all impurities. The sulphur is drawn off from the receiving vessels, and poured into cylindrical wooden moulds from which it is removed when cold in the form of sticks, which are the *Brimstone* of commerce. If in the process of distillation the sulphur vapor is conveyed into a large chamber which is kept cool, the sulphur will be deposited in a pulverulent state, in which condition it is known as *flowers of sulphur.*

Sulphur melts at from 220° to 230° F., and boils at 800°. It inflames at about 480°, burning with a pale blue flame, and the production of the suffocating sulphurous oxide gas $S O_2$. When exposed to the air it vaporizes more or less rapidly at almost all temperatures. Sulphur, from the low temperature at which it ignites, is used in the manufacture of gunpowder, of fireworks, and friction matches. The vapor which it produces in burning is used to some extent in bleaching. It is of some medicinal value, being employed especially for cutaneous diseases both in men and animals. Many of its combinations are very useful in the arts and in manufactures.

Sweet Herbs, are Thyme, Summer Savory, Marjorum, Balm, Basil and Sage, all members of the mint family, and used either green or dried, as a flavoring for soups and forcemeats.

Sweet Potato, (*Batatas edulis*) a trailing plant belonging to the order convolvulaceæ. The root is perennial, tuberous; tubers oblong, acute at each end, yellowish white or sometimes purple externally, yellowish within. The stem is four to eight feet long, slender and prostrate; leaves two to four inches in length. The plant is cultivated for its large, sweet, edible farinaceous roots, especially in the Southern States, where it takes the place of the common potato. It is also successfully grown in New Jersey and Southern Michigan. They are largely shipped from New Jersey and the South to Northern markets. It is cultivated largely in the tropics of both hemispheres, and is the potato of the old English writers. Its native country is uncertain, some referring it to India and some to Tropical America. Sweet Potatoes were among the presents carried by Columbus to Isabella from the newly discovered world. The best varieties in cultivation are the Nausemond, Red Skinned and Yellow Skinned.

Sword Fish, (Xiphias gladius) a name applied to fishes remarkable for having the upper jaw prolonged forward in the shape of a bony sword. The common sword fish ranges from our Atlantic coast eastward to the Mediterranean. It is from ten to sixteen feet long, is a very rapid swimmer, and is said to attack the largest whale with its sword. It sometimes strikes vessels with such force as to leave its sword embedded in the planks of the vessel. Its flesh is excellent food, and it is captured by the harpoon, affording an exciting and even dangerous sport.

Syrup, as used here, signifies the liquid which drains from refined sugar (see sugar). It is rendered of a proper consistence by reboiling and filtering through animal charcoal. Its color depends upon the amount of impurities still remaining. These syrups may be said to constitute a purified form of treacle ; the above applies to syrup made from the sugar of cane. But most of the syrups now sold consist of glucose or starch sugar, instead of cane sugar. From an article by R. C. Kedzie in the report of the State Board of Health of Michigan, for 1874, we select the following in relation to this class of syrups.

" The saccharification of the starch in France is carried on in large wooden vats, capable of holding 2,800 gallons. The contents of the vat may be heated by forcing in steam through a coiled steam pipe at the bottom. The steam pipe is perforated, to permit the steam to escape at many points into the contents of the vat. In France the steam pipe is made of lead; in this country I suspect they use iron pipes. When two tons of starch are to be converted into sugar, 32 barrels of water and about 80 lbs. of sulphuric acid are placed in the vat, and the whole heated to 212°, by forcing in steam. Two hundred pounds of starch are then mixed with 22 gallons of water and stirred up, and 4 or 5 gallons of this mixture are run into the vat. The temperature is kept up to the boiling point all the while, and successive charges of starch are run in till the whole amount is converted into sugar. The steam is then shut off, and chalk is added in sufficient quantity to neutralize the sulphuric acid, but if too little chalk is used, free sulphuric acid will be left in the contents of the vat. The sparingly soluble sulphate of lime is formed, and much of it settles to the bottom of the liquid; the clear liquid is drawn off and evaporated by steam heat till the proper density of syrup is secured, or until it will crystallize on cooling and standing for several days, according as they seek to make syrup or sugar.

This brief description will assist us to understand why certain impurities are found in these starch-sugar syrups. If iron pipes are used to convey the steam for heating the contents of the vat, the sulphuric acid will attack and dissolve some of the iron, and thus sulphate of iron (copperas) will appear in the syrup. If too little chalk is used, free sulphuric acid will remain in the syrup. The chalk being carbonate of lime, its use will explain why lime may be found in large quantity in the syrup. As chalk is insoluble in water, and sulphate of lime is very sparingly soluble, many persons would suppose that little or no lime would remain in these syrups. But we must bear in mind that sugar itself acts the part of an acid with many basic substances. Thus there are two well known salts formed by combination of sugar and lime, one containing one equivalent of lime to one of sugar; the other containing three equivalents of lime to one of sugar. These sucrates of lime have lost entirely the sweet taste characteristic of sugar, and have a bitterish taste instead.

Not only will sugar thus combine with lime, oxide of lead, oxide of iron, etc., but it will associate with itself sulphuric acid, and form a compound acid which comports itself very differently from simple sulphuric acid. This sucro-sulphuric acid forms a pretty large class of salts which are soluble in water, but especially soluble in solutions of sugar. Reagents which will readily precipitate sulphuric acid, and sulphates, e. g. chloride of barium, will not precipitate the sucro-sulphates.

Glucose has the same power as an acid substance as sucrose, forming a class of soluble glucosates. It will also associate with itself sulphuric acid, and form a class of gluco-sulphates of a like character as the sucro-sulphates. Undoubtedly a large part of the lime found in these starch-sugar syrups exists in the form of gluco-sulphate of lime. The sparing solubility of sulphate of lime in water is no guaranty that these syrups will not contain a large amount, because it may exist in the form of the soluble gluco-sulphate of lime.

One evil connected with the presence of lime in syrups is the destruction of a portion of the sweetening power of the syrup. One part of lime will destroy more than six times its weight of sugar, so far as any sweetness is concerned ; and the compound of lime and sugar is bitter.

In making my selections for examination, I obtained specimens only from those who are regarded as first-class tradesmen. If syrups bought at such places are adulterated, we may well suppose that the inferior class of dealers will have no better articles. Some have said that, undoubtedly, poor people who trade at small groceries are swindled in these syrups, but that the respectable class of citizens who patronize first-class grocers need not apprehend any such imposition. I determined to follow up " the respectable citizen" and see what syrups he obtained of " first-class grocers." Part of the specimens were obtained near home, but the most from abroad. I have examined 17 specimens in all, with the general result that 2 were made of cane sugar and 15 of starch sugar or glucose.

SPECIFIC RESULTS OF EXAMINATION OF TABLE SYRUPS.

No. 1.—Pure cane sugar syrup.

No. 2.—Starch sugar syrup. Contains some sulphate of

iron (copperas), and contains in each gallon 107.35 grains of lime.

No. 3.—The grocer called it "poor stuff." I have seldom seen an article that better sustained its recommendation. Made of starch sugar; contains plenty of copperas and 297 grains of lime in a gallon.

No. 4.—Nearly pure cane sugar syrup.

No. 5.—Starch sugar syrup. Contains copperas, and 100 grains of lime in a gallon.

Nos. 6, 7, 8.—All made of starch sugar. Contain sulphate of iron and plenty of lime.

No. 9.—All the members of a family in Hudson, Michigan, were made very sick by eating freely of this syrup. A starch sugar syrup; contains in the gallon 71.83 grains of free sulphuric acid, 28 grains of sulphate of iron, and 363 grains of lime.

No. 10.—Contains starch sugar, copperas, and lime— amount not estimated.

No. 11.—A starch sugar syrup. Contains in the gallon 141.9 grains free sulphuric acid, 25 grains sulphate of iron, and 724.83 grains of lime.

No. 12.—Contains starch sugar, seasoned with sulphate of iron and lime.

No. 13.—Starch sugar. Contains in the gallon 58.48 grains of sulphate of iron, 83.14 grains of free sulphuric acid, and 440.12 grains of lime.

No. 14.—Starch sugar. Contains in a gallon 80 grains of free sulphuric acid, 38 grains of iron and 262.48 grains of lime.

Nos. 15, 16.—Contain starch sugar, sulphate of iron, and lime.

No. 17. Starch sugar, sulphate of iron, and 202.33 grains of lime.

A very important element in this discussion is the great disparity in sweetening power between cane sugar and starch sugar or glucose. One pound of cane sugar has the same sweetening power as two and a half pounds of glucose. In these starch-sugar syrups, the public is not only treated with compounds loaded with foreign and injurious materials, but they are enormously cheated in the very thing they seek to buy, viz. the sweetness. Sugars and syrups are bought, not as articles of food solely, but entirely for *their sweetness*, and thus the buyer is largely defrauded out of the very thing for which alone he makes a purchase.

The thought of using such mixtures as a relish for our food is not very appetizing. Some of these drips seem to be made up of about equal parts of fraud and dirt! A facetious friend has quoted, in this connection, the old saying, " A man must eat his peck of dirt before he dies." If any one feels uneasy lest he be defrauded of " his peck of dirt," let him eat a few gallons of No. 11, and he may rest on his laurels for the balance of his days.

WHOSE FAULT?

The public will naturally ask, " Who is to blame that such disgusting and fraudulent mixtures are sold in the shops? I do not think that the retail dealers are " sinners above all that dwell in" Michigan in this respect. Most of them honestly suppose that they are selling a good article of cane sugar syrup, and are themselves surprised that so good looking syrups can be sold at so low a price compared with that of sugar—a price often less than that of the dark colored and strong flavored molasses which remains from the manufacture of cane sugar. The manufacturers are chiefly to blame in this matter, for they cannot be ignorant of the fraud in selling glucose for cane sugar; but even they will probably be surprised to learn how large a quantity of foreign materials is left in these syrups.

TESTS.

It is popularly supposed that an infusion of tea leaves will certainly detect the presence of starch sugar, by the dark coloration which it imparts to the syrup. Strong tea will give a re-action of this kind with a salt of iron— the same re-action which makes black ink; hence strong tea may be used to detect the presence of copperas in syrup; but it will give no reaction with grape sugar containing no iron.

In most of these syrups, lime is the largest adulterant aside from the starch sugar itself. Lime may easily be recognized in the syrup by a solution of oxalic acid. Dissolve one ounce of oxalic acid in a pint of rain water; if the solution is not clear, let it stand for a few hours till it settles, then pour off the clear solution into a clean bottle and label it OXALIC ACID : POISON. To test the syrup, place a tablespoonful in a tumbler half full of rain-water, stir it up, and add a tablespoonful of the oxalic acid solution. If there is much lime in the syrup it will show itself by a white precipitate, the amount of which will give some measure of the amount of lime present."

Tapioca, a starch obtained from the species of *manihot*, a shrub, native of South America. The expressed juice, after the manufacture of mandioca (which see) after being allowed to stand, deposits a white powder, which after being well washed and dried constitutes *Tapioca meal* or *Brazilian arrowroot.* When this meal is dried on hot plates, the grains partly burst, and the fecula agglomerates in irregular semi-opaque, gum like masses, and this is what is called *Tapioca.* There is a false tapioca found in the shops consisting of very small, smooth, spherical grains, which is sold as *Pearl Tapioca.* It is supposed to be manufactured from potato starch.

Tartaric Acid, is obtained from the crude tartar or *argol* deposited in the casks by fermenting wine. (See Cream of Tartar.) Argol is an impure bitartrate of potassa. To obtain tartaric acid, argol is dissolved in hot water, and pulverized chalk slowly added until effervescence ceases. By this process tartrate of lime is formed which settles to the bottom of the vessel, and bitartrate of potassa is reduced to the soluble tartrate which remains in solution in the clear liquid, with which it is drawn off, and to which is then added a quantity of chloride of lime, which causes the rest of the tartaric acid to enter into combination with the lime, forming another quantity of insoluble tartrate of lime. These two precipitates are then united, dried, and treated with sulphuric acid, which decomposes the salt, producing sulphate of lime, which is thrown down as an insoluble precipitate, and free tartaric acid, which remains in solution. This solution is drawn off and concentrated in leaden pans, until the tartaric acid becomes crystallized out. Commercial tartaric acid is apt to be contaminated by traces of sulphuric acid and lead. It is used principally in dye-

ing, and in the preparation of baking powders and effervescing drinks.

Tea is the prepared leaves of a small shrub, (*Camellia
Thea*), from three to six feet high, a native of Northern
India and closely resembling our common camellia. The
leaves are simple and feather veined, oblong or broadly lan-
ceolate, longer than wide, with serrate edges. The tree is
largely cultivated in China and Japan, from which countries the markets of the world are supplied with tea. The
first mention we have of the use of tea in China, was in
the fourth century, but by the ninth it was in general use.
The Dutch were probably the first to introduce tea into
Europe, about the beginning of the seventeenth century;
about the middle of the century the East India Company
began to import tea into England, and from being used
by a few hundred people at that time, it has now become
the common beverage to the millions of English speak-
ing people wherever they can obtain it. On its first introduction into England it sold as high as ten guineas a
pound, while at the present time good tea may be had
for two shillings. The preparation of tea from the tea
plant has been surrounded with some mystery on account of the distance at which it occurs, but the affair is,
however, very simple in all except what refers to minute
details in its preparation, which of course must vary in
different parts of the country. There is but one species
of tea plant, and from this, and probably from a variety,
all our different teas are obtained. The Chinese make
new plantations by planting the seeds at regular distances
from each other, and in about three years the plant yields
its first crop; in seven or ten years it is cut down and

shoots spring up in profusion from the old stump, and yield an abundance of leaves. The average product of a single plant seems to be about six ounces, and from an acre of ground about 320 pounds of dried leaves are obtained.

The leaves are picked by hand, and three harvests are generally made during the year; the first in April, the second in May, and the third in June or July. The first gathering is the most valuable, and consists only of the young and tender leaves which yield a fine young Hyson, with a thin leaf, and a large proportion of juice in relation to the solid substance of the leaf. This tea is difficult of preparation on account of its being liable to ferment, and on this account is not shipped in large masses, but is sent over-land in small quantities to Russia; also a good portion of the crop is kept for the use of the wealthy Chinese. The later pickings are less valuable, those of July being the least so. The leaves are now older and contain much more tannin, which gives an astringent and bitter taste to the infusion.

The difference in the manufacture of Black and Green teas consists in the leaves of the former undergoing a sort of fermentation before drying, while the latter are directly submitted to a high temperature in iron pans,—the idea that green tea is obtained by drying the tea in copper pans, being quite a fallacy. In making black tea the process is not unlike that of making hay. The leaves are placed in heaps, and allowed to undergo a certain degree of fermentation by which they assume a dark color, and become flaccid. They are then subjected to the operation of the twisters, who either twist them between thumb and forefinger, or place them on a table of split bamboo, where they are rubbed and rolled by the hands till the twisting is effected. From the twisters the leaves are taken to the drying room, and heated for some minutes in an iron pan. They are again subjected to the operation of the twisters, and then put in wicker cylinders and dried on a slow fire. This operation is repeated several times till they become black and crisp. For green tea the leaves are put directly into firing pans, over charcoal fires, and after a short time are removed and subjected to the operation of the rollers, who roll them in the different forms in which they appear in market. They are again put on the fire for drying, and the operation is repeated until they are dry and crisp, when they are stowed away for use or for market. The green teas of commerce are artificially colored by turmeric powder and a mixture of gypsum or Prussian blue, or of gypsum and indigo. Some of the teas are flavored or scented by placing among the leaves, during preparation, aromatic flowers of certain plants. Pekoes and Capers are the kinds most generally flavored. Of Black Tea we have the following varieties, *Bohea*, which is in the form of a small blackish leaf, dusty and of somewhat brackish taste ; it should be quite crisp and have a strong odor. *Congous* are of two kinds, one with a large leaf and but little dust, with a fine flavor, and the other with a small, wiry leaf and burnt smell. *Souchong* or English Breakfast is made from leaves of trees three years old, and from older trees when they are grown in very rich soil. But there is very little of this variety made, and that which is sold for it is simply a good quality of Congou. Genuine Souchong should be crisp and dry, not broken, of a pleasant, fragrant smell and free from dust.

Caper Souchong is so called from its being rolled up like a caper; it is of a fine glossy black color, heavy, fragrant smell, high flavor, and the infusion, of a bright reddish brown color. Padre Souchong, or Powchong, is a superior variety, of a fine taste, smell and flavor, with large leaves not strongly twisted and whole. *Pekoe* is made from the tenderest leaves of three year old plants gathered after the plants are in bloom. They are collected just as the buds have burst and made a shoot long enough for a sprig, when it is picked off. It is regularly curled and should never be broken. These teas are often scented and used to impart flavor to other teas. *Ball Tea* is a kind of Black tea made into balls about the size of a nutmeg and gummed together. *Oolongs* are black teas generally of the poorer kind, with a light colored infusion and penetrating flavor and well adapted for mixing with other varieties. Of Green teas we have, *Gunpowder*: should be round like small shot, with a beautiful bloom which will not bear the breath; it has a greenish hue and a fragrant, pungent taste. This kind of tea is often adulterated by inferior kinds colored, glazed, and manipulated to look like the Gunpowder with which it is mixed. When the leaf is open and loose, the outside of a darker hue, and the taste brassy and unpleasant, it should be rejected.

Imperial, much like Gunpowder only more loosely rolled and coarser. *Young Hyson* is of a fine blooming color, very dry, crisp, full sized grains and will crumble to dust on the slightest pressure. The infusion is of a light green color, an aromatic smell and strong pungent taste and the leaf should open clear and smooth without being broken or shrivelled, as this is an indication of age. The teas which give a high color to water should be rejected as they have been "doctored." *Old Hyson* consists of the largest, most irregular and worst colored of the leaves that are picked from the young hyson. Its infusion is of a pale yellowish green, of a delicate taste, with something of a burnt taste. Some of the Old Hyson is simply the true hyson, after becoming old, and, after repeated drying and freshing it up, is sent to the market a second time. *Twankay* consists of the broken and mixed leaves and is of inferior quality. *Japan Tea* is largely consumed in this country, and, as its name implies, is imported from Japan. It has an agreeable odor, is both colored and uncolored. In the cup the infusion should be of light color, fragrant, and, in the better qualities, of a mild and pleasant taste.

Most of our tea trade with China is carried on from the ports of Shanghai, Foo-Chow and Amoy. The tea is mostly brought over in steamers and reaches New York by the way of the Suez Canal, from Shanghai in from sixty to seventy days; by the way of San Francisco the time is shortened about twenty days. The Japan tea, by way of the latter place, arrives in about thirty-five days. For the year ending June 30th, 1876, there were imported into the United States 62,887,153 lbs., valued at $ 19,524,166. This would give about one and a half pounds for each person in the United States. Of this amount imported, Japan tea takes the lead. Tea prepared for shipping is more highly fired than that for home use; and

it is said that which comes across the Pacific is superior
to that from other routes. The tea sent to Russia over-
land from China is in the form of bricks. It is made by
mixing the dried leaves with some glutinous substance
and putting it in molds and drying it in an oven. Tea as
generally exported is packed loose in chests of wood
lined with sheet lead. In India the cultivation of tea is
being successfully carried on and considerable quantities
are imported into England. Tea dust has of late years
made its appearance in market but it cannot be recommended for either cleanliness, purity or quality. The
chemical composition of tea, in 100 parts, consists of
theine which is the essential principle, 2 to 3, caseine 15,
gum 18, sugar 3, tannin 26.25 starch, aromatic oil, 0.75,
fat 4, vegetable fibre 20, mineral substance 5 and water 5.

Tea is astringent and gently excitant, and exerts
a favorable influence on the nervous system; but
when taken in excess it induces nervous and dyspeptic
symptoms. Many large houses employ professional tea
tasters who prepare their samples from a uniform and
very small quantity, viz. the weight of a new sixpence,
which is infused for about five minutes in a covered
pottery vessel, with about four ounces of water, and,
in tasting, the tea is not swallowed. He must have a
sensitive and refined taste, and should be in good health,
to determine properly the flavor of the tea. Teas should
never be bought unless tested by steeping, as a fair style
tea may be a poor drawer, and the adulteration of tea
is more readily detected in this manner. That tea is
largely adulterated by the addition of leaves of other
plants, and by various mineral and organic elements is a

matter that is well known. At the Exhibition of 1876, in Philadelphia, a number of plants used in the adulteration of green and black teas were on exhibition. One of the British Consuls at Shanghai stated that at one time there were 53,000 pounds of willow leaves in course of preparation to mix with the tea for shipment in the ratio of from 10 to 20 per cent. The willow leaves cost about four cents a pound and no concealment is made of the business, which is regularly carried on. One of the most common forms of adulteration is the coloring or " facing" of teas. All our green teas are thus colored in order to conceal other leaves, and to meet the demands of the trade. This coloring is carried on in the United States and England as well as in China, though in the latter country the colored tea is never used. As before stated these coloring materials consist of Prussian blue, indigo, turmeric and kaolin; and steatite, graphite etc. are used to impart a glossy color to the leaves. Most of these coloring matters can be detected by the use of the microscope. Silica, metallic iron, old tea leaves and leaves of other plants are added to increase the weight. Strength is given to exhausted tea by the addition of tannin and soluble iron salts. " Lie Tea" used to adulterate gunpowder tea, consists of tea dust mixed with mineral substances and starch and gum, and then formed into little masses resembling tea; hot water will dissolve this gum and the grains will become liberated. Caper tea is a similar preparation and may be tested in the same way. Metallic iron may be detected by the use of the magnet; salts of iron by heating the powdered sample with acetic acid and testing by ferrocyanide of potassium. An English paper states that a sample of tea proved to be composed of the following substances ; iron, plumbago, chalk, china clay, sand, Prussian blue, turmeric, indigo, starch, gypsum, catechu, gum, the leaves of the cammelia, sarangua, elm, oak, willow, poplar, elder, beech, hawthorn and sloe.

In the steeping of tea the amount should be regulated by weight, as the bulk and weight are not convertible terms : a given bulk of Gunpowder is more than three times heavier than the same of Oolong. Soft or brook water is preferable to well water, and the water used should be newly boiled. The water should be applied to the tea while in a boiling condition, and the tea allowed to steep for about five minutes, when it may be served. Black and Japan teas require more steeping to extract their essential qualities than the green teas. In this country sugar and milk are generally added to the infusion of tea ; in Russia lemon juice is added, while in its native country the infusion of the tea is drank clear.

Tobacco, (*Nicotiana Tabacum*) an annual plant belonging to the Nightshade family. The stem is from four to six feet high, stout, becoming almost woody at base, paniculately branched above. Leaves from one to two feet long, and six inches in width, being smaller as they ascend. The flowers are in a loose terminal panicle, corollas funnel form, the petals rose colored, the calyx one third the length of the corolla ; the seed vessel or capsule is ovoid or sulcate on each side ; seeds many and small. The tobacco plant is a native of tropical America and was in use by the Indians when the country was first discovered. From America it was carried to Europe, where its use rapidly spread. It is now cultivated in all the countries of the world where the climate is mild enough for its growth. The great commercial supply is derived from the United States, where it is cultivated in almost every state in the Union, the middle and southern states producing the most. It is cultivated in the West Indies and is largely produced in central and southern Europe. It is cultivated by the natives of Africa, from the Mediterranean to the Cape of Good Hope. It is found all over Asia, the Indian Archipelago, Australia, and the islands of Polynesia, and it would be difficult to find a place where the weed is not found.

It is a strange commentary on human nature that this nauseous and powerfully narcotic plant, smoked by savages in the wilds of America, should have spread so rapidly not only among civilized races but also among those farthest removed from all civilizing influence. We are accustomed to wonder that the Chinese and other Asiatic races should be addicted to the use of opium, but the use of tobacco amongst us has become so common that we are liable to forget that it is of the same nature and more widely used. When tobacco was first introduced into the Old World it was received with a sort of enthusiasm, and Europeans, Africans and Asiatics began to smoke, chew and snuff. But its evil effects were soon apparent, and it began to meet violent opposition. Theologians called it an invention of Satan to prevent fasting; Church councils prohibited its use by the clergy. Two of the Popes punished its use by excommunication. Prussia and Denmark prohibited its use, whilst James of England wrote a pamphlet against it. But finding that nothing succeeded in checking its use, the governments turned it into a source of revenue, and would allow its cultivation and manufacture only under restrictions or monopolies and these still prevail in many parts of Europe.

The distinctive and valuable properties of tobacco are found mostly in the leaves, for which the plant is cultivated. By analysis chemists have found that in 10,000 parts of fresh tobacco there are 6 of nicotine, 1 of nicotianine, 287 of bitter extractive, 174 of gum, 26.7 of resin, 26 of albumen, 104.8 of a substance analogous to gluten, 51 of chloride of potassium, 9.5 of potash, 16.6 of malate of lime, 24.2 of lime, 8.8 of silica, 496.9 of lignine and 8,828 parts of water. The oil distilled from tobacco, and called tobacco oil, is a most virulent poison.

For the cultivation of tobacco a rich soil and favorable climate is requisite to grow it in perfection. The seeds are sown in beds to raise the young plants and these are transplanted to the open fields in April or May, and set in rows two or three feet apart one way to allow of being cultivated by a horse and plow. The cultivation must be thorough and the ground kept clean. As the leaves are the part desired, every effort is made to increase their size and perfect their growth. The plant is topped just before blooming, and the suckers broken off, as well as superfluous leaves removed. From three to four months are required to fit the crop for gathering. When the plant begins to yellow it is cut close to the ground, by raising the bottom leaves and cutting the stem with a tobacco knife. The plants are allowed to lie on the ground for a short time, to fall or wilt, when they are placed in small heaps of eight or ten plants in a heap, and thus taken to the drying house, or they may be speared, which consists in stringing the plants on a small stick, and then carrying to the house on these sticks.

In the drying house these sticks are hung on rafters about 12 or 15 inches apart, and the leaves, being smoothed down, are allowed to dry, pushing the sticks together as the leaves dry. This drying operation lasts some weeks, and in some houses artificial heat is used in the process. Sometimes the leaves are partially fermented before drying, and a second sweating afterward, before the final manufacture. During the process of partial sweating and drying is developed a powerful aroma, with strong narcotic and acrid properties. After the tobacco is cured and dry it is stripped; which operation can only be performed during mild and damp weather. It is taken off the sticks and laid in heaps, when the leaves are stripped from the plants and tied in bundles of small size; these bundles are formed by wrapping a leaf around the upper end of a handful of leaves, and tucking the end into the middle of the bundle. In a crop of tobacco there should be four sorts, second, bright, yellow and dull. When the tobacco is taken down the culler separates the leaves into the different sorts, and ties them into bundles, these being kept separate for convenience in bulking. This operation consists in placing the bundles in rows so as to allow free circulation of the air. After being bulked several times it is weighted down by sticks or logs, and is in order for packing. The best time for packing is during the mild, pleasant weather of spring or in summer. The crop is generally packed in hogsheads, and the brand and grade put on by a state inspector. In

Virginia and the adjacent States the hogsheads contain from 250 to 1200 pounds. The inferior tobacco of Maryland consists of stems, lugs, etc., packed for export, weighing but from 650 to 800 pounds per hogshead. Western tobacco reaches 1500 pounds or more. Leaf tobacco is also packed in bales of about 250 pounds weight for export, and manufactured tobacco in cases of about the same average weight. Lugs are the lowest quality of tobacco exported, and consist of stems, strippings and broken leaves. The best full leaves are commonly packed as wrappers, and are generally very high priced.

Manufactured tobacco is technically distinguished from both the whole leaf and cigars or snuff. It is generally made from common or inferior leaves. These leaves are placed on one another to form large cakes, and then cut by a machine, somewhat similar to our straw cutter, worked by horse or steam power. The machine can be regulated so as to cut either coarse or fine. The dark leaves, after being cut, are rendered still darker by the addition of syrups and liquorice; it is then pressed into cakes of various forms and sizes. The better sort of leaves are spun into rolls of different sizes; what is known as Negrohead consisting of large, coarse rolls, weighing from six to eight pounds. Pig-tail is also spun, but is made into fine rolls about the size of a pipe stem, all of these being flavored by the addition of sweetening. The outsides of these rolls are wrapped round with whole leaves. The style of plug known as Cavendish is first cut by machinery, and, being softened and flavored, is, by powerful pressure, formed into cakes and these packed into oak boxes or caddies and sent to market. It is used both for the purposes of chewing and smoking. The names Cavendish, navy twist, negrohead, etc., are standard names or brands by which the different forms of solid or pressed tobacco are known. " Fine cut" chewing is shredded and loose, and is cut by delicate machinery, generally from the better qualities of leaves, and flavored by the addition of sweetening. In fine cut the length of the shreds and a bright color, are tests of good quality. Smoking tobacco is made of all grades and styles but mostly from stems, broken leaves, and other inferior parts. In trade many names are given to particular styles, but these are continually changing. Killikinick, cut cavendish and the common cut leaf, embrace most of these classes. For these kinds of smoking the tobacco is granulated in a mill or shaved in a fine cutting machine. Most of the operations in the manufacture of tobacco are done by machinery. Shorts is a term given to the siftings of tobacco, and is used both for smoking and chewing.

SNUFF is made from the leaf stalks of the tobacco, or combined with leaves ; it is sometimes made with the addition of rosewood dust, salt and various drugs. The material is well dried before being ground, which is accomplished by mills. The old method was by grinding in small mortars, the pestles of which were moved by machinery. It is now ground by steam in iron mills. For the last half century, Scotch snuff has been the favorite, but the use of snuff is now declining. For the year ending June 30, 1876, there were manufactured in the United States, 3,317,086 pounds of snuff. The standard branches of snuff in market are the Maccaboy, originally from Martinique and Spain, Rappee, or the French, and that known as Scotch snuff. The revenue tax on manufactured snuff is twenty-four cents per pound. Snuff is largely adulterated both by other leaves and the addition of various drugs. It is doubtful if much adulteration takes place in our manufactured tobacco, beyond the addition of flavors and sweetening; the poorer sort of smoking may be adulterated. In England adulterations are extensively carried on, and stringent laws are passed for its prevention. The tobacco trade and manufacture is a source of great revenue to the government. All manufactured tobacco pays a tax of twenty four cents to the pound. The receipts from internal revenue on manufactured tobacco, cigars and snuff, as well as the taxes for dealers were, for 1876, $39,795,274. The amount exported for the year ending June 30, 1875, was 233,927,167 lbs, valued at $28,547,862. In England the cultivation of tobacco is prohibited by law, so that more revenue may be derived from this source. Most of our exported tobacco goes to Germany and the Low Countries; next, to England, France, Italy, etc.

Bremen is the greatest general tobacco market in Europe, and Liverpool next. The United States produces more than half of the tobacco consumed in the world. The average of the crop in the United States for the five years ending with 1875, was about 450,000,000 pounds. Cuba annually raises a large quantity of tobacco of superior quality and it is almost wholly consumed in the manufacture of cigars either at home or abroad. The tobacco plant is very severe on soil, rapidly exhausting the ground on which it is raised and large areas of land have been abandoned in the Southern States as worthless or worn out. Tobacco, used in whatever form, is undoubtedly injurious to the system, and if long continued must produce evil results. The evil is greatest with chewing, smoking next, and snuffing last. Tobacco is used to a slight extent in medicine.

Tomato, (*Lycopersicum esculentum*) an annual plant native of Tropical America, and now largely cultivated in this country and Europe. It was introduced into France from America under the name of Love Apples, and, coming into general use there, was brought back to this country. They are now extensively cultivated and eaten raw or cooked. They enter largely into the manufacture of soup, sauces and pickles. The fruit of the tomato is a true berry, from one to four inches or more in diameter, globose or flatly depressed, often distorted by large swelling ridges, red or reddish orange color when mature. Flowers from June to August, and fruits in August and September, in the north United States. The varieties in cultivation are very numerous and change rapidly. Among the best now in cultivation are the Canada Victor, Trophy and General Grant. Immense quantities of tomatoes are canned and consumed annually.

Tripe, an article of food prepared from the stomach and intestines, with the fatty structure attached thereto, of the ox and cow, and consists of the walls of these organs and the enclosed fat. It is prepared by thoroughly cleansing the organs from all impurities and gently boiling them in water for about an hour. It is food easy of digestion and of somewhat agreeable flavor. It is eaten in a fresh state, but is most commonly pickled, and is known as pickled tripe.

Trout, a name applied to a species of fish belonging to the genus Salmo, of the salmon family. The Great Trout of the Lakes (*S. amethystus*) is from twenty-four to sixty inches long, dark gray, with numerous light spots on the back and sides ; under part light ashy gray, or cream color. Its average weight is about five pounds, though it sometimes attains a weight of one hundred and twenty pounds. It is often called Mackinaw trout. It is found in the deep waters of the Lakes, and is mostly taken by gill nets, though they may be easily taken by the hook, as they are voracious and will bite almost any bait. These fish are largely eaten fresh, though they are salted and packed in kits and barrels similar to the mackerel. The Speckled Trout or Brook Trout, (*S. fontinalis*) found in the clear streams of northern North America, is from six to twenty inches long, horn color above, with irregular dark markings, and sides variegated with silvery white and yellow spots with vermillion dots. This fish is much sought after by anglers, and the flesh is considered as a delicate luxury.

Truffles, the common name for several species of fungi, of the genus *Tuber*, the most common being *T. œstivum*. They are roundish in outline, with black, wrinkled exterior, and brown and solid inside. In size they are from one to three or four inches in diameter. They are the most highly esteemed of all the edible fungi. Their manner of growth is peculiar, the entire life of the plant being passed at a depth of from six to twelve inches below the surface of the ground. Trained dogs and swine are employed to find the truffles, which they do by scent, and when they begin to dig for them the attendant drives them away and digs the truffle himself, with a trowel, rewarding the animal with a tid-bit of some other food. Truffles are found in calcareous soils, growing among the roots of oak trees. They are native throughout Europe, and occur to some extent in this country, but are cultivated only in France.

Tunny Fish, (*Thynnus vulgaris*) a large fish belonging to the mackerel family, and abundantly caught in the Black and Mediterranean seas, and to some extent in the Atlantic Ocean. The fish sometimes attains a length of twenty feet, and exceeds half a ton in weight. The flesh is eaten both fresh and salted, and is highly esteemed. These fish move in vast shoals, and, being surrounded with a net, are killed with the harpoon.

Turnips, the fleshy root of a variety of *Brassica campestris*, a biennial plant belonging to the Mustard family. It is a native of Europe, but is cultivated extensively in all cool, temperate climates, for food both for man and animals. Although highly esteemed by many as a table article, it does not take high rank as a food, from the fact of its containing the exceedingly large amount of from 87 to 92 per cent. of water. In England, turnips are one of the most important of field crops, being the forage plant most generally relied upon. The Swedish turnip, or Ruta-baga is a distinct variety, having an elongated root. There are also many sub-varieties both of these and of flat turnips. The varieties most commonly grown are the White Dutch, Yellow Aberdeen, Laing's and Improved American ruta-baga.

Vermicelli (see Macaroni).

Vinegar, the common name applied to a dilute and somewhat impure solution of acetic acid used for domestic purposes. Acetic is the most common of the vegetable acids, occuring in the juices of very many plants. It is composed of carbon. oxygen and hydrogen, its chemical formula being $C_2H_4O_2$. It is formed in the destructive distillation of wood, but the great source of it is from the oxidation of dilute solutions of alcohol. One part of alcohol and two parts oxygen form one part acetic acid and one part water, which may be expressed in chemical formulæ thus : Alcohol, C_2H_6O,$+2O=$Acetic acid, $C_2H_4O_2$ $+H_2O$. The oxidation of alcoholic solutions will not, however, take place from the simple presence of the oxygen of the air, but requires that some carrier for the oxygen, which shall yield the gas in a more potent form, shall be present. Spongy platinum and other similar substances will serve this purpose, but the more common agent is a species of fungoid plant, (*Mycodermi aceti*) which is commonly known as *mother of vinegar*. Its action is entirely similar to that of the yeast plant in the process of fermentation, it serving simply to take oxygen from the air and convey it to the alcohol in a condition such that its union with the alcohol may take place.

Vinegar in the United States is made principally from cider, although whiskey and other alcoholic liquors are also used to some extent, and in maple sugar making districts large amounts are produced from the last sap of the season, which is of poor quality for sugar. and is consequently boiled down to a proper consistency and converted into vinegar. In Germany and France almost all the vinegar used is made from the inferior grades of wine ; in England infusions of malt and soured beers are very generally made use of for the purpose. The flavor and quality of the vinegar depend to a considerable degree upon the material from which it is made, chiefly upon account of the presence, in varying quantities, of acetic and other ethers, together with small quantities of other compounds peculiar to the source from which it is derived. Wine vinegar is thus white or red, according to the color of the wine. Cider vinegar, made from sound and ripe sweet apples, by a good process, and without adulterations, is, without doubt, the most generally agreeable variety that is in use.

Wine, cider, and other alcoholic liquids may be converted into vinegar by simply adding to them a small quantity of vinegar or *mother* and allowing them to stand in casks in the sun in summer or in a warm place in winter where the temperature is kept at 75° F., or higher. The conversion may even take place without the addition of any mother or vinegar, but as the process is one of oxidation the presence of air is necessary and the process in casks must be slow because of the limited amount of air which can come in contact with the liquid. Vinegar is now mostly made by what is known as the *quick* or *German process*, which was introduced by Schützenbach in 1823, and consists essentially in exposing a large surface of the liquids at an elevated temperature to a constant current of air. The process is conducted in a tall cask or vat having a perforated false bottom, about a foot above the line bottom. Above this false bottom the vat is filled with beech shavings, which have been soured by soaking in warm vinegar for twenty-four hours, to within six or eight inches of the top, where a false top perforated with numerous small holes is placed. This false top is covered with cotton batting, and bits of it are drawn through the small holes in it, and the liquid is poured by a small continuous stream upon the cotton, from which it trickles slowly downward upon the shavings. A number of air holes about a half inch in diameter are bored in the sides of the vat just below the false bottom and as the oxidation takes place among the shavings the temperature is considerably raised which causes the air to rise and escape through glass tubes set for the purpose into the false cover whilst more air continually comes in by the the air holes below to take its place. If the temperature of the room is 75° or 80° F., the temperature inside the vat will rise to 95° or 100,° which will cause a constant circulation of air among the shavings, and, there being so large a surface of liquid exposed to its action, it will be converted into vinegar by being passed through two or three such vats. As the vinegar flows down and accumulates between the false and true bottoms, it is drawn off by means of stop cocks, and transferred to casks. Aside from the articles above mentioned, from which the better qualities of vinegar are made, a great variety of refuse articles, washings of sugar and molasses hogsheads, beer and similar liquids which have become sour, and in fact, almost everything which contains fermented liquor or a fermentable substance, is employed in the manufacture of this article.

From the high price of acetic acid, vinegar is often adulterated with sulphuric, muriatic, or nitric acids, and in some cases an article has been sold as vinegar in which not a trace of acetic acid was to be found, the sour element being one of the acids named, and flavor being given by the addition of ether, alum, red pepper, mustard, etc. Such an article is exceedingly injurious if taken into the stomach. Vinegar should contain from three to five or more per cent. of acetic acid, and no other acid should be present unless it be one derived from the fruit from which the vinegar is made. The specific gravity is sometimes used as a test of strength, but is not a good one, owing to the presence of other substances which affect it. The amount of acetic present is best learned by first testing for other acids and precipitating them, if present, and then finding the amount of a standard alkaline solution needed to neutralize the acetic acid present. When no other acid is present, the strength may be very closely estimated by tasting, after a little practice.

The presence of sulphuric or muriatic acids is best detected by boiling the vinegar with a little starch, and, after the liquid has become entirely cold, adding a solution of iodine, when, if the vinegar is pure, the blue iodide of starch will be formed ; but if muriatic or sulphuric acid be present, the starch will be destroyed and no blue coloration will appear. Free sulphuric acid if present will cause a white precipitate to be formed upon the addition of chloride of calcium to the vinegar. Free muriatic acid is in the same way indicated by the formation of a white precipitate upon the addition of nitrate of silver. Nitric acid is best detected by its forming a yellow color when the vinegar is boiled with indigo. The presence of red pepper, mustard, and similar substances is most readily detected by boiling the vinegar until much concentrated, when, if present, they may be detected by the taste.

Walnut, the name applied to the fruit and trees of the genus Juglans. *J. Regia* is the English walnut, a native of Persia, but probably so called as it was introduced from England into this country. The tree is from twenty to forty feet high, branched. The *fruit* is oval, mucronate, about two inches long, and one half inch in diameter ; the *nut* is smoothish or somewhat corrugated. This walnut is grown in this country to some extent but requires shelter, and the fruit scarcely ever reaches perfection. But large quantities are imported and these are highly esteemed. The young immature fruit is much used for pickling. Our common black walnut is *J. nigra,* a large tree from forty to eighty feet high, with spreading branches, often forming a rounding and rather open top. The kernel of the nut is very rich in oil and is esteemed by some persons. From the kernel of the English walnut an oil is extracted which is much prized by artists and varnish makers. The timber of the black walnut is very valuable and is extensively used by cabinet makers.

Washing Powders, Washing Fluid, Soap Powder, preparations for use in the laundry, designed to lessen the labor of washing. The essential elements in all these preparations are similar. A washing fluid may be formed of certain parts of soda, lime, ammonia, alcohol and water ; or of potash, borax, salt, soapwart and water. A washing powder may be the hydrous silicate of soda or potash, in dry, fine powder ; or it may consist simply of carbonate of soda deprived of its water by heat, under constant stirring. Soda-ash and lime may be mixed to render the soda caustic and then the whole is boiled in water. Carbonate of soda, or sal-soda is the main ingredient in all of these preparations.

Wheat, (Triticum vulgare) an annual plant belonging to the grass family. It has been cultivated from remotest antiquity, and, though never found in a wild state, is supposed to be a native of Asia. Wheat is probably the most valuable of all the grain growing grasses, and furnishes the food of all civilized men, especially in the temperate climes. It is used by being ground into flour and baked into bread. Cracked or prepared wheat is the grains removed of the outer husk or bran and coarsely broken. It retains the gluten of the wheat and is boiled and used like oat-meal. It is very nutritious and much recommended for invalids. The production of wheat in the United States, for 1876, was 250,000,000 bushels, of which 194,990,240 bushels were necessary for home consumption. Wheaten Grits, or Groats, are simply the grains of the wheat removed of its outer husk.

Wheat Flour, the crushed interior of the wheat grain after separation from the woody exterior portion or bran. The quality of a given sample of flour will depend upon the quality of the wheat from which it was made, the method of grinding to which it has been subjected, and the process and care employed in the separation of the bran and different qualities of flour. For a thorough understanding of the last named process it is first necessary to know the constitution and structure of the wheat grain, and what the process is intended to accomplish, together with some of the difficulties lying in the way. The wheat grain consists first of two outer, chaffy coatings, which are easily detached and are composed of woody fibre and silica; beneath these are two other coats more tenacious and closely adherent to the grain, and composed almost exclusively of woody fibre. These coats being entirely indigestible can furnish no nutriment to the system, and if it were possible to separate them entirely from the other parts of the grain they would have no value. Within these outer coatings there is first a layer of cells, which are filled with a number of albuminoid substances, the most important of which is gluten, together with a number of mineral salts, chiefly phosphates, of which the most abundant is phosphate of potassa; the phosphates of soda, lime, magnesia and iron, being present in small quantities. Within this covering which is known as the gluten coat, the entire central portion of the grain consists almost entirely of starch. Of these different constituents of the wheat kernel, starch is much the most abundant, making up usually about 70 per cent. of the entire grain; of gluten and other albuminoids, there is usually from 12 to 18 per cent., while the phosphates constitute but about two per cent. of the grain, the remainder being principally woody fibre. The phosphates are undoubtedly the most valuable, weight for weight, and the gluten next in value of these different substances.

We accordingly see that the more perfectly the outer woody coatings can be removed, and at the same time the larger the proportion of the gluten coat which can be retained in the flour, the better will be its quality. But it is evident that this will be a process of much difficulty as these coatings are very closely adherent, are both hard and firm as compared with the central, starchy portion, and consequently are, in grinding, reduced to much the same condition, being much coarser than the easily crushed starch.

The process of manufacturing flour generally adopted in this country is that known as *low milling*. The wheat is first thoroughly cleaned from other seeds, shrunken grain, etc., and is then passed through the smut machine, which, by centrifugal force, removes the smut and dust, which has accumulated upon the grain, and, at the same time removes much of the two outer coatings of the kernel. It is then conveyed into hoppers, which deliver it at a regulated speed to the mill stones, where it is ground. The stones in common use, are a kind of burr stone obtained from France. They are cut in the form of short cylinders and placed one above the other, having the two surfaces which are nearly in contact ground in grooves, in a peculiar manner, the general tendency of them being to run from the center to the circumference. The adjustment of the distance between the stones is a matter requiring care and experience, for, upon it the quality of the flour much depends. If too far apart the flour is not sufficiently finely ground, and the separation of the bran is difficult; if, on the other hand, they be brought too near together, the flour suffers from too great friction, and is liable to become so much heated as to soften the gluten.

The flour is conveyed from the stones to the bolting

apparatus for the separation of the bran and the various grades of flour. The bolting apparatus is of different character and complexity in different mills, some making as many as ten or eleven grades of flour besides the bran, whilst others separate only into flour, middlings or cannel, and bran. The bolt consists essentially of a long cylindrical frame covered with a kind of cloth made for the purpose. The frame being placed in a horizontal position is made to revolve about a central axis while the flour is conveyed into its interior. The middlings as obtained from the bolts consist of coarse, gritty flour and fine bran. At some mills the bran is separated from them by passing over a vibrating, gently inclined sieve, the holes in which are sufficiently large to allow all to pass through, but by a constant current of air blown up from beneath, the bran is prevented from passing through. By a similar process, together with a variety of qualities of bolting cloth, the numerous grades of flour produced in some mills is obtained.

The celebrated *new process* flour is obtained by slow grinding, thus giving a coarse product, the separation of which is effected by the air current, in connection with bolts and sieves. The middlings being then re-ground produce a flour rich in gluten and commanding the highest prices.

Self raising flour is made by thoroughly mixing with flour a quantity of bicarbonate of soda and tartartic acid or cream of tartar. When such flour is moistened and made into dough the tartartic acid acts upon the soda, setting free its carbonic acid, which causes the rising of the bread.

Flour is often adulterated by the addition of potato starch, white corn flour, rice flour, plaster of Paris, chalk, alum, sulphate of copper, etc. Such adulterations are made in a perfectly conscienceless manner by many of the bakers in our large cities. Alum is used to cause the flour to take up a larger amount of water and thus add to the weight of the bread made from it; potato starch serves the same purpose, and at the same time, adds cheaply to the weight of the flour. Sulphate of copper is used to give greater whiteness to the bread, whilst corn flour, chalk, plaster of Paris, and other things are used because cheaper, weight for weight, than wheat flour. When in flour these adulterations are usually easily detected; but after being baked into bread they are not so easily recognized, except by the quality of the bread.

Rice flour, potato starch, and corn flour, when present, may be easily detected before baking, with the microscope, from the difference in form of the starch granules. Plaster of Paris forms an insoluble residue when the flour or bread is washed in water. Sulphate of copper reveals its presence by the formation of a blue color when a little prussiate of potash is placed upon the moistened bread or flour, and in a similar manner the presence of alum is shown by a claret red coloration, when a solution of logwood is used in the same way. As all of the mineral adulterants used are heavier than chloroform, whilst flour is lighter, and none of them dissolve in this material, their presence may be easily detected by placing a small quantity of flour in a test tube, adding chloroform and shaking thoroughly, and allowing to stand at rest for some time, when, if mineral matters are present they will settle to the bottom of the tube, whilst the flour will float upon the chloroform.

Whiskey, a spirit distilled from grain. In Great Britain it is distilled largely from barley; in this country Indian corn, rye and barley are all used. Whiskey may also be distilled from potatoes or turnips. Whiskey generally contains about 50 per cent. of alcohol. England, Scotland and Ireland produce the most whiskey. In the United States the principal manufactories are in Illinois, Ohio, Indiana, Kentucky, (Bourbon whiskey) Pennsylvania and New York. Bourbon whiskey is prepared from a mixture of Indian corn and small grain, with about 10 per cent. of malt. Monongahela whiskey is made entirely from rye, mixed with 10 per cent. of malt.

The two operations in the manufacture of whiskey are the formation of the vinous mash and the distillation of the alcohol. The mash is prepared by grinding the grain with some malt, and making an infusion in the mash tub with hot water, which is constantly stirred; the wort is then drawn off and water added to extract the soluble matter of the grain. The mash is then allowed to ferment, and, sugar being formed from the starch, it is converted into alcohol by the fermentation. When it arrives at a proper stage it is distilled, and the alcohol separated from the other substances.

A large proportion of the whiskey used in this country is artificially prepared from the raw products of malt, or potato spirits, and reducing with water and adding certain substances to give the desired flavor; creosote being added to give whiskey flavor. Pure whiskey, when newly prepared, is nearly colorless, but when preserved in casks acquires a brownish color. Whiskey is largely consumed as a beverage, and is also the principal source for the manufacture of brandy. In 1875 over 61,000,000 gallons of distilled spirits were manufactured in this country, of which over 130,000 gallons were exported. The present revenue tax on proof spirit is ninety cents a gallon.

White Fish, (*Caregonus albus*) a fresh water fish, belonging to the Salmon family, found almost exclusively in the Great Lakes of North America. It is usually from sixteen to twenty inches in length, but varies much in size with the locality, in some places averaging no more than one and a half pounds in weight, whilst in other localities the average weight is four or five pounds, and it occasionally reaches a much greater size, even as high as twenty pounds in weight. It is bluish gray in color above, and white below. In form it much resembles the salmon, but is somewhat thicker, especially at the tail.

It is usually found in rather deep water, although approaching shoal water at times. It is taken in pound and gill nets, and in seines, but will not usually take the hook. It is the most important product of the great lake fisheries, the annual catch being estimated at 15,000,000 pounds, and reaching in value nearly $1,000,000. Great quantities are shipped and consumed while fresh, throughout the Western States, whilst others are salted and packed in kits and barrels for the market.

Whiting. The true whiting is a European fish, belonging to the Cod family and genus *Merlangus*. It is noted for the excellence of its flesh, which is more highly esteemed than that of any other member of the family. It is of a dark, almost black color above, and grayish beneath, has an average length of about fifteen inches, and weighs from one to three pounds. It is taken in considerable quantities in the seas of Northern Europe. The American Hake, and perhaps other members of the genus, *Merlucius*, are known in this country by the name of whiting, the one to which the name is more commonly applied (*M. albidus*) being from one to three feet in length, of reddish brown color above, and soiled white below.

Wine, the fermented juice of the grape. It should, therefore, contain the same elements that are found in the grape juice, subject to the changes of fermentation, and the effect of age and treatment. In the must, or grape juice, we find grape *sugar*, *gum* and *dextrine*, *vegetable acids*, such as *malic, citric*, and *tartaric; albuminoids, tannin, coloring matter; volatile aroma*, and *ash ingredients*. Of these, grape sugar is the most important, ranging from thirteen to thirty per cent. of the must. In the fermented juice or wine, are always found alcohol, grape sugar or glucose, bitartrate and malate of potash, tartrate of lime, chloride of sodium, tannin, various essential oils which give flavor, and ethers which give "bouquet" or aroma to the wine. The process of wine making varies in its details, in different countries, and even in different districts of the same country. In France and Germany the grapes gathered during the day, are generally pressed at night, and the juice at once set aside for fermentation.

The ripest and choicest grapes are set aside for the

finest quality of wine. The juice having been placed in the vat, produces a froth upon the surface during the course of the night, which is skimmed off and the process renewed with a second or third layer of froth. After the process of fermentation has fully set in, the froth all rises to the surface and is rapidly skimmed off, when the clear liquor is transferred to barrels, and set away to complete the process, and allowed to ripen. During the winter the wine is again racked off, and separated from the lees, by which further fermentation is avoided. In some wines this racking process is continued a number of times. When sparkling wines are made from black grapes, they are gently pressed so as not to squeeze out the coloring matter of the skin, and the residue is used in the manufacture of inferior wines.

In making common wines the grapes are trodden under foot, and allowed to ferment in the vat, and run off for further fermentation and ripening. When making colored wine the seeds and skin are crushed along with the grape. After the first run has been taken off, a second run is made, and the residue is again used in the manufacture of inferior wines, brandy or vinegar. The wine thus made varies according to the season, locality and age; but generally each vineyard retains its own peculiarities. The quantity of alcohol in the natural wines also varies very much ranging from seven per cent. to twenty-three per cent. in the stronger wines.

Wines are either red or white. Red wines are made from black grapes, fermented with their skins; and white wines are made either from the juice of white grapes, or from the juice of black grapes fermented without their skins. As to quality they are designated as spirituous, sweet, dry, sparkling, still, rough, or acidulous. *Spirituous wines* are made from the juice that contains a large proportion of sugar, and enough of the yeast principle to convert the sugar into alcohol, when the excess of the latter arrests fermentation. *Sweet wines* are formed when the sugar is present in large proportions, and but little of the yeast principle, by which the production of alcohol is less, and more, proportionately, of the sugar remains.

Dry wines are produced when the sugar and yeast principle are present in considerable amount, and in the proportion for mutual decomposition, when the wine will be strong bodied and sound without any sweetness or acidity. *Light wines* are made from grapes which contain only a small amount of saccharine matter, and therefore only a small quantity is formed. *Sparkling wines* are the result of bottling before fermentation is fully completed, and, the process proceeding slowly in the bottles, carbolic acid gas is generated, and the wine becoming impregnated with it, becomes effervescing and sparkling.

Rough or *Astringent wines* owe their flavor to the presence of tannin, derived from the husk of the grape. *Acidulous wines* are those containing carbonic acid, or an unusual proportion of tartar.

Wines of *France.* The principal wines of France are Champagne, Burgundy, Bordeaux, Rhone, of each of which there are several varieties. Champagne wines are of two kinds, the white and the red, and these are again distinguished as "still" and "sparkling." The champagnes are bottled wines, and when first bottled are placed on frames with the neck down. The lees are thus collected in the neck of the bottle, and after some time the bottle is uncorked and the neck emptied; it is then re-filled from another bottle and set away for the required age. Champagne is largely imitated, by forcing into sweetened still wines, or cider, such gas as is used in the preparation of soda water. Gas-generating powders are also added to bottled wine.

The *Burgundy wines* of the best quality are supposed to be the finest and most delicate red wines in the world, full of rich perfume, of exquisite bouquet, and fine purple color. They contain from fourteen to fifteen per cent. of alcohol. *Bordeaux wines*, known as claret, are produced on the banks of the Gironde, in the district of Bordelais. The best of the wines are of fine color and delicate flavor, light, less warm than Burgundy, with a violet perfume and rich purple hue. The varieties of claret wine are very numerous. The best *wines of the Rhone*, are those of Lyonnais, La Drome, Ardeche, Garel and Herault. Numerous varieties of wine are made in each of these localities, both red and white. The white wine of the Hermitage is said to be the first white wine of France, and will keep for a hundred years.

Wines of Spain. Sherry is the name by which the wines of Spain are most familiarly known. True Sherry is made in the vicinity of Xeres, about twenty-one miles north of Cadiz, it being shipped from the latter place; but there are many other wines of Spain shipped abroad under the same name. Sherry is not a " natural wine," but is formed by mixing different varieties. Malaga wines are similar to sherry, but inferior in flavor, and retain a sweet taste till they are two years old. Oporto or Port wine, is from Portugal, and is essentially a dry wine, mixed to suit the English market. Among the best wines from Germany are those produced on the Rhine and the Moselle. They are generally drier and more aromatic than the French, of perfect fermentation, with a slightly acid flavor. Hochheim, Marcobrienn, Rauenthal, Johannisberg and Steinberg well represent the different classes.

Madeira, is from the island of that name, is luscious and rich, with a pungent, aromatic, and nutty, bitter-sweet flavor. It is not considered to have reached maturity till it has been ten years in the wood, and twice that time in the bottle. Of American wines those of California bid fair to rival those of the old world, and judicious selection of the grape and improved treatment will attain the desired result. In some portions of the eastern United States wine is made from the Catawba grape, but, owing to the large proportion of malic acid, it is of inferior quality. From Hungary, a wine is exported of superior quality, known as Tokay. For the year ending June 30, 1875, there were imported into the United States, 6,731,593 gallons of wine in casks, and 401,849 dozen bottles of wine, representing a total value of $5,551,274. The total production of wine in the United States, according to the census of 1870, was 3,092,370 gallons, of which California has 1,814,656 gallons. Since then the production has largely increased, and also the consumption. Wine is also made from raisins, in Spain, Italy and Greece.

Yeast. In all preparations of yeast the essential element is the yeast plant, a microscopical fungus plant. It is owing to the presence of this plant that fermentation takes place in any material containing sugary matter. Fresh yeast may be obtained from breweries, and German, or Compressed yeast, is of great advantage, as it may be obtained fresh every day. It was introduced from Holland, where it was made at the large distilleries. In the distillation of whiskey from rye and barley after fermentation takes place, and the liquor is drawn off, large quantities of yeast remain in the vat, along with the undecomposed gluten of the barley and rye. From this residue; and from the addition of some potato starch, after a process of washing and settling, the yeast is obtained in a comparatively pure state.

It is then pressed in linen bags and is ready to be sent to market, where it appears done up in various forms. Placed in a cool place it will keep for several days. Yeast cakes and dry hop yeast are made by adding a portion of good yeast to rye or wheat flour, with the addition of a little salt; when risen it is stirred in with Indian meal; and when again risen it is rolled out thin, cut into small cakes and allowed to dry. Hops, or rather the extract of hops, is often added; when made perfectly dry these cakes will keep for six months. The yeast plants in these cakes become partially dried, and by soaking in warm water they are revived. Hot water will scald them and render the yeast germs inactive.

Table of U. S. Money.

10	Mills	make	one	cent,
10	Cents	"	"	dime,
10	Dimes	"	"	dollar,
10	Dollars	"	"	eagle.

Denomination of Coin.	Weight in troy grains.	Pure metal	Alloy.	Legal tender.
Gold.				
Double Eagle,	516.00	900	100	In all amounts.
Eagle,	258.00	900	100	"
Half Eagle,	129.00	900	100	"
Three dollar piece,	77.40	900	100 •	"
Quarter Eagle,	64.50	900	100	"
One dollar piece,	25.80	900	100	"
Silver.				
Trade dollar,	420.00	900	100	Not legal tender
Dollar,	412.50	900	100	Full legal tender
Half dollar,	192.00	900	100	
Quarter dollar,	96.45	900	100	
Dime,	38.58	900	100	
Copper Nickel.		Nickel.	Copper	
Five cent piece,	77.16	25	75	Not exc. 25 cts.
Three cent piece,	30.00	25	75	" " "
Bronze.		Tin & Zinc	Copper	
One cent piece, •	48.00	5	95	Not exc. 25 cts.

Miscellaneous Table.

12	units	make	1 dozen.
12	dozen	"	1 gross.
12	gross	"	1 great gross.
20	things	"	1 score.
24	sheets	"	1 quire of paper.
20	quires	"	1 ream
2	reams	"	1 bundle.
5	bundles	"	1 bale.
100	pounds	"	1 quintal of fish.
196	pounds	"	1 barrel of flour.
200	pounds	"	1 barrel of pork or beef.
100	pounds	"	1 firkin of butter,
14	pounds	"	1 stone of iron or lead.
21½	stones	"	1 pig.
8	pigs	"	1 fother.
2	weys (328 lbs.)	"	1 sack of wool.
12	sacks (39 cwt.,	"	1 last.
3	inches	"	1 palm.
4	inches	"	1 hand.
9	inches	"	1 span.
18	inches	"	1 cubit.
22	inches (nearly)	"	1 sacred cubit.
3	feet	"	1 common pace.

Pork, full weight, should contain 200 lbs., but the standard has been reduced to 190 lbs.; pickled beef, hams in barrels 306 and 220 lbs.; clear sides in bulk, in boxes 500 lbs., and in hhds. from 800 to 1000 lbs.

Weights of original Packages.

COFFEE.	lbs.
Brazil, bags, old style	160
" " new style.	132
Domingo, bags.	130
Laguira, "	110
Maracaibo, "	120
Ceylon, "	150
Manila, mats.	70
Jamaica, packages	200
Java and Singapore, bags	130
" " mats	60

SUGAR.	lbs.
Cuba, hhds	about 1,350
" boxes	400
Domestic, hhds	1,100
Java, baskets.	500
" bags	60
Manila bags	70
East India, bags	150
Brazil, bags	150

In transportation of freights, actual weight is generally given, but when that cannot be done, the following articles are estimated as follows:

Ale and Beer	320 lbs.	per	bbl.
" "	170	" $\frac{1}{2}$	"
" "	100	" $\frac{1}{2}$	"
Apples, dried	24	"	bu.
" green.	56	"	"
" "	150	"	bbl.
Barley	48	"	bu.
Beans, white.	60	"	"
" castor	46	"	"
Beef	320	"	bbl.
Bran	20	"	bu.
Brooms.	40	"	doz.
Buckwheat	52	"	bu.

Cider 350   "   bbl.
Charcoal.................................... 22   "   bu.
Clover Seed 60   "   "
Corn 56   "   "
" in ear.................................. 70   "   "
" meal 48   "   "
"   " 220   "   bbl.
Eggs 200   "   "
Fish.......................................300   "   "
Flax Seed 56   "   bu.
Flour......................................200   "   bbl.
Hemp Seed................................. 44   "   bu.
High Wines................................350   "   bbl.
Hungarian Grass Seed..................... 45   "   bu.
Lime 200   "   bbl.
Malt 38   "   bu.
Millet..................................... 45   "   "
Nails......................................108   "   keg.
Oats....................................... 32   "   bu.
Oil. 400   "   bbl.
Onions 57   "   bu.
Peaches, dried............................ 33   "   "
Pork 320   "   bbl.
Potatoes, common.........................150   "   "
"   "   60   "   bu.
"   sweet   55   "   "
Rye....................................... 56   "   "
Salt, fine 56   "   "
"   " 300   "   bbl.
" coarse 350   "   bbl.
" coarse 200   "   sack.
Timothy seed.............................. 45   "   bu.
Turnips 56   "   "
Vinegar...................................350   "   bbl.
Wheat 60   "   bu.
Whiskey...................................350   "   bbl.
One ton weight is.......................2,000 lbs.

Table showing the weights of various articles in different States.

ARTICLES.	Mich.	Mo.	N. Y.	Ill.	Ind.	Iowa.	Wis.
	lbs.	lbs.	lbs.	lbs.	lbs.	lbs.	lbs.
Barley...................per bush.	48	48	48	48	48	46	48
Beans................... "	60	60	60	60	60	60	60
Buckwheat.............. "	48	52	48	52	50	52	48
Broom Corn............. "	46	46	46	46	46	46	46
Blue Grass............. "	14	14	14	14	14	14	14
Bran.................... "	20	..	..	20	..	20	20
Castor Beans........... "	46	46	46	46	46	46	46
Clover Seed............ "	60	60	60	60	60	60	60
Corn, shelled.......... "	56	56	56	56	56	56	56
Corn, on ear........... "	70	70	70	70	68	70	70
Corn Meal.............. "	50	..	..	48	50	48	48
Coarse Salt............ "	50	50	56	50	50	50	50
Charcoal............... "	22	22	22	22	22	22	22
Coke................... "	..	..	..	40	..	..	..
Coal, Stone............ "	80	..	..	80	70	..	..
Cranberries............ "	40	..	..	..	..	..	..
Dried Apples........... "	22	22	22	22	22	22	22
Dried Peaches.......... "	28	33	32	33	33	33	28
Flax seed.............. "	56	56	56	56	56	56	56
Hemp seed.............. "	44	44	44	44	44	44	44
Hungarian Grass Seed... "	50	48	48	48	48	48	48
Irish Pota'es, heaping meas. "	60	60	60	60	60	60	60
Millet................. "	50	48	48	50	48	50	50
Malt................... "	38	..	..	38	38	38	38
Oats................... "	32	35	32	32	33	32	32
Osage Orange........... "	33	33	33	33	33	33	33
Orchard Grass.......... "	14	14	14	14	14	14	14
Onions................. "	54	57	57	57	57	57	57
Peas................... "	60	60	60	60	60	60	60
Plastering Hair........ "	8	8	8	8	8	8	8
Rye.................... "	56	56	56	56	56	56	56
Red Top Seed.......... "	14	14	14	14	14	14	14
Sweet Potatoes......... "	56	56	56	56	56	56	56
Timothy Seed.......... "	45	45	45	45	45	45	46
Turnips................ "	58	55	55	55	55	55	55
Wheat.................. "	60	60	60	60	60	60	60

Beef and Pork per bbl., net........................ 200 lbs.

Flour   "   "   .... 196 "

White Fish and Trout, " .... 200 "
Salt, per barrel.................................. 280 "
Lime, " .... 220 "
Hay, well settled, per cubic foot.................. 4½ "
Corn, on cob, in bin, " .... 22 "
Corn, shelled, " " .... 45 "
Wheat, " " .... 48 "
Oats, " " .... 25½ "
Potatoes, " " .... 38½ "
Sand, dry, " .... 95 "
Clay, compact " ..'................ 135 "
Marble, " .... 169 "
Seasoned Beech Wood, per cord.................5,616 "
Seasoned Hickory, " ....·····6,960 "

Foreign Weights and Measures,

Reduced to the standard of the United States.

Aham, in Amsterdam ....41 gallons
Almude, in Portugal..............................4½ gallons
Almude, in Madeira.......................... 4.68 gallons
Alquiere, in Maderia....................... .over 1½ peck
Alquiere, in Portugal ....1⅜ to nearly 1¼ pecks
Alquiere, in Bahia ....1 bushel
Alquiere, in Maranham..........................1¼ bushels
Alquiere, in Rio Janeiro and Pernambuco····1 to 1¼ bushels
Anna, of rice, in Ceylon.....................260 2-5 pounds
Arroba, in Portugal and Brazil ....32¾ pounds
Arroba, in Spain and Argentine Confederation····25 pounds
Arroba, in Spain, (liquid measure) 4..............46 gallons
Arroba, in Havana ....3.10 gallons
Arroba, in Malaga, of wine····:·············about 4½ gallons
Arsheen, in Russia ....28 inches
Bahar, in Batavia ....are 4½ piculs
Bale, of cinnamon, in Ceylon, net..............104⅜ pounds
Barile, in Naples ....equals about 11 gallons
Barde, in Leghorn, of wines·················12.04 gallons
Candy, Ceylon.................................515 pounds

Candy, Bombay ....560 pounds
Candy, Bombay (grain)..........................358 pounds
Candy, Bombay (rice) (nearly 25 bushels) .....215.93 pounds
Candy, Madras ....500 pounds
Cantar, in Levant contains 44 oakes...........118.80 pounds
Cantar, in Leghorn, of oil.....................88 pounds
Cantar, in Malta...............................171½ pounds
Cantar, in Naples ....106 to 196½ pounds
Cantar, in Sicily.....................175 to 192½ pounds
Carro, in Naples, of grain.....................52½ bushels
Carro, in Naples, wine.........................264 gallons
Catty, of tea, in China........................1½ pounds
Cayang, or Koyang, in Batavia.................3.581 pounds
Chetwert, in Russia...........................595 bushels
Fenega, in Spain.........................1.575 bushels
Fenega, Havana..............................1.123 bushels
Hectolitre, in France ....2.84 bushels
Killog, in France and Netherlands ....2.21 pounds
Last, in Amsterdam, of grain...................85½ bushels
Last, in Bremen, of grain......................80 bushels
Last, in Cadiz, of salt......................74 4-5 bushels
Last, in Dantzic, of grain.............nearly 93 bushels
Last, in Flushing, of grain....................90½ bushels
Last, in Hamburgh, of grain ....89.64 bushels
Last, in Lubec, of grain................over 91 bushels
Last, in Portugal, of salt.....................70 bushels
Last, in Rotterdam, of grain ....85.136 bushels
Last, in Sweden...............................75 bushels
Last, in Utrecht, of grain................over 59 bushels
Lispound, in Hamburg ....16 pounds 5 ounces
Lispound, in Holland ....18 pounds 4 ounces
Mark, Holland ....9 ounces
Maud, in Calcutta....................75 to 84 pounds
Maund, Bengal ....85.285 pounds
Maund, Bengal (Factory) ....74.667 pounds
Maund, Bombay ....28 pounds
Maund, Madras...............................25 pounds

Mina, in Greece ....2.205 pounds
Mino, in Genoa, of grain........................3.43 bushels
Mount, in France.....................................1 ton
Moy, in Lisbon....................................24 bushels
Moy, in Oporto....................................80 bushels
Moyo, in Portugal.................contains over 23 bushels
Moke, in Smyrna................................23 pounds
Ohm, Hamburg ....38.28 gallons
Orna, in Trieste, of wine......................14.94 gallons
Orna, of oil..17 gallons
Oalmo, in Naples ....is a little over 10 inches
Pfund, Austria and Bavaria....................1.235 pounds
Pfund, Bremen ....1.99 pounds
Pfund, Denmark...............................1.102 pounds
Pfund, Hamburg...............................1.068 pounds
Pond, Netherlands (metric)....................2.205 pounds
Punt, Russia.....................................9.028 pounds
Pecul, in Batavia and Madras.................135.68 pounds
Pecul, in China and Japan ....133½ pounds
Pipe, in Spain, of wine...................160 to 164 gallons
Pood, in Russia........is equal to nearly 36 pounds 2 ounces
Quarter, in England, of grain.....................8 bushels
Quintal, in Portugal ....89.05 pounds
Quintal, in Smyrna ....139.48 pounds
Quintal, in Spain.................................96 pounds
Quintal, in Turkey ....167 pounds 3 ounces
Rottoli, in Portugal ....12 pounds 4 ounces
Rottoli, in Genoa................................24 pounds
Rottoli, in Leghorn.............................23 pounds
Salma, in Sicily, of grain ....9.77 bushels
Salma, in Malta, of grain......................8.22 bushels
Scneffel, in Germany......varies from 1½ to nearly 3 bushels
Shippound, in Hamburg and Denmark...........331 pounds
Shippound, in Holland.................368 pounds 4 ounces
Staro, in Trieste.................................2¾ bushels
Tael, in China.....................................1½ ounces
Vara, in Rio Janeiro ....nearly 1½ yards

Vara, in Spain...................100 are equal to 920 yards
Werst, in Russia.....................................350⅔ feet

Avoirdupois Weight.

By this weight all articles in the grocers' trade are
bought and sold.

27 11-32 Grains . .	1 Dram,
16 Drams	1 Ounce,
16 Ounces . . .	1 Pound,
25 Pounds	1 Quarter,
4 Quarters or 100 pounds .	1 Hundred weight.
20 Hundred weight . .	1 Ton.

The grain avoirdupois, though never used, is the same as
the grain in troy weight; 7,000 grains make the avoirdupois
pound, and 5,760 grains the Troy pound.

Table of Liquid Measure.

4 Gills . .	1 Pint,
2 Pints . . .	1 Quart,
4 Quarts . .	1 Gallon,
31½ Gallons . .	1 Barrel,
63 Gallons . .	1 Hogshead,
2 Hogsheads . .	1 Pipe or Butt,
2 Pipes . .	1 Ton.

5 ounces Avoirdupois of water will make one gill. The
gallon of water should contain exactly 10 pounds of pure
water at a temperature of 62° F. the barometer being at 30
inches.

Table of Dry Measure.

4 Gills . . .	1 Pint,
2 Pints . . .	1 Quart,
8 Quarts, . .	1 Peck,
4 Pecks or 32 quarts .	1 Bushel,
8 Bushels . .	1 Quarter.

The legal bushel of the United States, is the old Winches-
ter measure of 2,150.42 cubic inches. The Imperial bushel
of England is 2,218.142 cubic inches, so that 32 English bushels are about equivalent to 33 of ours.

Value of Foreign Gold and Silver Coins.

ECUADOR............	Gold,	Half Doubloon...........	7	60 0
	Silver,	Quarter Dollar..........	0	18 7
EGYPT.	Gold,	Hundred Piasters.........	4	97 0
	silver,	Twenty Piasters	0	96 0
FRANCE	Gold,	Twenty Francs...........	3	85 0
	Silver,	Five Francs.............	0	93 2
	"	Franc...................	0	18 5
FRANKFORT ·······.	Silver,	Florin...................	0	39 5
GREECE.............	Gold,	Twenty Drachms...........	3	04 5
	Silver,	Drachm	0	16 5
GUIANA, BRITISH..	Silver,	Guilder	0	26 2
HANOVER...........	Gold,	Ten Thaler............ ···	7	89 0
	Silver,	Thaler (fine silver)······	0	69 2
	"	Thaler (750 fine)	0	68 0
HAYTI	Silver,	Dollar, (100 Centimes) ..	0	25 7
HESSE CASSEL......	Silver,	Thaler.................	0	67 5
	"	One-sixth Thaler........	0	11 0
HESSE DARMSTADT	Silver,	Florin, or Gulden	0	39 5
HINDOSTAN	Gold,	Mohur (E. I. Co.).......	7	10 0
	Silver,	Rupee.................	0	44 5
MECKLENBURG......	Gold,	Ten Thaler.............	7	89 0
MEXICO	Gold,	Doubloon (average).....	15	53 0
	Silver,	Dollar (average)········	1	00 7
NAPLES	Silver,	Scudo··················	0	94 0
NETHERLANDS	Gold,	Ducat··················	2	26 5
	"	Ten Guilders............	4	00 7
	Silver,	Three Guilders··········	1	20 0
	"	Guilder	0	40 0
	"	Twenty-five Cents.......	0	09 5
	"	Two and a half Guilders.	0	98 2
NEW GRANADA	Gold,	Doubloon, 21 carat stand.	15	61 0
	"	" including the silver,	15	66 0
	"	" nine-tenths stand ···	15	31 0
	"	" including the silver,	15	36 0
	Silver,	Dollar, usual weight.....	1	02 0
	"	Dol. or ten Reals, 1851...	0	93 0

NORWAY..........Silver, Rigsdaler.............. 1 05 0

PERSIA ....Gold, Tomann................. 2 23 0
                Silver,· Shaib Koran............. 0 21 5

PERU.............Gold, Doubloon, Lima, to 1833, 15 55 0
              "   "   Cuzco, to 1833....15 62 0
              "   "   Cuzco, 1837......15 53 0
            Silver, Dollar, Lima mint....... 1 00 6
             "   Dollar, Cuzco............ 1 00 8
             "   Hf. Dol. Cuzco, debased. 0 36 0
             "   Hf. Dol. Arequipa "   0 36 0
             "   Half Dollar, Pasco....... 0 49 5

POLAND............Silver, Zloty 0 11 2

PORTUGAL..........Gold, Half Joe (full weight)... 8 65 0
             "   Crown.................. 5 81 0
            Silver, Cruzado 0 55 2
             "   Crown of 1000 Reis...... 1 12 0
             "   Half Crown............. 0 56 0

PRUSSIA............Gold, Double Frederick 8 00 0
            Silver, Thaler, average......... 0 68 0
             "   One-sixth Thaler, aver'ge 0 11 0
             "   D'bl Thaler, (3½ Gulden) 1 39 0

ROME,............ Gold, Ten Scudi..............10 37 0
            Silver, Scudo 1 00 5
             "   Teston (3-10 Scudo) 0 30 0

RUSSIA,............Gold, Five Roubles............ 3 96 7
            Silver, Rouble................. 0 75 0
             "   Ten Zloty.............. 1 13 5
             "   Thirty Copecs........... 0 22 0

SARDINIA...........Gold, Twenty Lire............. 3 84 5
            Silver, Five Lire............... 0 93 2

SAXONY............Gold, Ten Thaler............. 7 94 0
             "   Ducat.................. 2 26 0
            Silver, Species Thaler.......... 0 96 0
             "   Thaler (XIV. F. M.).... 0 68 0

SIAM.............. Silver, Tical.................. 0 58 5

SPAIN,.............Gold, Pistole (Qr. Doubloon).. 3 90 5
            Silver, Pistareen (4 Reals Vellon)0 19 5

SWEDEN ....Silver, Species Daler 1 04 2
             "   Half Daler............. 0 52 0

TURKEY .... Gold,	Hundred Piasters........	4 37 4
"	Twenty Piasters (new)..	0 82 0
Silver,	Twenty Piasters (new)..	0 82 0
TUSCANY........... Gold,	Sequin..................	2 30 0
Silver,	Lepoldone..............	1 05 0
"	Florin	0 26 2
WURTEMBERG...... Silver,	Gulden, 1824.............	0 38 5
"	Gulden, 1838, and since..	0 39 5
"	Dbl. Thaler, (3½ Gulden.)	1 39 0

GERMANY.—The new German Empire has adopted a new and uniform system of coinage, which contemplates the gradual withdrawal of the coins of the various States composing the Empire, and the substitution of the new coinage as follows:

A pound of fine gold is divided into 130½ pieces, the one-tenth part of this gold coin is called a "Mark," and is subdivided into 100 Pennies, (Pfennige.)

A TEN MARK piece, the unit of the coinage is equal to 3½ South German Thalers, or 3 1-93 Bremen Gold Thalers. Its value is $ 2.43.

JAPAN.—The new system of coinage for Japan embraces four gold coins valued respectively at $ 20, $ 10, $ 5 and $ 2.

INTEREST TABLE.

INTEREST TABLE.
SIX PER CENT.

TIME.	$1	$2	$3	$4	$5	$6	$7	$8	$9	$10	$100	$1000
1 day.	0	0	0	0	0	0	0	0	0	0	2	17
2 "	0	0	0	0	0	0	0	0	0	0	3	33
3 "	0	0	0	0	0	0	0	0	0	1	5	50
4 "	0	0	0	0	0	0	0	1	1	1	7	67
5 "	0	0	0	0	0	1	1	1	1	1	8	83
6 "	0	0	0	0	1	1	1	1	1	1	10	1 00
7 "	0	0	0	0	1	1	1	1	1	1	12	1 17
8 "	0	0	0	1	1	1	1	1	1	1	13	1 33
9 "	0	0	0	1	1	1	1	1	1	2	15	1 50
10 "	0	0	1	1	1	1	1	1	2	2	17	1 67
11 "	0	0	1	1	1	1	1	1	2	2	18	1 83
12 "	0	0	1	1	1	1	1	2	2	2	20	2 00
13 "	0	0	1	1	1	1	2	2	2	2	22	2 17
14 "	0	0	1	1	1	1	2	2	2	2	23	2 33
15 "	0	1	1	1	1	2	2	2	2	3	25	2 50
16 "	0	1	1	1	1	2	2	2	2	3	27	2 67
17 "	0	1	1	1	1	2	2	2	3	3	28	2 83
18 "	0	1	1	1	2	2	2	2	3	3	30	3 00
19 "	0	1	1	1	2	2	2	3	3	3	32	3 17
20 "	0	1	1	1	2	2	2	3	3	3	33	3 33
21 "	0	1	1	1	2	2	2	3	3	4	35	3 50
22 "	0	1	1	1	2	2	3	3	3	4	37	3 67
23 "	0	1	1	2	2	2	3	3	3	4	38	3 83
24 "	0	1	1	2	2	2	3	3	4	4	40	4 00
25 "	0	1	1	2	2	3	3	3	4	4	42	4 17
26 "	0	1	1	2	2	3	3	3	4	4	43	4 33
27 "	0	1	1	2	2	3	3	4	4	5	45	4 50
28 "	0	1	1	2	2	3	3	4	4	5	47	4 67
29 "	0	1	1	2	2	3	3	4	4	5	48	4 83
1 mon.	1	1	2	2	3	3	4	4	5	5	50	5 00
2 "	1	2	3	4	5	6	7	8	9	10	1 00	10 00
3 "	2	3	5	6	8	9	11	12	14	15	1 50	15 00
4 "	2	4	6	8	10	12	14	16	18	20	2 00	20 00
5 "	3	5	8	10	13	15	18	20	23	25	2 50	25 00
6 "	3	6	9	12	15	18	21	24	27	30	3 00	30 00
7 "	4	7	11	14	18	21	25	28	32	35	3 50	35 00
8 "	4	8	12	16	20	24	28	32	36	40	4 00	40 00
9 "	5	9	14	18	23	27	32	36	41	45	4 50	45 00
10 "	5	10	15	20	25	30	35	40	45	50	5 00	50 00
11 "	6	11	17	22	28	33	39	44	50	55	5 50	55 00
1 year.	6	12	18	24	30	36	42	48	54	60	6 00	60 00

INTEREST TABLE.
SEVEN PER CENT.

TIME.	$1	$2	$3	$4	$5	$6	7$	$8	$9	$10	$100	$1000
1 day.	0	0	0	0	0	0	0	0	0	0	2	19
2 "	0	0	0	0	0	0	0	0	0	0	4	39
3 "	0	0	0	0	0	0	0	0	1	1	6	58
4 "	0	0	0	0	0	0	1	1	1	1	8	78
5 "	0	0	0	0	0	1	1	1	1	1	10	97
6 "	0	0	0	0	1	1	1	1	1	1	12	1 17
7 "	0	0	0	1	1	1	1	1	1	1	14	1 36
8 "	0	0	0	1	1	1	1	1	1	2	16	1 56
9 "	0	0	1	1	1	1	1	1	2	2	18	1 75
10 "	0	0	1	1	1	1	1	2	2	2	19	1 94
11 "	0	0	1	1	1	1	1	2	2	2	21	2 14
12 "	0	0	1	1	1	1	2	2	2	2	23	2 33
13 "	0	1	1	1	1	2	2	2	2	3	25	2 53
14 "	0	1	1	1	1	2	2	2	2	3	27	2 72
15 "	0	1	1	1	1	2	2	2	3	3	29	2 92
16 "	0	1	1	1	2	2	2	2	3	3	31	3 11
17 "	0	1	1	1	2	2	2	3	3	3	33	3 31
18 "	0	1	1	1	2	2	2	3	3	4	35	3 50
19 "	0	1	1	1	2	2	3	3	3	4	37	3 69
20 "	0	1	1	2	2	2	3	3	4	4	39	3 89
21 "	0	1	1	2	2	2	3	3	4	4	41	4 08
22 "	0	1	1	2	2	3	3	3	4	4	43	4 28
23 "	0	1	1	2	2	3	3	4	4	4	45	4 47
24 "	0	1	1	2	2	3	3	4	4	5	47	4 67
25 "	0	1	1	2	2	3	3	4	4	5	49	4 86
26 "	1	1	2	2	3	3	4	4	5	5	51	5 06
27 "	1	1	2	2	3	3	4	4	5	5	53	5 25
28 "	1	1	2	2	3	3	4	4	5	5	54	5 44
29 "	1	1	2	2	3	3	4	5	5	6	56	5 64
1 mon.	1	1	2	2	6	4	4	5	5	6	58	5 83
2 "	1	2	4	5	6	7	8	9	11	12	1 17	11 67
3 "	2	4	5	7	9	11	12	14	16	18	1 75	17 50
4 "	2	5	7	9	12	14	16	19	21	23	2 33	23 33
5 "	3	6	9	12	15	18	20	23	26	29	2 92	29 17
6 "	4	7	11	14	18	21	25	28	32	35	3 50	35 00
7 "	4	8	12	16	20	25	29	33	37	41	4 08	40 83
8 "	5	9	14	17	23	28	33	37	42	47	4 67	46 67
9 "	5	11	16	21	26	32	37	42	47	53	5 25	52 50
10 "	6	12	18	23	29	35	41	47	53	58	5 83	58 33
11 "	6	13	19	26	32	39	45	51	58	64	6 42	64 17
1 year.	7	14	21	28	35	42	49	56	63	70	7 00	70 00

EIGHT PER CENT.

TIME.	$1	$2	$3	$4	$5	$6	$7	$8	$9	$10	$100	$1000
4 days.	0	0	0	0	0	1	1	1	1	1	9	89
8 "	0	0	1	1	1	1	1	1	2	2	18	1 78
12 "	0	1	1	1	1	2	2	2	2	3	27	2 67
16 "	0	1	1	1	2	2	2	3	3	4	36	3 56
20 "	0	1	1	2	2	3	3	4	4	4	44	4 44
24 "	1	1	2	2	3	3	4	4	5	5	53	5 33
28 "	1	1	2	2	3	4	4	5	6	6	62	6 22
1 mon.	1	1	2	3	3	4	5	5	6	7	67	6 67
2 "	1	3	4	5	7	8	9	11	12	13	1 33	13 33
3 "	2	4	6	8	10	12	14	16	18	20	2 00	20 00
4 "	3	5	8	11	13	16	19	21	24	27	2 67	26 67
5 "	3	7	10	13	17	20	23	27	30	33	3 33	33 33
6 "	4	8	12	16	20	24	28	32	36	40	4 00	40 00
7 "	5	9	14	19	23	28	33	37	42	47	4 67	46 67
8 "	5	11	16	21	27	32	37	43	48	53	5 33	53 33
9 "	6	12	18	24	30	36	42	48	54	60	6 00	60 00
10 "	7	13	20	27	33	40	47	53	60	67	6 67	66 67
11 "	7	15	22	29	37	44	51	59	66	73	7 33	73 33
1 year.	8	16	24	32	40	48	56	64	72	80	8 00	80 00

TEN PER CENT.

TIME.	$1	$2	$3	$4	$5	$6	$7	$8	$9	$10	$100	$1000
4 days.	0	0	0	0	1	1	1	1	1	1	11	1 11
8 "	0	0	1	1	1	1	2	2	2	2	22	2 22
12 "	0	1	1	1	2	2	2	3	3	3	33	3 33
16 "	0	1	1	2	2	3	3	4	4	4	44	4 44
20 "	1	1	2	2	3	3	4	4	5	6	56	5 56
24 "	1	1	2	3	3	4	5	5	6	7	67	6 67
28 "	1	2	2	3	4	5	5	6	7	8	78	7 78
1 mon.	1	2	3	3	4	5	6	7	8	8	83	8 33
2 "	2	3	5	7	8	10	12	13	15	17	1 67	16 67
3 "	3	5	8	10	12	15	18	20	23	25	2 50	25 00
4 "	3	7	10	13	17	20	23	27	30	33	3 33	33 33
5 "	4	8	13	17	21	25	29	33	38	42	4 17	41 67
6 "	5	01	15	20	25	30	35	40	45	50	5 00	50 00
7 "	6	12	18	23	29	35	41	47	53	58	5 83	58 33
8 "	7	13	20	27	33	40	47	53	60	67	6 67	66 67
9 "	8	15	23	30	38	45	53	60	68	75	7 50	75 00
10 "	8	17	25	33	42	50	58	67	75	83	8 33	83 33
11 "	9	18	28	37	46	55	64	73	83	92	9 17	91 67
1 year.	10	10	30	40	50	60	79	80	90	$1	$ 10	$100

Weights and Measures,

AS RECOGNIZED BY THE LAWS OF THE UNITED STATES.

Bush.	Lbs.	Bush.	Lbs.
Wheat	60	Blue Grass Seed	4
Shelled Corn	56	Buckwheat	52
Corn in the ear	70	Dried Peaches	33
Rye	56	Dried Apples	24
Oats	32	Onions	57
Barley	48	Salt	65
White Beans	62	Stone Coal	88
Irish Potatoes	60	Malt	30
Sweet Potatoes	55	Bran	20
Castor Beans	46	Plastering Hair	8
Clover Seed	60	Turnips	55
Timothy Seed	45	Unslacked Lime	30
Flax Seed	56	Cornmeal	48
Hemp Seed	40	Fine Salt	55
Millett Seed	50	Hungarian Grass Seed	54
Peas	60	Ground Peas	20

	Africa.	Tenn.	Virginia.
Peanuts, per bush.	32 lbs.	28 lbs.	22 lbs.

A box 24 by 16 inches, 22 deep, contains 1 barrel.

A box 16 by 16½ inches, 8 deep, contains 1 bushel.

A box 8 by 8½ inches, 8 deep, contains 1 peck.

A box 4 by 4 inches, 4½ deep, contains ½ peck.

A box 4 by 4 inches, 4-10 deep, contains 1 quart.

TARE.

The subject of tares is one of much importance to the retail grocer, and he should be allowed tare on goods the same as the jobber. Of course where less than an original package is bought no tare should be expected. We give the rates of tare as prescribed by the government, and also rates as given by the wholesale trade in New York City.

Rates of Tare

PRESCRIBED BY THE GOVERNMENT.

Almonds, in bags	2	per cent.
" in bales	2½	"
" in frails	8	"

Alum, in casks ....10 per cent.
Alum coarse or ground, in sacks.............. 2 lbs. per sk.
Barytes, in sacks............................ 3 per cent.
Cassia, in mats............................. 9   "
Cheese, in casks or tubs....................10   "
Chiccory, in bags............................ 2   "
Cocoa, in bags............................... 2   "
   "   in ceroons............................ 8   "
Cinnamon, in bales........................... 6   "
Coffee, Rio, in double bags.................. 2   "
   "   in single bags.................... 1   "
   "   all other, actual tare, in single bags.
Coperas, in casks ....10 per cent·
Currants, in casks,.........................10   "
Hemp, Manila in bales....................... 4 lbs.pr. bale
   "   Hamburg, Leghorn, Trieste, in bales..... 5   "
Indigo in ceroons...........................10 per cent·
Melado, in ceroons..........................11   "
Nails, in bags.............................. 2   "
   " in casks.............................. 8   "
Ochre, dry, in casks........................ 8   "
   " in oil, in casks.....................12   "
Paris White, in casks.......................10   "
Pepper, in bags............................. 2   "
   " in double bags....................... 4   "
Peruvian bark, in ceroons...................10   "
Pimento, in bags............................ 2   "
Raisins, in boxes...........................25   "
   "   in casks............................12   "
   "   in half boxes.......................27   "
   "   in quarter boxes....................29   "
   "   in frails............................ 4   "
Rice, in bags 2   "
Spanish Brown, dry, in casks................10   "
   "   in oil, in casks.................12   "
Sugar, in bags............................. 2   "

Sugar, in bbls ······························10 per cent.
"   in boxes·····························14   "
"   in hhds ·····························12½   "
"   in mats.·····························2½   "
Salt, alum, coarse or ground, in Sacks,········2 lbs. per sack
Salt, fine, in sacks·························3   "   "
Tea, China or Japan, duty on net invoice weight.
Tea, all others actual tare.
Tobacco, leaf, in bales····················12 lbs. per bale.
"   "   in bales extra covers········12 lbs.   "
Whiting in casks.························10 per cent.

Rates of tare given by the wholesale dealers in New York city.

ARGOLS—Actual tares.

BARLEY, &c,—Come 100 lbs. in keg—all net.

BIRD SEED—2 per cent.

Butter—1 lb. on tubs as soakage; 2 lbs. on firkins; pails net weight.

CALIFORNIA HONEY—In cases, weighing 70 to 75 lbs.

CARAWAY SEED—2 per cent.

CHEESE—Always net or marked tares.

CHICCORY—Casks, marked tares, with 10 per cent. additional.

CITRON, and all Peels—2½ lbs per box.

COFFEES—1 per cent. on everything except as below. Jamaica and St. Domingo, 2 per cent; Savanilla, in double bags, and Laguayra, in heavy bags, 2. Costa Rica, in heavy bags, 2 per cent. Old Government Java, in bags, 2 per cent. Mexican Coffee—In bales, 15 lbs. Mocha Coffee—½ bales, 6 lbs.: ¼, 4lb: ½, 2½ and 3 lb.

CURRANTS—Bbls. 27 to 29 lbs average; in box, 4 lbs.

DATES—In frails, 9 per cent.

FIGS—Drums, 10 per cent; in kegs, 10. Layer figs—boxes, 12.

HOMINY—200 lbs net

LENTILS—2 per cent.

MOLASSES AND SYRUPS—Always allow ½ gallon out.

NUTMEGS—Cases and casks, marked tares.

Nuts—2 lbs per bag.

PRUNES—German, 4 lbs per box. French—marked tares. Turkish, in casks, marked tares.

RAISINS—Sultana, in boxes, 10 per cent.

RICE—4 lbs per bag; tierces, 10 per cent.

ROCK CANDY—in boxes, market tares.

SAL SODA—Casks, 7 per cent.

SODA—English, marked English tares.

SPICES—2 per cent. except Cinnamon and Cloves.

Cassia—9 per cent. on bales and mats; and 1½ lbs. extra for bale; cases, 17 lbs.

Cloves—9 lbs per bale.

SUGAR—Hhds, 12 per cent.; Refined Sugars, always *net* or marked *tares*. Boxes 15. Mats and bags—5 per cent. Barrels—Demarara, except where marked net, 12 per cent.

The per cent. for bags and mats with the trade applies only to East India sugars. On bags and mats imported from other countries the tare is according to agreement between buyer and seller.

TAPIOCA—2 per cent. SAGO—2 per cent.

TEA—Invoice weight ascertained as follows:—Three to four pkgs. are taken from out of each 50 or 60 (usually those numbered the same), the tea turned out, and the pkgs. weighed; the average of the three or four is taken as the tare of the whole.

VALENCIA RAISINS—5 lbs. per box, usually.

CREDITS.

In the buying of goods on time the length of credit varies with the articles bought, and with different houses. The general custom of wholesale houses may be stated as follows:

GROCERIES—Cash in 30 days, except as follows:

TEA—4 months net, or 3 per cent. off for cash in 10 days.

COFFEE—Mostly 30 days, except to jobbers, who settle by note, which can be readily sold.

RAW SUGAR—Cash in 7 to 10 days; discount 2½ per cent.
REFINED SUGAR—30 days net, or ½ per cent. off for cash in 7 days.

SPICES—10 to 30 days.

RICE—First hands pay cash in 10 days; dealers sell for cash, 10 to 15 and up to 30 days the extreme.

FOREIGN FRUITS—Usually 30 days; to jobbers 60 days for note that will sell readily, or one per cent. off for cash.

DOMESTIC FRUITS—10 to 15 and sometimes 30 days.

PROVISIONS—Nominally cash in 7 days; generally 20 up to 30 days the limit; cash in less than 7 days ½ per cent. discount.

BUTTER AND CHEESE—Cash or 10 days; dealers pay cash. Cheese for export due each week or steamer day.

EGGS—Cash or 7 days.

DOMESTIC LIQUORS—30 days to 4 months, according to grade. Cheap goods are generally sold on close profits and will not bear time.

IMPORTED BRANDIES—10 to 30 days; sometimes months, but depends on the price.

FINE WINES AND LIQUORS—4 months, except champagnes, which are net cash to 30 days.

TALLOW—Cash in 7 days.

OILS—Most oils are sold at 7 to 10 days net cash; sometimes 30 days· to out-of-town buyers of quantities of sperm, olive and other expensive oils, 90 days to 4 months.

TOBACCO—To export trade cash in 10 days; domestic manufactured tobacco 10 to 30 days.

GRAIN—Cash in 7 days.

HOPS—First hands pay cash; brewers buy on an average at 3 months.

Wholesale grocers put in many small items on 30 days for which they pay cash, and then again they get 60 days on some goods for which they get paid in 30 days, so that in these respects the two about balance each other.

INDEX.